APPROACHES TO COMPUTER WRITING CLASSROOMS

SUNY series, Literacy, Culture, and Learning:
Theory and Practice

Alan C. Purves, editor

APPROACHES TO COMPUTER WRITING CLASSROOMS

Learning from Practical Experience

edited by
Linda Myers

State University of New York Press

Published by
State University of New York Press, Albany

© 1993 State University of New York

Printed in the United States of America

For information, address State University of New York
Press, State University Plaza, Albany, N.Y., 12246

Production by Dana Foote
Marketing by Bernadette LaManna

Library of Congress Cataloging in Publication Data

Approaches to computer writing classrooms : learning from practical
   experience / edited by Linda Myers.
       p.   cm. — (SUNY series, literacy, culture, and learning)
   Includes bibliographical references and index.
   ISBN 0–7914–1567–8 (hc : acid-free). — ISBN 0–7914–1568–6 (pb :
acid-free)
   1. English language—Rhetoric—Study and teaching.   2. English
language—Computer-assisted instruction.   I. Myers, Linda, 1961–
   II. Series.
PE1404.A65 1993
808'.042'0285—dc20   92–32896
                                                          CIP

10 9 8 7 6 5 4 3 2 1

*This volume is dedicated
to honest, open willingness
for progress*

CONTENTS

ACKNOWLEDGMENTS

I thank all authors contributing to this special volume for the creative and scholarly excellence of their presentations and for their conscientiousness regarding our revision and publication schedules. I am especially grateful to Anthony McDonnell, whose time, advice, and support encouraged me to produce this book.

INTRODUCTION

Linda Myers

Instructors across the country, excited about the possibilities of combining technology with writing instruction, are obtaining monetary support for the construction of computer classrooms. For this task, they have plenty of guides to grant writing and people from whom to gain advice regarding computer equipment. What they lack, however, is a strategy for designing the actual learning environment.

Once funding is acquired, the technologically complex nature of computer composition generates many questions about electronic facilities. What is the next step? How do I plan an electronic classroom, and what equipment goes into such a facility? What options already exist? What mistakes have others made that I can avoid? More importantly, which room design will best suit the pedagogical goals of my institution and its instructors? And ultimately, what are some possible alternatives for future classrooms? This book specifically addresses these concerns. The strategies within this volume comprise an essential, comprehensive menu, an assortment of actual experiences from which readers can gain insights into designing their own computer-assisted writing environments.

From these models, readers can see what options might be considered with electronic writing environments. Those who are just beginning the process of room design and construction will find valuable guidance in these essays. Those who wish to renovate their rooms also will find helpful ideas here. And those who are generally pleased with their room designs may find useful means of reviewing and perhaps refining their designs.

Readers can approach these essays along two different but intersecting routes—classroom layout and pedagogical method. Because some essays detail the design and construction of specific computer composition classrooms or labs, readers can compare their own available space to the spaces actually used by the authors. Because other essays describe the practical teaching

applications suitable for particular environments, readers can compare pedagogical goals and adopt a design suitable to their pedagogy. Finally, several
essays emphasize electronic networks, networks that model the author's re-
conceptualization of electronic learning environments and envision teaching
that transcends the walls of the traditional classroom.

To insure approachability and comprehensiveness, a variety of tenured,
associate, and graduate student instructors from a variety of educational institutions—private, public, and community—were invited to detail the
planning and structure of their classrooms and the way that structure affects
their teaching. The essays move from explicit discussion of room design and
construction, through pedagogical descriptions and concerns, to theoretical
hypotheses for future learning environments. This book does not advocate
any particular pedagogy, software package, or hardware system, but rather
provides a collective experience from which the reader can learn and thus
create the environment that suits his or her needs without recreating others'
past mistakes.

The essays are personable, informative, and as jargon-free as possible.
Important computing terms are defined briefly the first time they appear, and
in the Glossary. Change never occurs in a uniform, predictable manner, particularly in academe, which is filled with a profusion of variants reflective
of change. Content and style are not standardized within this text. Thus, the
essays may seem irregular at times, inconsistent in voice and style or redun-
dant in emphasis. Each instructor presents her or his design as she or he decides is best. This variety reflects the irregularity of change, and any overlap
demonstrates the importance of the design elements that have worked well in
several schools.

Although this book attempts to be generic regarding specific products
and other details, each college and university has selected either Apple or
IBM-compatible products, and some have decided upon software packages.
Such choices do not influence the room design as a whole, nor does this book
attempt to advocate any particular hardware configuration or software system. Thus, hypertext environments are not singled out for discussion, because software is not the focus of this text. Any of the configurations
presented may house any software decision. Similarly, virtual reality classrooms are not discussed within this volume.

Virtual reality technology has created an irreversible research momen-
tum, but there has been no clear connection to writing. While virtual reality
may indeed serve to release imagination, it involves no actual writing, and
therefore no critical reading, on the part of the student. The goal of the
writing classroom is to create physical space for reflective, critical writing.
Some feel that technology is desired to relieve, if not supplant, the teacher's

burden.[1] This is not what we in English desire; at least, I sincerely hope it is not. We seek room designs that allow access, not substitution. The teaching of writing is as personal as the act of writing itself. This personal connectedness is what our classroom structures need to foster.

Good theories are eminently practical. In this collection, learning methods are discussed by instructors alongside their ideas for room construction. Each instructor has a firm theoretical foundation and has written a practical essay at my request. By reading about the instructors' experiences within the particular environments, we see more than various structural designs; we also see pedagogical theories in practice.

AN OVERVIEW OF THE BOOK

The initial essay, by Trent Batson, traces the problematic history of teacher-centered classrooms and offers new student-centered, interactive design concepts. Batson's historical overview of design processes includes traditional classrooms, the entrance of computers, and the introduction of networks. This detailed synopsis suggests theoretical implications to remember while reading the practical description of the networked ENFI (Electronic Networks for Interaction) writing environment in which Batson currently teaches. Such implications include support for change in current composition theory, dualistic thinking about teaching and learning, environmental versus presentational design approaches, detailed description of ENFI's effect on teaching, physical setup, technical design considerations, and the network's social factor.

Much electronic instruction emphasizes collaboration, supporting the current composition theory that writing is interactive. The expansion of networked instruction from teacher-student to student-student is Fred Kemp's emphasis in the second essay. In his argument for networks, Kemp laments that in English departments, rooms never intended for computers are assigned to be computer-based classrooms. Kemp discusses physical considerations of a networked classroom, costs, behaviors associated with computer-based facilities, the "virtual" environment of networked computers, and how computer use depends upon the instructors' understanding of how computers affect writing pedagogy.

Gail Hawisher and Michael Pemberton, in the third essay, analyze the results of an electronic writing classroom design survey. The survey seeks to "identify some of the questions worth asking." Responses from the editorial board of *Computers and Composition* and their colleagues provide insightful answers from a cross-section of instructors from four-year institutions and community colleges across the country. Considerations focus around public versus private spaces, and the roles of instructors and students. Hawisher and Pemberton conclude with a presentation of intriguing proposals for tomorrow's learning space.

The fourth essay, by Deborah Holdstein, raises essential questions regarding the design process: What are the needs of the students in the writing program at my particular institution? Can lab assistants teach the software so that I can teach writing? How can I convince my department chair and my colleagues that the computer should be used throughout the writing curriculum? What should the room look like? How can I make the room reflect my pedagogy? After construction, what other support and alliances will I need? Along with possible solutions for these concerns, Holdstein emphasizes important alliances that composition and English faculty must forge in order to form a learning environment that is successful both functionally and pedagogically.

In the fifth essay, Barbara Sitko examines the logic behind the planning of the lab she uses, instructional expectations, implementation of these plans, and the actual results. Sitko specifies the physical structure of the lab: equipment, locating the facility in adjoining rooms, layout and furniture, temperature control, and security, as well as the lab's virtual structure: links between file servers, use of course sections as shared writing groups, and software support.

In the sixth essay, Cynthia Selfe, Richard Selfe, and Johndan Johnson-Eilola, tell a story about the process of building models. These instructors present their past model of room design strategy, their colleagues' commentary about this model, and how the model worked—and didn't work—in practice. The opportunity to design another computer-assisted classroom provided these instructors with a chance to reconceive their model. They present a "less linear, more robust" model of how computer-supported writing facilities are designed and redesigned on a daily basis, along with practical applications using hypertext, Storyspace, laserdisks, CD-ROMs, and high-end multimedia programs.

After instructing in electronic environments for a number of years, Carolyn Handa received the opportunity to serve on a committee charged with designing the electronic learning space for writing instruction that she describes in the seventh essay. Handa describes her shift in pedagogical stance caused by instructing in an electronic room. This shift caused her to set new goals which she strove to meet by serving on the planning committee. Handa's detail regarding layout, hardware, software, and even how to form an aesthetically pleasing environment emphasizes that the "classroom's design should reflect a student-centered pedagogy."

The eighth essay, written by Robert Green, discusses a way for those on a tight budget to encourage collaboration without the use, and cost, of a network. With use of computer projection systems, the lab at Green's institution can make each computer a "platform" to support effective peer response. While detailing his lab's design history, instructional uses of space, and ultimate benefits for the student and for the instructor, Thomas offers his experience with major instructional problems.

In the ninth essay, Valerie Balester's description of three rooms traces the physical and pedagogical evolution of room design from a traditional "row" approach to an innovative "cluster" design. Each plan—from the proscenium, through the perimeter, to the cluster—corresponds to a theoretical, pedagogical strategy. Balester also highlights networking and the importance of a room design that makes the best use of software capability.

In the tenth essay, Lisa Gerrard proposes criteria for an ideal computer classroom, able to accommodate multiple, and sometimes contradictory, space requirements. Gerrard's comparisons among three lab/classroom experiences provide a valuable overview of the advantages and disadvantages of various room designs. Gerrard emphasizes the benefits of a cooperatively planned room and suggests alliances to form and opinions to solicit before actually designing the space.

Karen D'Agostino received the opportunity to enter the room-design process. In the eleventh essay, D'Agostino offers a comprehensive, detailed discussion of her training and preparation for electronic classroom instructing, and the way in which her ideas regarding room design and pedagogical goals were formed while she was instructing in an electronic room. A firm belief that students need access both to computers and to each other guides D'Agostino's arrangement of computers, tables, and chairs, as well as her decisions regarding software selection. This essay concludes with helpful warnings about potential problems such as maintenance contracts and lack of developmental teacher training.

Gordon Thomas concludes the essay collection with reflections on lessons he has learned through teaching experiences in a computer lab. Thomas's reflections cover the three phases in which his room developed: establishing a permanent facility, developing pedagogical advantages of word processing for composition and revision, and integrating the full power of Unix-based hardware and software into course work. Thomas concludes with helpful recommendations about hardware, lab administration, and ways of adapting to continually changing circumstances.

The sheer number of assumptions, expectations, questions, theories, pedagogies, methods, approaches, complexities, and continual changes rel-

evant to the construction of electronic writing classrooms prevents instructors—regardless of their excitement about computers—from easily sitting
down and sketching out a classroom design. This book provides design options, experiences, and fundamental concerns that, once considered, will
enable instructors to pick up their pencils.

NOTES

1. Rheingold 19, 49.

Historical Barriers to Intelligent Classroom Design

Trent Batson

THE WRITING PROGRAM AT
GALLAUDET UNIVERSITY

Though Gallaudet is unique in enrolling mostly deaf students—deaf education being its mission—it supports a traditional writing program with some additional features.

Most deaf people write and read with more difficulty than do hearing people. Many are skilled readers and writers, of course, but they tend to be the exception and not the rule. As a result, about half of incoming Gallaudet students, though bright and capable by any intellectual measure, need more work in writing and reading than the average first-year college student.

In fact, it was because of the need for this extra attention and work that ENFI was started at Gallaudet in 1985. We have remedial writing courses to help students write and read at the college level; we also require that all students (except those in honors English) take two years of English. All writing and reading teachers are part of the English department. About half the members of the department have used one of our computer labs in their teaching.

At the University of Pittsburgh, in the Tower of Learning, a number of model classrooms were constructed years ago to represent traditional classrooms one would find in countries throughout the world. In these, appointments, trim, floors, wall furnishings, window treatments and layouts create striking cultural statements. However, as different as the rooms are physically, they are all alike in their assumption that the teacher will stand at the front of the room. All are based on the traditional idea that the teacher "has" knowledge that is then passed on to students.

Though the rooms are striking, even more striking is the realization that these centuries-old classroom designs from countries such as Poland, Spain, France, Scotland, and Russia could as well be, essentially, classrooms being built in schools and colleges right at this moment. Naturally, the lighting and ventilation and other amenities in today's classrooms are doubtless more ergonomic, but it does seem curious that with the changes in our understanding of learning we wouldn't see a concomitant revolution in basic classroom design.

Did we, as educators, get burned so badly by the open classroom of the '60s and '70s that we now have returned, shaken, to the classrooms we knew (and hated) in our childhoods? Or is it that most educators believe the classroom to be a neutral stage on which any kind of drama can be enacted? Give us the right props, set design, and dialogue, and we can create whatever reality is necessary?

And yet, one need only listen to an interior designer to get a glimpse of how a professional understands the impact of space on how people act, react, and interact. A psychotherapist places chairs, pictures, couches, desks all in a precise design to elicit certain reactions (and considers color and light and heat and noise and myriad other factors). Store designers know that a good design will make sales more likely; shopping malls across the street from each other sometimes demonstrate the power of design: One we know of is nearly empty while its near neighbor, sharing the same name, is one of the busiest in the world. They differ only in design and layout.

Businesses have found that office layout and design, use of music, even aromas, can affect productivity by significant percentages. It is not only commercial space, or therapists' offices, then, but work space that must be carefully considered.

THE CLASSROOM AS CHAPEL

We teachers, then, are surrounded, daily, by reminders that the way space is designed has a profound and wide-ranging influence on how people respond, how they think, how their emotions play out, how they work, and certainly, therefore, how they learn. Yet we seem to have some kind of mental glitch about classrooms. It is as if the classroom were a church, where tradition and creed are placed above practical experience. In fact, the design of the classroom suggests that when we think about teaching, we fall into centuries-old churchly habits of mind. We sometimes refer to knowledge within our domain as "canonical." Many teachers tend to follow the pulpit model of teaching, standing at the front, their knowledge being delivered ex cathedra. Students are sometimes graded not entirely on their intelligence and learning but on the basis of a moral code: "class participation" (allegiance), "regular attendance" (obedience), high scores on pop quizzes (speaking the creed; correct thinking), and so on. Are we teaching thinking or doctrine?

It was not that long ago—a couple of centuries—that most teachers were clerics. Colleges in America were founded to train ministers. A degree from Harvard was a divinity degree. Those who were literate were also religious. Even today, many colleges and universities retain their religious affiliations, and teaching is still thought of as a "calling." The belief that all knowledge came from God and was passed on by the teacher to the passive receptacles sitting in the classroom may have passed, at least in our conscious thoughts, but in many ways we still conduct classes, particularly writing classes, as if the belief in knowledge from on high were still alive and vital.

The written word, even as late as the mid nineteenth century, was regarded as divine, and not to be used frivolously.[1] It could be argued that English teachers then were, and perhaps even now are, as interested in guarding the sacred as in enlightening minds. (The question I am asked most often about teaching in our computer lab is, "But, how do you correct the student's writing on the computer?" Error in writing, is perceived similarly to sin: If allowed, and not corrected immediately, it will become a habit. We have no similar perception about "error" in speaking, but instead have faith that young people will gradually improve in their speech regardless of the travesties of teenage talk).

Given the religious roots of modern classroom design, it is not too surprising to find that classrooms today still retain the aura of the divine origin of knowledge and the divine nature of writing—the Word as the embodiment of God's grace. When one is thinking of education as transmission of the one true faith, one may be excused for resisting changes in room design that might encourage freethinking.

I doubt that most composition teachers actually still make the *conscious* connection to divine origin, but while that explicit belief held sway, which continued for thousands of years, ways of thinking about teaching were strongly influenced by religious belief. It's these secondary, derivative assumptions still hanging around today, the quasi-clerical image of the English teacher, and the cultural perceptions and expectations arising from that image, that make it difficult to think objectively about how we teach writing. Without such objectivity, it is hard to consider classroom design intelligently.

AN EXAMPLE OF CLASSROOM DESIGN

How do classrooms get designed? The 12 August 1991 *New Yorker* magazine gives us one example:[2]

Here, in schematic plan, is the New York City public-school classroom as it has existed for most of the century:

And here, in schematic plan, is a design for one of the new New York City public-school classrooms—a design that will probably last into the new century:

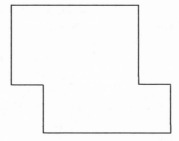

And in more or less schematic plan—or, at least, in stripped-down, instant oral history—is the story of how that little asymmetrical push off center happened and what the people who did the pushing hope its consequences will be for New York City schoolchildren.

One of the things special to the New York City public-school system is that its schools have usually been built to the design of a simple, easily reproducible template, known as a "prototype," which, of course, saves the city the expense of coming up with a fresh set of architectural plans every time it needs a new school. The first prototype was devised around 1898, by C. B. J. Snyder, an architect who was the city's first Superintendent of School Buildings. It was a so-called cookie-cutter plan—a single design that could be, and was, reproduced all over the city. Other prototypes, which included a U-shaped design, were devised in the nineteen-thirties, and some less wide-ranging prototypes have been developed since, as the need arose. Then, in the mid-eighties, certain farseeing folks at the Board of Education realized that there was going to have to be a new generation of schools, and that the city would need entirely new prototypes.

Rose Diamond (Office of Strategic Planning . . .): "In the mid-eighties, we saw that we were severely overcrowded, and needed new schools. . . .

"We put out an R.F.P. . . . and started taking architects around to look at schools that were working and to figure out why they were. The first school we took them to was my old school—P. S. 85, in Queens, which goes back to the twenties. It has big, generous windows and nice detailing, but the most perceptive architects began to see that the design of its classrooms was what really made the school work."

Peter Samton [one of the architects]: "Among the things that impressed me—really stayed with me—from my time studying science at Stuyvesant [High School] was the way the cell is such a fundamental aspect of all that happens in life. And the classroom is the cell of the school system. Our firm studied the classroom carefully, and we decided to try to design the school around the classroom instead of wedging the classroom into the prototype school."

George Luaces [another architect]: "In the nineteen sixties, the 'in' thing in educational design was the open classroom. There was a movement—it began in California, of course—that was predicated on infinite optimism. You never knew, these educators thought, what the school would be or what it could become— how many students there would be, or what they would want to do. And the idea was that a teacher should be able to change the personality of the schoolroom to match his or her own personality. So they built enormous open floor spaces, with movable partitions. Well, it worked in Beverly Hills, but it was a disaster in New York. Kids needed to focus, and the open classroom wouldn't let them. In the open classroom you would sometimes have three classes going on, and one disruptive or unhappy student could destroy the day for all three classes. So, very early in the process, even before we had the job, we started playing around with a simple square classroom shape."

Peter Sampton: "And we said, 'what if you just give a jolt to the square?' That happened very early in the design process—in the first couple of weeks. It solved so many problems at once. A whole handful of problems solved with a single jolt! You could turn one of the protruding ends of the new shape into a bay window, which would enable you to have a lot more light in the classroom. You could have little bays to put the independent-study groups in, and a little niche to put the computers in. But at the same time the teacher would remain the real focus of the room, instead of being only a bit player. Just that simple change in shape—dividing the classroom in half and pushing the halves off center—could have big consequences for New York schools."

Rose Diamond: "Everybody at the Board of Ed liked the idea of this new classroom. We showed it to teachers and principals, and they were all crazy about it. Then, sort of surprisingly, the legislature came through with the [funding] . . . and we had new classroom prototypes ready for the new authority. The designs were ninety per cent complete"

Peter Sampton: "Building out from that little asymmetrical cell, we decided to take six elementary-school projects that we'd been assigned and apply to them a whole new kind of modular plan for elementary schools in New York.

. . .

Rose Diamond: "New schools will be opening next year as the end result of a process that started in 1988. That's unbeliev- able in New York City. And they're great schools, too—not quick, thrown-together designs but models for the future. It's unbelievable."

Peter Sampton: "One of the interesting things about the new classroom is that, although it includes computers and televisions and bay windows, the focus of the schoolroom is still the black- board. A teacher up there with a piece of slate and lump of chalk. Well, not slate—our blackboards are actually porcelain enamel, which is less brittle than slate."

Rose Diamond: "We try not to call them blackboards. Chalk- boards."

We aren't provided enough information in this little sketch to seriously critique New York's design process. What does it mean, for example, that a school is "working"? Or what kind of predesign study did the architects con- duct, and who was consulted? And so on. But a couple of things seem clear enough: No one questioned the basic assumptions of traditional education (direct, personal control by the teacher is the only approach), and computers are largely peripheral to the real business of learning (they are to be put off in their little "niche"). It also seems clear enough that educators were con- sulted only after the basic design had been pretty much decided upon; edu- cational researchers don't seem to have been consulted at all. The architects are delighted that they've managed to keep education the way it's always been. And New York City has a new classroom that seems set for the next one hundred years.

Would an office space, a research lab, or a store be designed on the basis of architects' memories from their childhood? Would the designers feel triumph about keeping the design basically the same as it's always been?

With centuries of associations behind it, the traditional classroom is not easy to alter. For most teachers, it is a simple given. We accept the class- room as the college or university built it. Universities have not traditionally consulted instructors about classroom design, and even when they do, con- siderations are given over to sight lines, seating capacity, acoustics, HVAC, chalkboard color, audiovisual connections—all legitimate, of course—but normally those involved in the design do not get into considerations of how we conceive of learning. No matter how richly appointed, most classrooms in the end still adhere to the traditional concept of teaching.

ENTER THE COMPUTER

But fortunately for the students, the computers may not remain quietly closeted in their niche. At least at the college level, computers, particularly those that are networked, are causing a little perturbation in the centuries-old grip of the traditional classroom. The sacred classroom, standing firm in the face of modernity, meets the smart machine, secular to its very silicon heart.

Attendant to the computer is a whole culture alien to the hierarchical classroom New York's classroom architects celebrate. The computer is nothing if not a Trojan horse. Cramped within this particular Trojan horse are the three horsemen of the apocalypse for the traditional classroom: communication, communication, and communication. From a networked computer in the classroom/lab, a student can often connect to Internet and communicate with others throughout the world, or she may work with a real-time group-discussion tool, and, once at home, she can continue to communicate with other students, and even the teacher, through e-mail or conferencing. In all these cases, the student communicates not indirectly through the teacher, but directly with the world. Once students have broken the hammerlock teachers now enjoy over communication in the classroom (study after study shows how central and crucial the teacher is to all communication in the traditional classroom), maintaining the creed—the creed of correctness—grows impossible. (Not that the computer classroom leads to *incorrectness*, but that correctness, or effectiveness, is arrived at by the individual student, under her own motivation rather than being pulled there by the teacher.)

In other words, the computer network revolution we witness today on college campuses may involve deeper issues than many participants realize. The deepest issue may be over the very essence of the enterprise: Will education move more away from the lingering effects of its religious roots and toward the pragmatism and individualism that is one outcome of computer networks? Or will educators largely reject full implementation of computer networks in education, relegating the computer to a support function where it may merely help to perpetuate the sanctity of the creed or the hierarchical nature of the traditional classroom? For, as many commentators on the computer revolution have pointed out, computers can be used either for liberation or for control.

Design can only reflect how we see our enterprise. If we see it as mostly to make sure our students write *correctly* (teachers acting as the guardians of standards), we will feel quite comfortable in one of the chapel-like classrooms in ivy-covered halls on thousands of campuses. In contrast, if we see it as mostly to make sure our students write *effectively*, we will want nothing more than to break out of the chapel, giving our students the chance to discover their own authentic voices. And computer networks give us an additional nudge away from the classroom as chapel. Because computer networks create such a powerful virtual space and elicit quite unchurchly group behavior, it is hard to think of the classroom in quite the same way as we always have. We may think of it now more in terms of supporting various group collaborative interactions.

SUPPORT FOR CHANGE IN CURRENT COMPOSITION THEORY

If we look at the trends within the field of college composition during the past several decades—increased attention to the whole process of writing, including the thinking that goes on before words are put to paper (or to screen); increased awareness of writing as communication, not as composing a certain model of correctness; increased attention to the social context within which writing occurs (audience and purpose); increased awareness of the extent to which all writing is collaborative—we'd have to conclude that the traditional top-down model of teaching writing is inconsistent. On the one hand, we're moving radically toward an anthropological/linguistic conception of the composing process, but on the other, we have a classroom/chapel that puts the lie to this conception. Our conceptions have outstripped our physical environment. Students hear about the new concepts of writing but, sitting in the traditional classroom/chapel, still spew out doctrine (the five-paragraph essay they learned in high school).

DUALISTIC THINKING ABOUT TEACHING AND LEARNING

What would a classroom freed from religious roots look like?

The architects quoted by the *New Yorker* reflected the dualistic thinking about education that keeps us trapped in a rut and that makes the move to computers difficult. According to this dualism, either there is teacher control or there is chaos. The classroom without walls was predicated, the architect said, on "infinite optimism." The belief that students might learn without the control, the "focus," of the traditional walled-in classroom, was written off as flaky thinking of the sixties. Back to basics—the three Rs and all that.

But as many teachers know, it's only when students are doing something, when they are active, that they learn much. Teachers need to set up activities that themselves are instructive. Some educators have carried this idea to the level of complete individualized education, self-paced but teacher-monitored. Yet, removing social interaction in this way seems wrong to many teachers who recognize its power to leverage learning. Establishing group activities, collaborative activities, seems not only to be an effective means to get students engaged, but also to be good training for the way people work throughout life.

In other words, there is a middle ground between the teacher telling knowledge and students going off helter-skelter into chaos. The middle ground is the environmental approach. The teacher creates an environment—activities, perhaps, or an experience—that is structured with a sequence of experiences for groups of students. This environment itself teaches—or it allows the students to learn.

ENVIRONMENTAL VERSUS PRESENTATIONAL

If the predominant thinking about learning focused on the power of the environmental approach, and not the presentational approach (the effectiveness of which many researchers question), we doubt that so much emphasis would be placed in classroom design on keeping the teacher at the center of the classroom; instead, designers would be studying how best to support various groupings, to communicate in a variety of social settings, and to support the creation of activities in different subject areas.

The presentational approach, popularized in the media (Robin Williams in *The Dead Poets' Society*), shows a teacher at the front of the room, either failing to deal with the apathy or hostility of students, or finding some hidden dramatic talent at a telling moment, delivering a great truth, and the students all nodding or looking wide-eyed, their minds now enlightened. This popular culture model, unfortunately, also seems to permeate the thinking of those who design classrooms and even those who teach in them. If the teacher is not *presenting*, the students are not learning.

A colleague once told me about the time he had set up his class with a task, as he was accustomed to doing, and, finding that they worked quite successfully without his intervention, went out into the hall for a drink of water. While out there, he encountered the chair of his department, who said, "Don't you have a class now?" "Yes, I do," our colleague replied, "I've left them working." The chair looked at him with questioning eyes, obviously thinking our colleague was being irresponsible, and said, "Well, perhaps you'd better get back in to check on them." My colleague was sure the chair's estimation of him had dropped substantially.

Even the students are caught up in the presentational cycle; after all, it allows the students to remain passive. They have been so indoctrinated into the hierarchical notion of learning that education seems to be simply finding out what the teacher wants you to know, memorizing that, and spilling it back out on tests or in papers. Working with peers may then seem a waste of time, since their peers know no more than they do. Never mind that the lecture method over a full semester is a questionable approach, especially in a writing class, it is what students are used to.

Trying to move from presentational to environmental in the traditional classroom is indeed a struggle. Such a move seems radical in that setting. However, move the class into a computer lab, and behavior and expectations change. In the lab, for a number of reasons, it is the presentational, not the environmental, approach that seems odd.

THE MEANING OF *ENVIRONMENTAL*

What does *environment* mean? We think of it as a physical thing, but it is not always so. We sometimes refer to an "environment of fear" on city streets. Or to an "environment of wealth" in someone's grand home, an "environment of corruption" in someone's political tenure. Our terminology shows how a physical environment can create a psychological environment. A doctor may display family pictures in his or her office so that patients will develop the sense of an "environment of trust," knowing the doctor is human too.

In a business writing course, we might create working teams, three or four separate "corporations," each team competing with the others to come up with well-described and imaginative solutions to cases. This is creating a competitive environment that may share some attributes with life in the business world. If the parameters and goals of this environment are realistic enough, the environment created by the teacher allows the students to learn. Their learning does not depend on the teacher talking directly about relevant ideas, but on their experience in working through the problems. The environment leads to learning; the focus is on learning rather than on teaching.

THE ENFI ENVIRONMENT

Within a networked computer lab, instant communication in writing with people both inside and outside the lab is possible. This ability allows for a variety of virtual environments to be created. One of the most powerful of these environments is created by real-time group written discussion, an approach to teaching composition known as ENFI (Electronic Networks for Interaction).[3] This means that a computer network allows students and teacher to work in text, both to do writing work and to communicate. They still meet in a classroom, still communicate orally as well, but the network supports extensive group collaborative work in writing.

There are numerous reasons why this move to concurrent group writing is advantageous, so let's just assume for the moment that the ENFI classroom is one model for the composition class of the future. Since ENFI is already used by some instructors on more than a hundred campuses, this assumption is not too far-fetched. (The use of computer networks in business and research settings to augment meetings is growing, as well).

Once people who are gathered in a computer lab start communicating through the network as a group, they move *psychologically* out of the room and into some virtual space. Events in the lab at this time are much less intrusive than if the same group were engaged in an oral discussion.[4] A different environment, a virtual environment, has been created. In this environment, students can focus on the creation of text and ideas in ways that are not possible in the traditional classroom environment, even if the normally dominant teacher participates on the network with the students.

ENFI'S EFFECT ON TEACHING

How should composition be taught in an ENFI lab (taking ENFI as a type of network-supported collaborative approach to teaching writing)? First, it should be apparent that a lot more writing work will occur in such a lab than in the old talk-dominated traditional writing classroom. In fact, it may be that the *main* activity in this lab will be writing and not talking, since much of the discussion will be in writing, not in speech.

Once a teacher learns how to work in this new network environment, it may be that work that used to occur outside of class can take place in class instead. Students can do their prewriting work as a group in class, even working into their first rough drafts. The teacher will work as a modeler and coach, much as an art teacher might in an art studio, or a science teacher in a lab. Since students do all of their prewriting work right in the lab (and do only drafts outside of class), and since this writing is always present for the teacher—she watches all students write on the network—the teacher has full and current knowledge of how her students write. Thus, her evaluation of the students' writing is simplified. She has a daily record of each student's progress in writing. She can come to know how each student works out ideas in text and understands text, and can see students' progress toward a finished draft. Therefore, she may be able to spend less time on paper grading and, since the class is a lab session, less on class preparation as well.

At the same time, the class has the option of communicating as a group outside of class time, assuming the campus has a campuswide network. Class discussion, therefore, can take place during out-of-class time.

These changes from traditional writing-class procedure, very superficially described here, suggest that the normal scheduling of composition class might profitably be altered. If much of the work of the class that used to occur out of class now occurs in class instead, the hours in class should be increased and the hours out of class diminished. The traditional assumption is that for every hour spent in class, students will spend two doing homework. We think the network-based classroom requires a reversal of this assumption: not three hours in classwork and six in homework (for a total of nine), but five in classwork and four in homework (also for a total of nine). Those five in-class hours would be divided as follows: four for lab, one for lecture/discussion. On Monday, say, the class would meet for a regular lecture/discussion class; on Tuesday and Thursday, the class would meet for two hours each day in the computer lab and carry out the work talked about on Monday.

While it is difficult to alter class time, adding both hours and credits, I have found over the years of working in a networked writing lab that this work will benefit greatly from more time. One hour of writing work in a lab is certainly not enough time, and seventy-five minutes are barely enough. Two hours is really an ideal time span for writing work in a networked lab. This work is highly productive, so it is worth endorsing with extra time and credits.

We have, then, three phases of class interaction: four hours of lab work where the whole group works collaboratively on specific group tasks using the network, with the teacher setting goals, parameters, time limits, and performance expectations; also four hours of homework for reading course assignments, preparing drafts of individual compositions, and engaging in class discussion via the campus network; finally, one hour of lecture/discussion.

THE PHYSICAL SETUP

It might seem, at first, that the one hour of lecture/discussion could occur in a traditional classroom, but even during that hour the instructor will need to demonstrate concepts, using computers to display visuals at the front of the room and the network to distribute materials. While it would be ideal to set up a separate computerized presentation room, it is probably unrealistic to expect that most campuses would do so in the immediate future, because of the expense of duplicating computer installations. Therefore, in the interim we'll assume that the lecture/discussion session will meet in the same lab as the lab sessions.

The lab, then, will have multiple purposes. It will have to support teacher-led collaborative work on the network, small-group collaboration and critiquing, individual composing, and oral lecture/discussion. Needed in the room will be printing/publishing and display capabilities. Ideally the display would be hypermedia based.

During sessions in the lab, the teachers and students would alternate between oral and text interaction, or, in other words, between being off and on the network. While this might seem to require merely looking up from the screen to engage in oral interaction, it involves more than that. For effective oral interaction, we have to consider sight, sound, and distance. The computer lab creates problems in all three areas:

1. *Sight.* Computer monitors are inevitably between people, unless they are placed against the wall, an arrangement that is undesirable for other reasons (it makes it nearly impossible to have an oral discussion about something on the screen, an occasion that comes up quite frequently). However, when the monitors are in front of the students when they face toward the teacher, they are like the famous newspaper over the breakfast table: Though communication signals can get past them, their existence seems to obliterate any real person-to-person contact.
2. *Sound.* The many hard surfaces of the machinery, and their fans, create acoustical problems, so that teachers find themselves shouting to be heard in a class of only twenty students; in turn, students' spoken responses are often lost.
3. *Distance.* Because of the size of the machines and the greater space needed to type with two hands rather than writing with one, the average space occupied by each student is much greater in a computer lab than in a traditional classroom. Therefore, the students are spread out, diminishing the social and psychological density of the group. The more spread out physically a group is, the less cohesive it feels—a literal and psychological reality.

On the surface, therefore, it would seem that a computer lab would discourage oral interaction, except perhaps between neighbors. Yet our model proposes that a majority of the work of the course will occur in this difficult communication situation (difficult except through the wires). How can we resolve this conflict?

First, the computers should be formed in a *U* shape, or in an arena form, so that eye contact is possible between all participants. Ideally, monitors could be lowered into desks to make sight lines unobstructed, making not only faces visible, but bodies as well, since we read many signals from

body language. Furniture exists to allow monitors to be permanently recessed, or permanently on top of the desk surface; furniture allowing monitors to be pulled up or pushed down is, at this moment, either custom made
or very expensive. I hope, however, that this option becomes more readily
available. Monitors that are permanently recessed beneath a glass working
surface require a positioning of the head that is hard to maintain for long
periods of time. I also hope that *all* school desks might someday include a
network terminal, either with or without a CPU, but I don't see that yet on
the horizon.

A current compromise is a desk that allows the support surface for the
monitor to be cranked up and down. Also, now that the standard arrangement seems to be for the CPU to be installed tower-style on the floor, leaving
only the monitor on the desktop, the monitor is lower and less obtrusive than
when the monitor sat on top of the CPU. The cranking down and the reduced machinery on the desktop both make uncluttered sight lines at least
a possibility.

Addressing acoustical problems is less straightforward. Psychologically,
the improved sight line makes it *seem* as though people are easier to hear, but
computer noise and the proliferation of hard surfaces still make hearing each
other difficult in a computer lab. However, one way that we've addressed the
acoustic problem is by reducing the size of the computer furniture, thereby
bringing everyone in the room closer to each other. This is, of course, also a
way of addressing the social density problem (if there is too much distance
between people, group cohesion suffers, and discussion is hard to maintain;
in most computer labs, distances are just beyond the critical density point,
and monitors are visually distracting).

Another consideration is displaying information to the group either
through a large-screen computer or with a projector. While LCD projectors
that work in conjunction with overhead projectors work well with small
groups in dark rooms, for the typical class of twenty or twenty-five students
either large-screen monitors or a VIDEO projector is necessary. Naturally,
every lab should also be equipped with whiteboards.

Our primary criterion is that the lab support *multiple means of interaction.*
If the lab is the classroom, it must be able to support the activities of both.

TECHNICAL DESIGN CONSIDERATIONS

Light in a computer lab is problematic: It is less essential for seeing
one's work, of course, since computer screens provide their own backlighting,
but a room without much light creates psychological barriers to learning. A
room without windows has a similar problem. However, with strong ambient

light from room lights and windows, the problem of reflection on the screens crops up. And, too, monitors must face either toward the windows or at right angles to them; if windows are behind the monitors, students will have problems with light flooding their eyes, making it hard to see the screens.

For use of the computer projector, lights should be dimmable. Ideally, lights in different parts of the room could be dimmed independently.

Power sources need to be plentiful to allow for different configurations within the lab; cooling in both summer *and* winter may be necessary. A raised floor, providing the ability to run wires out of sight, is a blessing. Naturally, static-free carpeting is critical, as are dust-free whiteboards.

THE SOCIAL FACTOR

At some sites, computer labs have become gathering places for students. How much should departments encourage the use of computer labs as social centers? One way of thinking about this issue is to see the boundaries between "class time" and "out-of-class time" as an artifact of the old classroom/chapel. If the computer lab dissolves these boundaries, dissolving, also, teacher authority, some teachers might feel alarmed; but if, in dissolving the boundaries and the authority, the lab extends the *influence* of the teacher, and the *interaction* of teacher and students, it can hardly be a pernicious effect.

SUMMARY

Throughout this chapter, I've argued that the physical environment people work within has significant effects on how people work. I've suggested some concrete considerations in design of computer labs that I think would help move writing instruction toward a realization of the research trends of the past twenty years in composition studies, particularly the emphasis on collaboration. These suggestions are based not only on theory, however, but on the many years' experience I've had working within my own computer lab, talking to people working within labs at other campuses, and working on other campuses myself (as trainer, consultant, and visiting professor).

The emerging consensus I sense within the computers-and-writing community about computer lab design is not what we would have predicted in the early 1980s, when we thought of stand-alone applications and of the computer as supplemental to the main business of teaching writing. But now, not only has theory matured, but the technology itself influences our thinking as we discover how groups of people respond to advances in technological capabilities. Particularly as we move more in the direction of collaboration through local-area networks—ENFI—we find that the technology is pushing us toward a particular design imperative. This imperative is for an "open collaborative environment."

The "open" in this phrase means that not only does the technology need to be open to reconfiguration (of network and peripheral connections as well as software), but so does the space. The primary working group in a writing class may be the whole class, two smaller groups, triads, dyads, or even individuals; communication may be through the wires, or it may be through the air. So, the lab needs to be open to all these people configurations. In addition, it must take into account the need for technical support and for monitoring the lab, meaning that various people may have offices in the lab. Also, because of the many resources that computers provide, people will be visiting the lab during nonclass hours. Labs are often open, in the literal sense of *open,* from early in the morning until late at night. Unlike typical classrooms, which are abandoned when classes are not in session, computer labs are generally abuzz with activity at all hours, and this fact must be considered in the design process.

The "collaborative" in "open collaborative environment" suggests that the lab should be used to encourage working together, because current writing theory indicates there is value in doing so and because many writing jobs require it.

The term *environment,* as I've used it in this chapter, has three meanings:

1. The physical environment
2. The task environment (as in the "environmental," as opposed to "presentational," approach to teaching)
3. The virtual environment that people move into when communicating on the network—a kind of imaginative immersion in the computer screens leading students and teacher to ignore the physical reality around them

What I'm suggesting is that the open collaborative environment be designed with all three meanings of the word in mind. It should be a pleasant, flexible physical environment that supports the environmental approach to teaching and also encourages development of the virtual environment (imaginative space) that is the lifeblood of ENFI.

Computers can save us from the associational heaviness of the traditional classroom. In designing computer labs we can finally break from the medieval mindset in classroom design and develop working spaces that are in tune with learning theory and with how people actually work today.

NOTES

1. Herman Melville, for example, felt constrained to pose his novels about the South Pacific as actual accounts, not as fiction.

2. "The Talk of the Town" section, 22–24.

3. ENFI is a generic name, and was the original name, describing use of synchronous (real-time) networks to teach composition in college. On many campuses where ENFI ideas are used, the term *interchange* is used instead, since the name of the software used is *Interchange*. It's hard to predict which name, one of these two, or some other, will eventually become the standard way to describe network-based writing classes.

4. I've found, over the years, that students in our lab work on unperturbed when we bring in visitors to view the classes in session; in a traditional classroom, a visitor would be eyed curiously and the dynamics of the classroom altered substantially.

2

Student to Student: Putting Computers in Writing Classrooms

Fred Kemp

THE TEXAS TECH COMPUTER-BASED WRITING PROGRAM

The Texas Tech Computer-based Writing Instruction Research Project uses two networked classrooms (one DOS-based and the other Macintosh-based), some forty-eight computers networked to Novell and AppleShare servers, to support a range of writing courses including freshman composition, creative writing, and technical communication. The principal pedagogy the classrooms employ is ENFI (Electronic Networks for Instruction) and real-time electronic collaboration pioneered by Trent Batson at Gallaudet University in the early 1980s. The software that supports this pedagogy on both DOS and Macintosh computers is the Daedalus Instructional System, classroom E-mail, and synchronous discussion software that privileges the classroom publication of student text and peer critiquing. In addition, both classrooms have access to Texas Tech's mainframe computing facilities and national Bitnet and Internet capabilities, a valuable communications resource that graduate classes in rhetoric and composition often employ.

ARGUMENT FOR NETWORKS

The computer is usually seen by those who think of it in instructional terms as a means of providing the student with self-paced instruction. Generally this self-paced instruction is assumed to be remedial in nature, the sort of drill and practice that gives slower students exercise in rules and procedures. Other instructors, perhaps a shade more sophisticated in their understanding of what microcomputers can do, see computers as essentially writing tools that, particularly in word processing's ability to facilitate revision, make academic writing itself less bothersome for students. A third group of instructors find that special computer-driven text formats, such as hypertext, open the door to inventive new ways of generating and juxtaposing ideas. A fourth group, the "networkers," have come to an appreciation of computers as communication and publishing devices.

The manner in which computers are placed into a computer-based writing facility depends to a large extent on which of the above four positions is privileged by the facility's director. This is not to say that reasonable and informed instructors must choose one and exclude the others, or that all can't be given some credence in a computer-based writing program. But it has been my experience that people who turn to computers for instructional support (often courageously so) have from the start a particular idea of how those computers are going to be used, and often this initial idea stresses self-paced work.

Of the four emphases I described in paragraph one, the first three are basically self-paced uses of the computer, and the fourth, which relies on networks, is basically a collaborative use. This distinction is an important one. Self-paced users interact with the computer and the software: A single student operates in terrain the programmer has defined within the operating environment of a single computer in order to fulfill purposes the programmer has anticipated. Collaborative users, on the other hand, do indeed sit at computers, but the nature of what they are doing is determined not so much by the hardware or software, but by the responses of a human reader reading the student's text on another computer. Computers used collaboratively in a networked classroom employ "computer-mediated communication" as the basic instructional principle. Such computers function as "text telephones," means of moving student text from writer to reader instantly, conveniently, and cheaply. Perhaps a less radical way of conceiving of classroom computer networks is to think of them as electronic publishing devices that allow student writers to become "published" writers in a flexible range of distribution formats.

The design of a computer-based writing facility, or what a director will do with the computers he or she is about to buy, is to a large degree dependent upon the above predilections. If the computers are to support drill and practice for remediation, then it may be best to scatter computers throughout learning support centers across campus, putting five or six of them up against various unused back walls. Such centers operate as walk-on facilities, usually in conjunction with on-site human tutors and designed to support a self-paced acquisition of remedial skills. I have seen such learning support centers defined as writing centers or learning labs and located in every conceivable nook and cranny on campus. Instructors can assign individual students time or "modules" in a particular piece of software, and students can come to the center after class, sign in, and perform the time. If, on the other hand, computers are seen as mainly writing tools, then they can be collected in large computer centers managed by computer science majors and shared with programmers and business software users. Or they can be placed in dormitory lounges for easy access. These uses of computers, as self-paced learning or writing machines, dominated how microcomputers were used in most institutions since their arrival in the late 1970s to the mid 1980s.

These days, however, if the computers have been purchased by or assigned to an English department, the tendency is to collect them into a classroom. If they are to be used as self-paced devices, however, a number of instructors may respond negatively to "wasting" class time for any general self-paced activity. It is an almost universal and quite logical presumption that class time should be devoted to activities that require the class to be in the same place at the same time. The only justification for students coming together at 10:00 A.M. in order to perform drill and practice on computers or write drafts in Microsoft Word is that they may need technical assistance. In this case, as instructors rightly bemoan, writing instructors become mere computer or word processing technicians. The complaint I have heard over and over in my years of experimenting with computer-based writing instruction is, "I am no longer teaching writing. I am teaching computers and word processing."

So where one places computers in an English department has a lot to do with how one intends to use them. If a director is going to put a class-size number of computers in a classroom and expect that entire classes will use that facility either full-time or part-time, then he or she must be ready to justify that arrangement in terms of why the entire class must meet together in a single place at a specific time to do its computing. And that justification, I believe, cannot be based upon the need for technical help.

Let me digress only briefly and discuss what, indeed, a "class" is. Often the classroom teacher is so close to the classroom itself that he or she assumes that nature has ordained that classrooms should be constructed like shoe-boxes and students should sit in certain places or positions passively awaiting information. I believe that the physical arrangement of student desks and the teacher's desk and the blackboards and podiums encourages an instructional attitude that privileges one set of classroom methods over another. If the teacher can see the classroom itself, and the class itself, as malleable structures, something that came to be in response to historical requirements and can therefore be altered in response to new historical requirements, much of the confusion about how networked computers should be placed and used can be avoided.

A class is a group of students who gather to receive instruction. It is, to a large extent, a product of the sudden increase in mass instruction in the early 1800s, a technical accommodation to large numbers of students from the rising middle class who suddenly wanted the kind of instruction previously available only to those wealthy enough to afford private tutors. So what had previously been a fairly Socratic form of personal instruction became, because of social exigencies, either lectures to numbers of students or rote recitations. Discipline, never that much of a problem in tutorial situations, became paramount, and classroom decorum and instructor authority assumed a new importance. Students came together in a single place at a specific time because that was the only way to come under the authority of the instructor, and what was conducted in such classes was a kind of transference of ideas and information from the master to the students. That kind of instruction could not have been done in any other way.

The modern writing classroom, one presumes, should be less oriented to lecture and rote recitation and more oriented to the social dynamic of group discussion and question and answer and peer modeling and so forth. "In-class essays" and other forms of individual work are rightly judged perversions, to one degree or another, of what class time should be spent at. Often such in-class individual work seems necessary because of a presumed modern inability of the instructor to force students to work competently on their own. But class time should be spent doing something social, something that requires the participation of the group.

I mention all this to caution the director of a computer-based facility against promoting computer classrooms as "writing labs" or "practice labs" in which writing classes will be spending much classroom time. Most instructors will accordingly see the computers not as adding value to their instruction, but as something that takes away from intuitively valuable class time. If computers are conceived as simply writing machines or drill machines, having students write or drill during class can be interpreted as a squandering of precious class time.

When computers are used as collaborative devices, however, a strong claim can be made that class time is inherently social and that the collaborative activities conducted require meeting in a single place at a set time.

Students using computers with a network pedagogy are not operating in their own intellectual space exclusively, but are having to anticipate and conform to the expectations of peer readers who are reading their text almost immediately. Instructors still experience considerable dislocation, however, since the networked computer-based classroom is powerfully student-centered and becomes an eye-opener even to those who previously considered themselves student-centered instructors.

Class interaction in a networked classroom employing a network pedagogy takes place largely in a "virtual reality" defined by the network file server. However the computers are placed, the uninformed observer will see nothing more than students typing at keyboards (often furiously) and staring into monitors. The informed observer, however, will "see" a number of messages and file transfers occurring continually among the students, a great amount of text written, sent, and read across a multiplicity of classroom virtual, or invisible, channels.

PHYSICAL LAYOUT OF THE NETWORKED WRITING CLASSROOM

Even though, in a networked classroom, the student interaction is largely virtual and occurs across the wires in the virtual space provided by the file server, there are some less pedagogical and more physical reasons why computers should be placed in one arrangement or another. In almost all the cases I have observed, the computer-based classroom has been built "from the room in." Almost always in English departments, out of administrative necessity, rooms never intended for computers are assigned to be computer-based classrooms, and the placement of the computers becomes based more on the nature of the furniture acquired and where the wall plugs are located than on concerns more properly arising out of the nature of computer-based instruction.

The major physical difficulty of any computer-based classroom is what to do with the wires. In a computer-based writing classroom that is networked, there is yet another set of wires, and this set must connect all the computers in the room. The room's electrical circuitry must be inspected by a responsible electrician who can verify that the computers will not continually blow circuit breakers. All wiring between the wall sockets and the computers themselves should be of the proper size and kept off the floor in a professionally responsible fashion. Heartbreak occurs when a student accidentally kicks a cable and brings down six computers, thereby losing an hour's work for six students.

All the data cables should be secured in a reasonable manner and continually checked for crimping and cramping. Wires that are bundled with tape can eventually be smashed between the edges of tables or the edge of a table and a wall and, as computers are shifted with normal use, drag upon data plugs and sockets. This causes bent connector pins and considerable headache and some cost. I would suggest that wood spacers be used when utility tables are located close together with wires dropping down between them. These are two pieces of board nailed in the shape of a *T* and slipped between tables to make sure the table edges are not forced together, cramping the wires. For the usual ad hoc arrangements forced upon English departments, I would recommend that the wires and cables be secured to the utility tables or furniture by standard cable brackets that can be purchased in any hardware store. Any securing of wires in this fashion, however, should be done with the certain knowledge that it is temporary. Just as with the technology and the pedagogy itself, the ways in which these classrooms are set up will change with experience, and it would not behoove a facility director to secure either computers or wires too permanently.

In my experience, the best and least-obtrusive network wiring is Ethernet thinwire, though the cost of Ethernet cards for each computer may be prohibitive for some facilities (currently, 1991, about four hundred dollars per card). Other kinds of wiring can be just as effective. Macintosh computers can be networked with their slower but still usable built-in LocalTalk connectors and wiring for about forty dollars per computer. Ethernet connections throughout a classroom, a building, and a campus can provide a number of instructional uses that are not always apparent at the outset of a computer-based writing facility. I believe that in just a few years there will be demonstrated extraordinary advantages to having all microcomputers and mainframes in an institutional setting able to exchange files and electronic mail.

The major concern with wiring, of course, is that it not cross the floor in an area open to any foot or wheel traffic, for all sorts of obvious technical and safety reasons. This means that a facility director must do one of three things: (1) pattern workstation tables in such a way that cables can reach the walls without having to cross open spaces, (2) run conduit poles to the ceiling so that cables can be run there, or (3) drill holes in the floor so that cables can be run beneath. I have seen all three options and personally believe that the second is unsightly and the third is expensive and restrictive. Raised temporary cable conduits (plastic or rubber) can also be run across the floor, but they are aesthetically unappealing and not at all secure.

If the director chooses the first option, patterning workstation tables in such a way that cables can reach the walls without having to cross open spaces, then workstation arrangement is obviously restricted. The two patterns I've seen that demonstrate a hidden wire arrangement I call the "periphery" pattern and the "row" pattern. The periphery pattern simply has workstation tables placed flush to the walls in a rectangle, the computer screens facing inward, and the students' backs to the center of the room. The row pattern extends parallel lines of tables out from the walls in a gridiron. This pattern can more closely approximate the look of a traditional classroom, with all the students facing one end of the room. Or, as in one of our computer-based classrooms at Texas Tech University, the tables can extend from the wall in double rows with pairs of computers back to back and pairs of students facing each other.

If the director chooses to run wires along the ceiling or under the floor, and the room has the floor space, then other arrangements are possible. In another computer-based classroom at Texas Tech, we have arranged computers in "islands" of two back-to-back utility tables, each holding three IBM PS/2 Model 25 computers and an Epson printer. Two students sit on one side of the island, and the third sits on the opposite side. While definitely providing a classroom look different from that of a traditional classroom, the island approach has been criticized by at least two Texas Tech instructors as being isolating. There is, according to Barb Rodman and Lady Brown, something facilitating in having students at workstations lined up in a row, with "row buddies" available up and down the line for quick consulting.

It is my personal belief that networked computer-based writing classrooms need not try for any special "look" or unusual station arrangement. Since the principal vehicle of student interaction will be the "virtual" communication possible over the network, the physical arrangement of computers is secondary (given, perhaps, the qualifications of the two instructors above, that a line of computers encourages students to glance at neighboring monitors and help with software functions). If the instruction emphasizes the proper assignments, the students will be doing very little face-to-face communication and a great deal of text communication through the network. The netware (network management software) that manages student interaction seems more important to me than the physical arrangement of the computers.

In terms of the room environment, however, I do believe that windows are important, and since computer security is always a concern, I would recommend that the computer classrooms be located above the first floor. The computer screen, in my estimation, is an involving object, even obsessive. In terms of student engagement in the tasks the instructor assigns, this is a good thing, but it seems necessary that a good amount of daylight and outside view be available to allow some variety. However, computer screens should be perpendicular to windows, so that students don't have bright sunlight directly behind them (to create screen glare) or in front of them (to compromise retina adjustment to a relatively darker screen). Rooms should have adequate air conditioning, especially if they are somewhat small, for both the comfort of the students and the longevity of the equipment. In the computer-based classrooms I have supervised in Texas, we have inevitably had to use fans during the summer months. Chalkboards create a particular kind of dust harmful to computers.

An important advantage to the periphery workstation arrangement is that when computers are placed with their backs against the walls and their monitors facing inward, quite often a space is left free in the center of the room into which supplementary tables and chairs can be placed. This allows students to turn easily from their screens to face into the center of the room for classroom activities not requiring the computer. Instructors who feel uneasy about using computers exclusively or who want to supplement computer-based instruction with face-to-face activity or lectures find this arrangement helpful, although many of the computer facilities I've visited don't have the necessary room. Then too, some facility directors like the periphery arrangement because the backs of the computers, with their ugly wire connections and card slots, are hidden from view. The periphery arrangement also allows instructors to stand in the middle of the room and tell simply by glancing about which students are encountering trouble entering the right program and bringing up the right screen. On the other hand, some instructors prefer the row arrangement because it comfortably duplicates the traditional classroom and provides them a sense of continuity with precomputer classrooms. This unfortunately tends to encourage such instructors to attempt to pull student attention from the monitors to themselves, standing as usual at the "head" of the class, and places the instructors in competition with their own equipment, a situation distressingly common.

In any case, I would not have the instructor challenge the inherent "decentering" workshop tendency of the computer-based classroom by having a single machine defined as the "teacher's computer," or if there were such a designated computer, I would not place it in any special location or on a raised platform or provide it any special monitoring capability. In the classrooms I supervise I strongly encourage the instructors to be up and about the room, working constantly one-on-one with the students as they seek to solve writing or critiquing problems.

If, as I have yet to find in an English department, the facility director is allowed to define the shape and size of the room and the character of the furniture, then I would recommend the following. An ideal computer-based classroom would be roughly twice the size of the normal classroom. The computers should be located in one half, and the other half should contain little more than a rug and a set of padded, movable chairs. In the computer half of the room, the computers themselves should be set in furniture that sinks the keyboards, boxes, and monitors in such a way that students can establish eye contact across a table simply by lifting their eyes from their monitors. Computers could be arranged in the computer half of the room in a periphery arrangement, in rows, or in islands, according to a vote of those instructors using the room. The noncomputer half of the classroom should be free of blackboards, projection equipment, or teacher's desk. Presumably, collaborative text activity would occur on the computer side of the classroom, and the face-to-face interaction that some feel so necessary would occur on the chair side of the classroom.

Some people believe computer projection equipment (which projects computer images onto a public screen) is important. Since I tend to deemphasize anything in a networked computer-based classroom that centers attention on authority, I feel projection equipment in a collaborative classroom to be of secondary importance, though convenient when showing outsiders the software or methods.

CLASSROOM BEHAVIORS ASSOCIATED WITH COMPUTER-BASED FACILITIES

One of the difficulties experienced by instructors moving from a traditional classroom into a computer-based classroom, even only on a part-time basis, is that classroom decorum changes. The classroom center shifts dramatically from the instructor to the student and the computer, from a central authority to task-driven writing. Even in classrooms using the row pattern of workstation placement, which can duplicate the seating arrangement in the traditional classroom, the instructor has a great deal of difficulty taking and holding the attention of the students. The computer monitors interfere with the students' vision, the whir of computer fans interferes with what the instructor is saying, and—probably most important—the compelling interactive nature of the computer makes the instructor a poor competitor for attention.

Those instructors who want to retain a measure of the usual classroom authority would be advised to use the periphery pattern, which allows students to turn completely from their computers to listen to the instructor. An instructor who wishes to address a class as a whole should ask the students to darken their screens or turn off their computers altogether. Otherwise, and this is inevitable, the instructor will begin to hear the stray keystroke and notice students' eyes turning back to their monitors, even in the midst of a fascinating lecture.

The computer-based classroom of whatever design practically forces new classroom behaviors on the instructor. The student who enters a classroom filled with computers realizes that something new is afoot. Once the student has assumed (however moderately) an active control over a computer, a return to the usual passivity of the traditional classroom is practically impossible. This is especially true if the computers are networked and the students are engaged in sending messages or academic text to each other. The instructor should recognize that the nature of the instructional activity has been changed and that he or she can be more effective in one-to-one discussion with specific students as the class progresses rather than in addressing the class as a whole.

In the more successful computer-based classes that I have observed, the students' classroom activity is task oriented. A task list or set of assignments has been prepared beforehand by the instructor and given to the students either in hard-copy form or on-line through the network. The students enter the room, turn on their computers, log on to the network (if necessary), and begin performing the classroom duties provided by the instructor. Instructions and any pedagogical "content" that might otherwise have been delivered orally to the class as a whole can be included in the assignment text. The instructor, therefore, is free throughout most of the class period to move from student to student, to solve writing and software problems, and to monitor individual progress either by reading student files and messages off the network or by simply reading electronic text over the student's shoulder.

A number of instructors feel uncomfortable handling the class this way, more like test proctors than teachers. Such instructors often feel that they have become superfluous, a mere supplement to a classroom dynamic that is proceeding largely without them. Casual observers see it the same way, often questioning whether the computers haven't "taken over" the instructors' work and reduced instruction to automated busywork.

The opposite is true. The skill needed to prepare and coordinate classroom tasks that will satisfy instructional goals while keeping students active is considerable. The successful instructor must know the equipment, the software, and the pedagogy with an operating thoroughness few traditional instructors have had to enlist in the preparation of lectures, classroom discussions, and writing assignments. Then too, considerable skill is required in knowing when and how to intervene as the individual student goes about completing writing tasks. The computer-based writing classroom is often seen by many as little more than a typing class, with the instructor roaming about the room chatting informally and unproductively with this student or that; in fact, the students in such a class are continually wrestling with writing or reading problems, and the instructor is continually intervening to resolve individual problems in such a way that the resolution will stick with the student long after the class or semester has ended.

THE ADVANTAGES OF COMPUTERS IN INSTRUCTION

The students in most traditional classrooms spend their time passively listening to lectures or to a few of their fellow classmates support a classroom discussion. Even when a classroom discussion or question-and-answer session reaches an unusual level of excitement, the majority of students are merely listening, and I would suspect from twenty years of experience that their "listening" is more demonstration than real. The hated "pop quiz" often reveals a depressing inability in most of the students to summarize discussions and lectures even immediately after the fact. I suspect that one reason why high school and college students exhibit such poor levels of learning even after many years in the classroom is that they are seldom engaged by what is going on: They attend class as generally pacific but uninvolved aliens.

Engagement by an individual, I believe, requires a measure of individual authority, a perceived ability to manage some elements of a situation. The computer can distribute that authority, for while instructors (at first anyway) often feel a diminishing of hands-on classroom authority in the computer-based classroom, the students feel just the opposite. The computer is not a television that one turns on, adjusts the volume on, and then sits back to contemplate. Nor is a computer a listening station in a language lab. The computer demands constant operating attention and management, even for the simplest word processing functions. Screens are scrolled by command, features invoked by command, words written, erased, or moved by command. The command nature of handwriting, while infinitely more complex than using keystrokes or a point-and-click mouse to manipulate software functions, is nevertheless invisible to students who have been handwriting nearly all their lives, just as language use itself is largely invisible to them. But the management of a computer is self-conscious, visible, initially frustrating, and eventually compelling. The student is making something happen again and again.

Just as important, the computer "exposes" or distributes student writing in various ways. Text is clearly visible on a computer screen as the student is writing, which allows teachers to observe the writing process from a moderate distance and other students to collaborate on a piece of text. Two or three students sitting in front of a screen discussing the best wording in a paragraph is a simple but powerful means of conveying the idea that text is changeable, versions are negotiable, and writing decisions can be proposed and defended by openly stated criteria.

Even more powerful is the ability of the computer to duplicate or transfer student electronic text easily and cheaply. A three-page essay can be copied to another diskette in a second. A networked classroom can distribute twenty copies of that essay almost as quickly. In a noncomputer classroom, the distribution of a three-page essay among a class of twenty could involve considerable work with mimeo stencils or copy machines. Reading the essay aloud involves, again, the passive listener mentioned above and a considerable amount of classroom time. Putting the essay on overhead transparencies and lecturing or holding a classroom discussion involves, again, the student passivity described above.

Electronic text, either by copying from diskette to diskette or by posting to a network, can be distributed rapidly and for no cost (other than the cost of the original equipment) again and again, allowing for a text-sharing instruction impossible otherwise. Students can write, share that writing, and peer-critique that writing over and over in an electronic environment with little management and almost no cost. In a computer-based classroom, student text itself can become the medium of instruction in a way prohibitively difficult otherwise.

INSTRUCTIONAL PARTICULARS

Assuming that the classroom is networked and there exists some form of "shareware" that allows students to move and distribute their own writing easily, what happens in a typical class? In simplest terms, the student fulfills an "assignment cycle," part of which is performed out of class and part of which is performed in class. The typical assignment cycle I require includes (1) communal invention, (2) drafting, (3) peer critiquing, (4) revising, and, of course, (5) evaluation. If you substitute prewriting for communal invention and a teacher's draft review for peer critiquing, this cycle would be like the pattern of activity that many process-oriented instructors emphasize in a theme assignment: prewrite, write, revise, hand in.

The networked computer, however, encourages a much more powerful social element in the assignment cycle. Prewriting becomes communal invention, and revision becomes a function of peer review. The change is significant, for the preponderance of activity in a networked classroom shifts emphasis from writing as an isolated act to writing as a rhetorical and social act, and the shift powerfully supports progress in writing ability.

For instance, communal invention is performed by having an electronic classroom discussion through networked computers. Students type in comments that are displayed immediately in a text stream on every monitor in class. It is like contributing to a conversation and having instant access to the transcript at the same time. After twenty minutes or so, each student is given the electronic file of the discussion and told to review it and extract an issue that is important both to her and to the class at large (as revealed in the tenor of the discussion). From this file the student develops a topic and thesis. The assignment supports the concept that writing is inherently and uncompromisingly a social act and that ideas spring not from some deep interior well, but from our daily discourse.

The idea that revision should be a function of peer review is an equally powerful manifestation of writing perceived as a social act. Often students write for teachers in order to satisfy what they presume to be the criteria put forth in class by the teacher and textbooks. Usually these "criteria" are badly understood and awkwardly applied, almost universally resulting in the generic complaint, "I just don't know what she wants!" As instructors we know (or think we know) what good writing is; no matter how plainly we state it, however, the criteria for that good writing never seem to get through. We have tried a variety of ways to get the message across. One of the most effective has been draft comments, the process of having students turn in drafts for instructor review prior to final review or grading. But having to respond to student drafts places a heavy work burden on instructors, and the result is often that students "fix" only those things the instructor circles and do not commit themselves to the general review of a document that the word *revision* conjures up in the minds of writing instructors.

The networked writing classroom directs student writing to other students, not to the teacher. The ability of electronics to duplicate and transmit lots of writing among computers means that what Student A writes can be read almost instantly by Student B, by Student B and Student C, or by the class as a whole. One student, two students, or half a dozen can respond to that text almost immediately, in text, directly to the writer. The writer can, maybe ten minutes after "posting" a draft into a network computer directory or folder, receive three critiques discussing tone, organization, validity of the ideas, or any other aspect of the draft the instructor has emphasized for critical evaluation. Often these critiques are crude, off the mark, just plain wrong. The writer must decide if what his peers are saying is right or not, and whether change is in order. If the instructor says "Fix it," then the student simply fixes it. When a peer says "Fix it," the student must make a decision. The "fixing" process is no longer a half-conscious response to an adult command, but something that needs decision.

There is no doubt about it: Peer critiquing is messy and troublesome. Students balk at it; instructors have to run around the class answering all kinds of crazy questions. Of course, writing itself is a messy process not at all as neat as many teachers of writing would like to have it. The networked classroom recognizes the messy nature of writing and the writing decisions required of good writers and attempts to let individual students arrive at a personal understanding of writing problems and the problems associated with satisfying a readership.

The students in my networked classes, therefore, spend most of their time in electronic classroom discussion or in reading peer drafts and sending peer critiques. Outside of class they extract issues from the electronic discussions and write their drafts. I provide them "content" in the form of essays regarding developing and supporting theses, organization, the use of detail, and so forth, all provided in electronic form in their assignment tasks or in broadcast e-mail messages.

COSTS

It is not a cliché to say that costs are changing rapidly. They are, and always downward. Regardless of this, in order to put the classroom arrangements I have been discussing into a cost framework (however fragile), I will mention a few current (1991) estimated prices. I could purchase a functioning twenty-one-station networked classroom of Macintosh Classics running an AppleShare network and wired with Apple LocalTalk for about $25,000. My own classroom of twenty Mac IIcx computers with color monitors running an Appleshare network and wired with Ethernet thinwire cost about $110,000 in 1990. A network of twenty IBM PC/2 Model 25s running Novell Netware and Ethernet thinwire should cost about $35,000. A classroom of fifteen IBM PC/2 386 computers running Ethernet on IBM's LANkit network costs about $55,000. An adequate data projector, for throwing monitor images onto a public screen, costs about $1,200. Ethernet cards for networking with ethernet thinwire cost about $400 each for Apple or IBM-compatible, and a network using Ethernet requires a card for each computer. The cost of the wire itself and the T-connectors is negligible. I would estimate that the pedagogical software (word processing, E-mail, etc.) necessary to run an effective networked computer-based classroom would run from $5,000 to $10,000.

In reality, the mix of computing power and equipment cost is constantly in flux, and what can be done and how much it costs will change dramatically in a matter of a year or two. As in society itself, the technology in the classroom refuses to stand still for our comfort. This fact should not preclude some kind of action now, for if indeed prices drop tomorrow and capability increases, the same will undoubtedly be true the day after that, and the day after that. Somewhere along the line, those who recognize the need to get on the merry-go-round simply need to jump aboard and manage the changing nature of the technology from that point on. At some point a prudent conservatism becomes paralysis.

CONCLUSION

Computers have changed everything. Many people, perhaps most, don't like that idea. They don't want life-long suppositions threatened. But the electronic transmission of data is rapidly changing the idea of what information is, of what knowledge is, and what it is we are to teach in our classes. I submit that our principal duty as writing instructors is to allow our students to experience what it means to write well, and what it takes to write well. We've tried for 150 years to get that point across as an explanation, a set of guidelines, a set of abstract criteria for our students to follow. "Be concise." "Compound sentences require a coordinating conjunction." "Paragraphs should follow a pyramid structure."

Such an approach I call a "deductive" approach, a "top-down" description of what a writer "should do" to be a good writer. Better, I think, is an "inductive" approach. Let writers write to readers, a range of readers, and suffer their criticism. Let writers learn what to do and what not to do by experience, get "burned" for a blaring tone, get "praised" for the precise term. The instructor is vitally important in the process, because instruction becomes not simply a pronouncement of the right way to do things but the encouragement of an environment that allows and even privileges good writing processes. This environment must allow the easy distribution of student text and the notion that student writers have authority (some) over what and how and when they write. Networked computers support this environment in ways impossible otherwise.

But the virtual environment of networked computers must be supported by the physical environment of the computer-based classroom. Time and again I have had described to me the presumed "failures" of computers in classroom situations, which were actually, upon closer examination, the failures of people to manage the software, pedagogy, and instructional environment. Crimped wires and blown fuses and lectures shouted over tall monitors and whirring CPU fans have ruined many potentially good classes and soured many instructors and students on using computers. Instructors who plug computers into traditional classroom arrangements and attempt to maintain traditional classroom emphases in a computer-based classroom find themselves competing with, rather than complementing, their own equipment. To my mind, therefore, as I have indicated above, where computers go depends exclusively upon how they are to be used, and how they are to be used depends upon the instructors' understanding of how computers affect writing pedagogy.

3

Integrating Theory and Ergonomics: Designing the Electronic Writing Classroom

Gail E. Hawisher and Michael A. Pemberton

THE COMPUTER WRITING PROGRAM
AT THE UNIVERSITY OF ILLINOIS

The Department of English at the University of Illinois, Urbana-Champaign, was one of the first in the country to establish a computer-supported writing program, which it called "Computer Rhetoric." In 1984, Computer Rhetoric, the university's advanced first-year composition course, began in a networked environment and was taught to six sections of incoming students on IBM-XT computers. The philosophy underlying the program from its inception was that computers are most effective when instructors and students use them to write. Today the writing program is served by both IBM and Macintosh classrooms that house diverse writing courses. The Writers' Workshop, the writing tutorial facility, also makes computers available for consultations between students and teaching assistants. Because the university is fortunate to have many computing facilities in dormitories and other areas on campus, the writing program has always used its computer facilities as classrooms rather than as writing labs. For this reason, we have continuously tried to find a pedagogically sound class-

*room design that will best serve students and instructors. As this book
goes to press, and new IBMs for a hypermedia facility are about to
arrive, we are still searching for the best arrangement.*

15 August 1984—three years almost to the day since IBM introduced
its first personal computer, and the English department at the University of
Illinois was waiting for its shipment of IBM-XT personal computers. These
computers were to outfit two classrooms that would serve first-year composition classes, and none of us in the department had ever taught writing with
computers before. We had some ideas, though, about how they might be
used, and we also had some vague notions about how the computers should
be arranged for optimal teaching. We envisioned an arrangement in which
the students could see their instructors and one another, and in which their
instructors could in turn see them. A circle seemed like a good idea, but we
thought the wires coming from the back of the machines would somehow preclude that. What we didn't realize at the time, however, was that we would
have virtually no say in how the computers would be arranged, that the technical team from the computer services office would dictate the design of the
rooms. Thus, we ended up, finally, with a chain of computers lined up side
by side against four walls in each room, with students facing the screens and
sharing nothing but their backsides with the rest of the world.

15 August 1990—six years after Apple introduced its Macintosh, and
the English department at the University of Illinois was waiting for its shipment of Mac IIcx's. These computers were earmarked for a professional writing classroom that would serve a mixture of classes ranging from technical
writing and first-year composition to advanced expository writing and a de-
scriptive grammar course. Some of us had taught in electronic settings now
for six years, in different universities with different arrangements, and we had
definite ideas as to how the computer workstations should be organized in
classrooms. We wanted the computers to be arranged in clusters so that students might work more easily in groups, and we knew that this arrangement
was possible if we planned carefully for the cabling, extensions, network connections, and placement of file servers and printers. The technical team
from computer services was willing to work with our designs, and the recommendations we made were quickly put into effect. Thus, we now have a
new computer classroom with several "pods" of three Macintosh computers
grouped together, and most of the students are able to see one another and
the instructor most of the time.

These two scenarios suggest, if nothing else, that those of us working in computers and composition studies have become more sure of ourselves over the years—that today we tend to argue assertively for classroom designs that seem to serve our purposes best as instructors of writing. No longer do we feel inclined to let technology (or hardware specialists) drive our curricula, and no longer are we likely to assume that technological resources and pedagogical principles are mutually exclusive and independent. In general, we try to find ways to integrate our tools with our teaching, and, in the final analysis, we believe that our teaching philosophies are more important than the technology (Selfe, 1989).

Yet even today many of us working in these environments do not always have the opportunity to implement innovative, pedagogically driven designs in our computer classrooms. Often our computers, after being delayed for some reason, finally arrive for installation unexpectedly, forcing us to compromise and give up some of our ideas for sound pedagogical design. And even when we are able to arrange the electronic classroom as we wish, it may not work out quite as we expect. In the second scenario above, for example, we didn't realize that the two-page monitors would hide a short person so that he or she must peer around the screen to see other classmates or else choose to sit at another computer. Although we're not sure how we might have circumvented this problem, the final arrangement is not exactly what we desired.

Despite our best efforts to arrange the classroom into effective learning spaces, we failed to achieve the intended outcome regardless of the considerable planning we brought to the task. In some of our more lighthearted moments, we are able to see these difficulties as proof of one of Murphy's corollaries: Every solution merely masks a new, unforeseen problem. But more seriously, we believe these difficulties offer further evidence that we need to articulate the issues that are at stake in designing electronic writing classes and to decide what features of design create the kinds of arrangement that are conducive to learning. And finally, we must ask the difficult question: As we move increasingly to a time when text exists more frequently in electronic than in print form, does classroom arrangement ultimately matter?

In an effort to define the issues surrounding electronic classroom design and to identify some of the questions worth asking, we contacted members of the editorial board of *Computers and Composition* and asked them to complete an open-ended survey concerning the design of their electronic writing classrooms. We also asked them to distribute the survey to colleagues, from their own as well as other institutions, who were working in computer-intensive writing classes, so that our sample would include other knowledgeable computer-using instructors. We wanted to know what factors they thought important in design, what compromises they made and why, and what their ideal classroom might look like if they didn't have to deal with the sorts of constraints that inevitably seem to thwart their best efforts. We also wanted them to describe the worst of the classrooms they had taught in, thinking that this might help us determine, by default, the features that they prized. As we discovered, there is some consensus among computer and composition specialists about classroom ergonomics, but certainly no uniformity in their opinions.

Members of the editorial board of *Computers and Composition* seemed good candidates for our questions, since the policy of this journal has been to appoint to the board those scholars and teachers who have a great deal of experience working in electronic environments. With few exceptions, board members and their designates have been teaching writing in electronic class-rooms for five years or longer, and many of them have also designed their departments' computer facilities. We believe that this group of scholars and teachers represents as concentrated a nucleus of computer expertise in writing classes as exists in the United States today. Although we make no claims that our survey is in any way statistically valid, we do think that the respondents' answers are representative of the problems and questions we face today in working in electronic environments. Over twenty of the board members and their designates returned questionnaires, and all are currently writing instructors at community colleges or four-year institutions, representing a broad cross-section of such institutions throughout the country.

From their completed questionnaires and from articles and texts that we've read highlighting classroom design, we have been able to infer several different perspectives that seem to grow out of divergent views on a number of issues germane to the arrangement of space within electronic writing class-rooms. The issues we will focus on in this essay are (1) public versus private spaces, and (2) the roles of the instructor and students.

PUBLIC VERSUS PRIVATE SPACES

Writing as a communal versus an individual activity is a crucial issue to resolve when structuring writing activities in any writing classroom, but it becomes even more important in a classroom that is at once equipment ori-ented and writing oriented. Computers, as we all know, demand attention when they are turned on, and sometimes it takes an act of will (or coercion on the part of the instructor) to get students to turn away from them. For this reason, they can foster individual, solitary activities and inhibit group inter-actions unless the students are using software that is specifically designed to get them to work together. Even so, writing instructors in electronic class-rooms, regardless of their pedagogical philosophies and theoretical perspec-tives, would argue that it is important to provide both private and public spaces for working writers.

Expressivists would tend to privilege personal discovery and self-expression, activities that require the private activities of reflection and introspection, but they would also maintain that ideas are frequently gener-ated, and new insights realized, by bouncing thoughts off others in communal activities. Cognitivists would stress the problem-solving nature of writing ac-tivities and the periods of sustained attentional focus that individual writers require to solve them. But by the same token, they would also recognize that individual writers are not likely to have a full range of strategies appropriate to solve all writing problems and would, therefore, find valuable the oppor-tunity to exchange views with other writers. Social constructionists would stress the communal and collaborative aspects of writing and the need to es-tablish a clear sense of audience and discourse community, but they would also realize that no writing is entirely collaborative. At some point, individ-ual writers must produce individual pieces of text, and private spaces where this writing can be produced would, accordingly, be a necessity.

This conflict between the need to provide public access and private space to writers we found to be one of the most perplexing problems facing instructors designing electronic classrooms. Virtually all of our respondents commented on the need to foster group activities, but they had diverse opin-ions— often directly contradictory—about how best to achieve this commu-nity. The arrangement and placement of computer terminals were deemed crucial to the formation of the productive, mutually supportive social milieu that teachers wished to establish in the classroom, but which arrangement seems best to achieve such an environment remains open to serious debate.

With a few notable exceptions, the two classroom designs most fre-quently argued for are the "perimeter" design, with students and computers lined up against the walls of the classroom, and the "pod" design, with stu-dents clustered together in communal work spaces of three or four computers. Interesting variations on each type of arrangement were cited by our respon-dents, and proponents of one model tended to be especially good at pointing out the weaknesses of the other.

Those arguing in favor of the perimeter model point out the ease with which students (and instructors) can move around in the wide open space in the center of the classroom, facilitating group discussions and the sharing of on-screen texts. Emily Jessup (University of Michigan, Ann Arbor) refers, for example, to "the ability to have discussions/eye contact" within such a room arrangement, a point also noted by Diane Thompson (Northern Virginia

Community College), who says, "If computers are on [the] periphery, then students can: a) work in groups at a single computer, [and] b) turn to the center and function as a talking, hearing, interacting class." Catherine Smith and Don Wagner (Syracuse University), in fact, like the perimeter design best of all possible arrangements: "It's easy . . . to navigate in and adjust student arrangement for various instructional media especially for projections and computer-mediated presentations. Also, when team-teaching (two classes can easily pair up on machines), the perimeter model becomes flexible." Several respondents touched on the importance of such flexibility in the classroom, pointing out the need for movable/rolling chairs that allow students to congregate at a few terminals or turn their attention to the center of the room for whole-class discussions. Because of the flexibility this model provides, many of our respondents found that it allowed the opportunity for both private space and public forums, thereby meeting the changing needs of their students at different points in the writing process.

A number of other instructors, however, dispute the purported strengths of the perimeter model, pointing out—ironically—its inflexibility. Ron Fortune (Illinois State University) liked the perimeter model least of all, "because students faced into the walls, which made things difficult when they were not working on computers and we were trying to discuss something or trying to work in small groups." Eileen Schwartz (Purdue University, Calumet) concurs with this opinion, noting that, in the perimeter model, "students . . . can communicate only with those seated next to them," a point also mentioned by Cynthia Cochran (University of Illinois, Urbana-Champaign). We suspect, however, that this latter phenomenon is merely an artifact of convenience, not a necessity determined by the room design. With the proper encouragement and sufficiently mobile chairs, students could move easily to a station across the room and confer with another student there. Besides, regardless of the room arrangement, students will always feel inclined to confer with their closest neighbor(s).

On the other hand, a good many of the instructors we surveyed argued, often quite strongly, for the pod design in their electronic classrooms, though they frequently noted that they were often unable to implement these designs due to factors outside their control. Among the proponents of the pod model was Doug Hesse (Illinois State University), who prefers a room arrangement of "star-shaped" clusters, which "foster interaction and naturally break into groups for peer work." Emily Jessup, too, refers to clusters as her ideal arrangement, particularly because they "facilitate group work, but retain the possibility for easy discussion," and Lisa Bayer (Southern Illinois University) similarly believes that clusters "would encourage small group interaction and allow the instructor to move among the students more easily." Most of these

clustered classrooms also provide a number of open tables, without computers, that can be used for whole-class work, small-group discussions away from
terminals, or just private space where a writer can "spread out" and work
with reference materials and hard copy. By providing this sort of alternative
space in addition to the clustered sets of terminals, instructors feel that they
meet the varying demands of their students and the writing act.

Alternatively, some of our respondents felt the need to point out the
problems they either encountered or foresaw with a podlike room arrangement, most often touching on the issue of "sightlines" in the classroom.
When one places computers into formations that encourage inclusion and
small-group interaction, one invariably engages in an act of exclusion as
well. For all those within the group, there must be those outside the group.
Ron Fortune points this out in his remark that even though he preferred to
arrange his classroom terminals in clusters, "even this arrangement proved
awkward at times. When the class as a whole was discussing something,
students in different parts of the room could not always make eye contact
very readily."

The fault, of course, lies in the dominating physical presence of the
computer and its monitor on the table, taking up valuable space and block-
ing other students (and often the instructor) from view. If this were our only
concern, we could solve the problem with a focus on furniture and an outlay
of funds. Trent Batson (Gallaudet Univeristy) argues that, "ideally, one
could recess the monitor into the desk so that sight lines are clear and face-
to-face discussion is easy. Some standard computer desks now come with the
monitor recessed behind a glass plate so that the desktop is flat and usable for
regular work. The custom furniture at the University of Arizona allows students to lower their monitors into the desk and then cover them." But is this
a practice we wish to encourage or facilitate? On the one hand, we can look
at the CPU-monitor barrier in a negative light: It inhibits free interaction
among students, hinders whole-class discussions, and presents visibility problems for instructors. But on the other hand, we can look at the barrier this
places between the student and others in a positive light: The barrier helps
to create a private space for writers, isolating them from distractions and allowing them to focus on their texts. As always, the resolution of this issue
should be a matter for the individual instructor to decide based on his or her
pedagogical philosophy and theoretical perspectives on how students best
learn to write.

Yet despite our best intentions, as instructors we are not always able to
implement the theory-driven decisions we make; all too often, despite our
assertiveness about what we consider to be the "best" room design, we find
ourselves at the mercy of budgets, electrical regulations, and inherited room

layouts. Ellen Barton (Wayne State University), who works in a room with terminals in facing rows, refers several times to the electricity requirements that mandated such an arrangement as well as the monetary factors that prohibit making any major changes. Michael Spitzer (New York Institute of Technology) also refers to electrical and network wiring demands that necessitated the arrangement of computers in front-facing rows in his classroom. (Front-facing rows had the greatest consensus for "least liked" arrangement of computers in a classroom, yet many of our respondents indicated that this was the arrangement they were currently using or had used at some other institution.) Commentary by Linda Stine (Lincoln University, Pennsylvania) on her own classroom arrangement makes, we think, a significant point about room arrangement and the ergonomic/pedagogical issue of public and private space. Her classroom "was set up as a lab, with no input from teachers who would eventually use it as a classroom. The room divider was put in, originally, so that students could be working in the lab and staff training on mainframe terminals could be going on at the same time on the other side. In other words, efficiency, not pedagogy, was the driving force behind lab design." Other respondents refer obliquely to these matters as well. In talking about the perimeter design of his computer classroom, Steve Bernhardt (New Mexico State University) refers to "available space" and the "economy of the periphery" as two of the most important factors that influenced arrangement, and his remarks were by no means unusual.

We would argue, therefore, that the evidence presented here requires us to issue a word or two of caution: On the one hand, we all need to beware of retroactive rationalization, of justifying the value of a particular classroom design merely because it is the one we happen to be "stuck" with; yet, on the other hand, we should not allow ourselves to be too-hastily convinced that alternative classroom designs are necessarily superior to the ones we are currently using. We need to reflect seriously on our roles as instructors, and the students' roles as writers and learners, and decide whether the use of computers tends to change the relationships among students and among students and instructors. And, furthermore, if changes do indeed occur, we need to examine the various classroom arrangements in light of these changes and decide how each may or may not support the kinds of changes we like to see occurring.

THE ROLES OF INSTRUCTORS AND STUDENTS

Some research suggests that computers can be used as catalysts to de-center authority in writing classes and to encourage students to assume active, thinking roles as writers (Cooper and Selfe, 1990). When students participate in computer conferences, for example, they tend to respond to their fellow classmates frequently, and the instructor often becomes one participant among many in the writing class (Batson, 1988; Barker and Kemp, 1990; Hawisher, 1992). This kind of environment can, the argument goes, be used to encourage students to share their writing with peers and to respond to peers with greater frequency and confidence in their own abilities as student writers (Hawisher, 1988).

Although much of the recent research regarding the decentering of authority in electronic classrooms has focused on networks or the computer conference as the catalysts that may bring about more active participation on the part of students, others have made similar observations of stand-alone computer environments (Hawisher and Selfe, 1991). In such settings, instructors often remark on new cooperation in writing classes where teaching and learning are shared by both instructors and students and where conventional notions of the instructor as dispenser of knowledge have been altered. Indeed these observations from both networked and stand-alone computer environments largely reflect a shift in theoretical perspectives in which writing instructors have come to understand knowledge as made, not found, and as the product of conversations and reading among students and among students and instructors (Bazerman, 1980). As these changes in the thinking and behavior of writing instructors and students become prevalent in electronic writing classes, however, it becomes incumbent upon us to consider them in light of electronic classroom design. One might argue, for example, that the placement of computers, students, and instructor is moot; if one intends to conduct a writing class in which authority is distributed among students and instructor, classroom design, electronic or otherwise, will not prevent the instructor from doing so.

Many of the issues relating to instructor and student roles in the electronic writing class hinge on where the instructor is situated in the classroom. The place that the instructor chooses to occupy ultimately makes a statement about how he or she perceives not only what it means to teach in a writing class but also what it means to be a student. In conventional classrooms, expressivists, seeing their role as one in which they nurture students and encourage them to find meaning within themselves and to be able to express this meaning to others with an authentic voice, might arrange desks in a circle, with their desk unmarked. Students, along with the instructor, who would also participate in the act of writing, would share their ideas with the instructor and their fellow classmates in like fashion, with little difference expected in the behavior of instructor and student. Although cognitivists and social constructionists might construe their instructor roles in slightly different terms—the cognitivist as one who helps students define relevant problems and possible solutions, and the social constructionist as one who provides an appropriate social milieu for meaningful discussion—each might opt for a similar arrangement in a conventional classroom, at least insofar as the marking of a desk is concerned. Since these instructors more often than not understand their roles as facilitators rather than as authorities, an unmarked space for the instructor is appropriate, in that it reflects a pedagogical and theoretical perspective that values student talk at least as much as instructor talk. Thus the unmarked desk, arranged with others in a circle or perhaps in clusters or pairs, reflects a view that privileges both student and teacher contributions, making little distinction among them. Interestingly, however, unless computers are recessed into desks, a "discussion circle" is difficult in an electronic classroom (students can't see over the computers) and often defeats the openness that the circle invites in a conventional classroom.

In order to better understand how writing instructors understand their roles and "situatedness," within the electronic classroom, we turn again to the surveys considered earlier. Several respondents seemed to indicate an instructor station, not because it was desirable, but because it was already set up in the electronic classroom they were using; others clearly wanted an instructor station marked. Classrooms normally have a set space defined, usually in front, for the teacher, and it is from this space that instructors carry out their role as teacher and class manager. Tradition and convention have more effect on our behavior as writing instructors than we are sometimes willing to admit, and room arrangement in electronic settings is not exempt from convention. A few of the instructors wanted an instructor station for specific reasons: Some wanted students to be able to come to their station for conferences while others in the class worked on their writing independently, and some wanted access to specialized software that wasn't available at other computers. There were, however, also one or two respondents who found the placement of a specific instructor station in conflict with their goals as teachers. And still others believed that their original instructor arrangement was an appropriate one that had, for one reason or another, changed over the years.

Joy Peyton (Center for Applied Linguistics), who has worked with the ENFI (Electronic Networks for Interaction) project at Gallaudet University and who studies ENFI realizations at other sites, makes some important observations regarding classroom arrangement and instructor role. Both she and Trent Batson (Gallaudet University) note that at Gallaudet they arranged the computers in a circle with the instructor a part of the circle so that they might "create a feeling of community." As a result of expanding the number of computers, however, and because of the general lack of space, they were soon forced to have circles within circles, with the teacher now strategically placed in front in an outer circle. Peyton notes that another ENFI site on campus that was not set up in such a way as to foster community has become "more community-oriented than the computers in a circle facing each other." In this second classroom where computers are arranged peripherally along the walls, teachers and students are able to use the open space in the middle of the room for small discussion groups in ways that are not possible with the current circle arrangement. Batson readily admits that the first classroom has outgrown the advantages of the original circle. He does, however, make the important point that class interactions are changing and will continue to do so. In his opinion, "Alternating between computer work and face-to-face communication will become a norm in writing classrooms, so that having the computers facing the wall, turned away from a central point, although providing efficient use of space, will prove cumbersome." The peripheral arrangement is not always conducive to the kind of face-to-face discussion Batson envisions.

Interestingly, however, in an ENFI classroom where the bulk of communication takes place over a synchronous network, regardless of where his or her place may be in the physical space of the room, the instructor is always one of many in networked discussion. Research suggests that networked discussion is less likely to be dominated by any one person than is the case in face-to-face discussion (Chesebro and Bonsall, 1989; Feenberg, 1987; Hiltz and Turoff, 1978), and this of course is the case in the ENFI classroom. Since a less prominent position for an instructor within a classroom, then, is often reflected in networked discussion, featuring the instructor prominently within the physical space of a classroom may nullify some of the possible benefits that networked discussion can encourage.

Peyton believes that the majority of instructors working within ENFI environments try to make their presence less prominent in ENFI classrooms. She writes that from her research (Bruce and Peyton, in press), she has concluded that "all of the [ENFI] sites are interested in minimizing the visibility of the teacher, making the teacher less a leader and more part of the community, so in all cases but NYIT [New York Institute of Technology] the teacher station is just one among many and does not stand out. For some reason, at NYIT the teacher station is on a raised platform at the front of the room." According to Peyton, most of the ENFI arrangements reinforce the idea that instructors are situated in a physical and pedagogical environment in which they learn with and from their students. We see the search for the "invisibility" of the instructor as part of a theoretical perspective and philosophy of teaching that is in keeping with current social-constructivist views on learning and knowledge making, one that many of the respondents adhere to and that is reflected in their responses. Yet it's interesting that despite this predominant theoretical orientation the physical environment may be arranged in such a way as to mirror tradition and convention within American classroom settings, with the instructor situated on a platform with desks bolted (or wired, as is the case with computers) in place below. Ideas for what's pedagogically important don't always conform to the physical arrangement of the furniture and hardware. For whatever reason, as Peyton notes, the physical ENFI configuration may get played out in instructors' electronic classrooms differently from what one might expect. We imagine that the reason for the raised platform in the NYIT classroom is not unlike the reason Eileen Schwartz (Purdue University at Calumet) presents for her preferred placement of the instructor station. She writes that ideally she'd like a classroom in which "the teacher station stands alone at a spot where the teacher can have an unobstructed view of all students while seated at the console." In this way the instructor is able to make eye contact with all the students and is anything but invisible. At other institutions, however, instructors planned for invisibility.

At the University of Massachusetts, Amherst, those who designed the computer-equipped classroom tried, also for pedagogical reasons, to avoid any arrangement that featured the instructor at a separate and specified workstation. Charles Moran (University of Massachusetts, Amherst) stipulates that a primary consideration at his institution was the elimination of a teacher's station; he suggests that for them this was a design feature that they could control, and a significant one at that. The pedagogical intent was to make the instructor no more prominent than the students, to avoid what Barker and Kemp (1990) have called the "proscenium classroom," in which teachers talk in front of the classroom and students listen. In this instance, then, the physical arrangement of the classroom and the position that the instructor occupies (any computer in the class that's available) reflects the view that the instructor is one writer among many within the electronic environment, a view in keeping with both social and expressive views of writing. When we consider the placement of the instructor overall, however, it would seem that the physical location varies tremendously within electronic environments and often, for whatever reason, may or may not be in keeping with the pedagogical philosophy of the institution's writing program.

Another consideration involving the role of the instructor but also relating to the role of students is the issue of "mobility," that is, the ease with which the instructor and students can move around the classroom for various purposes. Two predominant views seem to prevail among the respondents, with the first relating primarily to the instructor and the second to the students. Each view, moreover, seems to regard the role of instructors and students in a slightly different light. Instructor mobility, for example, allows the teacher to be at the student's side at a moment's notice to help with various problems. Steve Bernhardt (New Mexico State University) writes that one reason he doesn't like computers arranged in rows is that it inhibits his movement and that he "can't see the screens or get attention." "Being able to see the monitors" is an important consideration he takes into account in setting up a computer classroom. In a more extended article on the subject of classroom design, Bernhardt (1989) writes that "the major drawback to [computers arranged in rows] is that it places the computer between the teacher and the student" (99). He goes on to state that "this creates a physical barrier, one that can be quite formidable with large computers with large CPU's, or monitors" (99). Certain arrangements, in other words, hinder the instructor's mobility, as well as sight lines with students, and prevent the instructor from having ready access to the students and their screens. Ed Kline (University of Notre Dame) also arranged the new facility at Notre Dame in such a way that the teacher can move around easily and thus "see what is on the student's screen." Eileen Schwartz (Purdue/Calumet) similarly notes that an arrangement should provide "aisle space . . . generous enough for teachers to move freely between rows," reinforcing this notion of the importance of mobility in facilitating the instructor role.

Other instructors were more concerned with the students' ability to move easily around the classroom. Ron Fortune (Illinois State University) notes that he has "tried to make the students as mobile as possible within the space constraints imposed by the room," since in his view good "instruction often depends of the mobility of students (both visually and physically)." Christine Neuwirth (Carnegie Mellon University) argues for the importance of students' being able to "form into a circle for a discussion or into rows for viewing an overhead presentation." Along with several other respondents, she cites chairs on casters as being one way to facilitate this increased student mobility. In these instances instructors are arguing for the importance of mobility for face-to-face group work and discussion, especially among students. Other respondents wanted mobility for everyone: Stating it simply, Dawn and Raymond Rodrigues (Colorado State University) argue that they arranged their perimeter classroom as they did because they "wanted ways around the classroom." In other words, both students and teachers need to be able to get up and confer with others easily. However, at other institutions, different decisions have been made with an eye toward facilitating networked rather than face-to-face discussion. At the University of Minnesota at Minneapolis, Terence Collins and his colleagues decided that for networked discussions, mobility and open sight lines distracted students and impaired productive on-line group work. Thus he and his colleagues had carrels constructed to shelter the students and reduce mobility, along with face-to-face, student-to-student interaction, so that written communication would take precedence over oral discussion.

We believe that at some point the issues regarding mobility actually break down along the lines of whether instructors desire a student-centered or a teacher-centered classroom. Despite the teacher-centered classroom's being out of favor within the profession (Lloyd-Jones and Lunsford, 1989), both types of classrooms at different times and for different purposes offer distinct advantages to students and instructors. There are times when it is important that the instructor make eye contact with students in an effort to understand how much the student might be understanding or how satisfied or frustrated the student might be with a particular software program or piece of writing. We suspect from the surveys that, although instructors theoretically privilege one type of classroom over the other, in practice they go back and forth between the two modes, depending not only upon their goals for the particular day but also upon the type of facility in which they are teaching. As Charles Moran (University of Massachusetts, Amherst) notes, "The room's architecture carries some force, limiting what you can and cannot do in a classroom—just as the proscenium classroom facilitates some behavior and limits others." Whether or not the design of the classroom facilitates eye contact, communication, and ease of movement about the class clearly influences instructional approaches. And, more importantly, these factors influence the degree of success an instructor might have with a particular approach in teaching writing.

SOME FINAL COMMENTS

What seems clear, then, is that the issue of ergonomics in a computer classroom will remain a perplexing one for some time to come. The wiring requirements and sheer physical bulk of computers that are currently utilized in electronic classrooms, most often Macintoshes and IBM PCs, impose restrictions on what it is possible to do with them, where it is possible to put them, and how it is possible to arrange them. The difficulty of arrangement is further exacerbated by conflicting theoretical beliefs about how writing classes should be taught and the fluctuating need for public and private spaces as writers compose. What works well at some times for some pedagogies and some writing needs does not work well for other pedagogies and other writing needs at other times. Given the present state of technology and the differing views among instructors about what is most important in writing instruction, the notion of a "best" ergonomic design for an electronic classroom must, apparently, remain an elusive ideal.

Nevertheless, a few relatively minor technological advances could help to bring this ideal closer to reality. Central to many of our respondents' comments was the need for flexibility in the electronic classroom, the ability for students and instructors to shift position, focus, and location as classroom activities required. This flexibility is largely hampered by three factors: the need to secure computers to tables for theft prevention, the need to hard-wire computers into LAN connections, and the ponderous mass of the computers themselves. Most, if not all, of these problems, we feel, could be ameliorated by the widespread use of laptops in the classroom as well as some minor advancements in laptop technology. Laptops eliminate the bulkiness problem; they can be picked up and taken anywhere—inside the classroom or out. They are, accordingly, perfectly suited for maintaining both private and public spaces as writing situations require. Their small size also resolves the problem of maintaining sight lines in class. They are easy to see over on tabletops, and their LCD screens can be folded down flat if necessary. Eventually (we hope), the cost of laptop computers will decline far enough that it will be feasible for all students to own them individually. Once this occurs, we can require laptops for certain classes in much the same way that physics and chemistry classes require students to own hand calculators today. At that point, our security problem will disappear.

Connectivity is a more complex problem but not an insurmountable one. Hard-wired network connections to a fixed server could be installed in a classroom, with serial- or parallel-connection plugs available at several stations to hook into appropriate laptop ports. Assuming compatible computers and software, students should be able to plug into a network for communal computer activities and disconnect when they wish to work on their own. At some time in the future, in fact, it is possible to visualize "cellular computers" whose network connections are established via electromagnetic transmission and are free of the need for any hard-wire attachments at all.

And this leads us to our final point: Although we believe that classroom design today is an important factor to consider in designing electronic writing classes, we also believe that design is an issue that might become less important in the near future. A few years ago, for example, when University of Illinois students won an Apple competition, Project 2000 (Young et al., Academic Computing, 1988), which challenged students to envision how computer technology might be used in year 2000, their depiction of a Tablet computer seemed somewhat farfetched. The Tablet could be carried in one hand and used to connect students visually and aurally with their various classes on campus. In addition to being able to write their notes and papers on the Tablet computer, students could also attend classes through Tablet, with their written compositions, for example, being submitted and returned to them electronically. They would also hold individual conferences with their instructors through Tablet in much the same way that many writing instructors use E-mail connections today. The scenario University of Illinois students devised for Tablet seems only steps away from reality on many of today's campuses. At the University of Texas, students began to sense the impact of these new electronic connections after attending a writing class that is predominantly on-line. Jerome Bump (1990) notes that when queried as to room arrangement in computer writing environments, many of his students felt that "the arrangement of the room [had] very little to do with the class because there is no speaking or visual contact necessary" (63). Another more recent view takes the argument for a virtual classroom environment one step further. Charles Moran (1992), for example, argues that "brick and mortar classrooms" are expensive and that our students and budgets might best be served with electronic classrooms that are virtual— that is, that exist only in the memories of the computer. Staffing and maintaining a computer classroom that is used for only part of a day might not be the most efficient way to allocate important resources. Thus the physical arrangement of a writing class becomes increasingly less important as a greater number of electronic connections and options are made available to students and their instructors.

August 15, 1999, Another Scenario—two years after Apple-IBM introduced its cellular computer and the English Department at the University of Illinois is waiting for the new tablet-sized computers to arrive. These 16-ounce computers are to be distributed to students through their first-year composition classes. It has taken some time to work out the network architecture so that when students sign on, icons for their classes appear on their screens. By clicking on the appropriate icon, students receive a voice message from each instructor, apprising them of the first meeting for their various classes during the semester. August 15, 1999 also marks the English Department's first attempt to teach writing in a virtual environment where students will meet frequently with their classmates and instructors over a network, in addition to several face-to-face meetings. As we wait, we wonder whether we have scheduled our meetings appropriately and whether the hypertext databases we constructed will serve our students' writing as well as their print-based research has served them previously. We wonder whether we will be inundated with the students' e-mail messages and whether we will miss seeing them three times a week. We also wonder whether the network architecture will give the students the cross-disciplinary opportunities we planned for them—whether they will write easily about their reading in political science in their first-year rhetoric classes. Thus, the Department of English at the

University of Illinois begins its entrance into the twenty-first century with all the excitement and trepidation it experienced fifteen years earlier, when the personal computer first entered the university's first-year writing classes.

REFERENCES

Barker, Thomas T., and Fred O. Kemp. 1990. "Network Theory: A Postmodern Pedagogy for the Writing Classroom." In *Computers and Community*, edited by Carolyn Handa, 1–27. Portsmouth, N.H.: Boynton/Cook.

Batson, Trent W. 1988. "The ENFI Project: A Networked Classroom Approach to Writing Instruction." *Academic Computing.* 2 (February/March): 32–33, 55–56.

Bazerman, Charles. 1980. "A Relationship between Reading and Writing: The Conversational Model." *College English* 41 (February): 656–61.

Bernhardt, Stephen A. 1989. "Designing a Microcomputer Classroom for Teaching Composition." *Computers and Composition* 7:13–26.

Bruce, Bertram, and Joy Peyton. N.d. *A New Writing Environment and an Old Culture: A Situated Evaluation of Computer Networking to Teach Writing.* New York: Cambridge University Press. Forthcoming.

Bump, Jerome. 1990. "Radical Changes in Class Discussion Using Networked Computers." *Computers and the Humanities* 49:49–65.

Chesebro, James W., and Donald G. Bonsall. 1989. *Computer-mediated Communication: Human Relationships in a Computerized World.* Tuscaloosa: University of Alabama Press.

Cooper, Marilyn, and Cynthia L. Selfe. 1990. "Computer Conferences and Learning: Authority, Resistance, and Internally Persuasive Discourse." *College English* 52 (December): 847–69.

Eldred, Janet. 1989. "Computers, Composition Pedagogy, and the Social View." *Critical Perspectives on Computers and Composition Instruction,* edited by Gail E. Hawisher and Cynthia L. Selfe, 201–18. New York: Teachers College Press.

52   APPROACHES TO COMPUTER WRITING CLASSROOMS

Feenberg, Andrew. 1987. "Computer Conferencing and the Humanities." *Instructional Science* 16:169–86.

Hawisher, Gail E. 1992. "Electronic meetings of the minds: Research, Electronic Conferences, and Composition Studies." *Re-Imagining Computers and Composition: Teaching and Research in the Virtual Age,* 3dited by Gail E Hawisher and Paul LeBlanc, Portsmouth, NH: Boynton/Cook

Hawisher, Gail E. 1988. "Research Update: Writing and Word Processing." *Computers and Composition* 5 (April): 7–23.

Hawisher, Gail E., and Cynthia L. Selfe. 1991. "The Rhetoric of Technology and the Electronic Writing Class." *College Composition and Communication* 42 (February): 55–65.

Hiltz, Starr Roxanne, and Murray Turoff. 1978. *The Network Nation.* Reading, Mass.: Addison-Wesley.

Jennings, Edward M. 1987. "Paperless Writing: Boundary Conditions and Their Implications." In *Writing at the Century's End: Essays on Computer-Assisted Composition,* edited by Lisa Gerrard. New York: Random House.

Lloyd-Jones, Richard, and Andrea Lunsford. 1989. *The English Coalition Conference: Democracy through Language.* Urbana, Ill: National Council of Teachers of English.

Moran, Charles. 1992 "Computers and the Writing Classroom: A Look to the Future." In *Reimagining Computers and Composition Studies: Teaching and Research in the Virtual Age,* edited by Gail E. Hawisher and Paul LeBlanc. Portsmouth, N.H.: Boynton/Cook.

Selfe, Cynthia L. 1989. *Creating a Computer-supported Writing Facility: A Blueprint for Action.* Houghton, Mich.: Computers & Composition Press.

Young, Luke T., et al 1988. "Academic Computing in the Year 2000." *Academic Computing,* 2 (May/June): 8–12, 62–65.

4

I Sing the Body Electric: The Near-Literary Art of the Technological Deal

Deborah H. Holdstein

The writing program at Governors State University features courses in writing at the graduate and undergraduate levels, notably Advanced Writing, Rhetorical Theory and Practice, and the Seminar in Advanced Composition and Rhetorical/Critical Theory. The director also provides academic leadership for the competency examination in writing, required of all new students at GSU.

THE WRITING PROGRAM AT GOVERNERS STATE UNIVERSITY

Let us go then, you and I,
When the evening is spread out against the sky
Like a patient etherised upon a table;
. . .
Oh, do not ask, 'What is it?'
Let us go and make our visit.

(T. S. Eliot, "The Love Song of
J. Alfred Prufrock," 11. 1–3, 11–12)

My references to Whitman and Eliot suit the purposes of this essay far more appropriately than might seem immediately apparent. The poem's archaic use of "electric" is useful here: Whitman's "body electric" suggests an interconnectedness, the essentially collaborative nature of all things—no news to composition specialists who acknowledge the virtues of collaboration not only among our students but also among our colleagues. Eliot's "Prufrock," on the other hand, reveals the isolated modern, timid in the face of life, of all things. In issues related to computers and composition, both visions are true. And given the complex circumstances within writing programs and the larger, still more complex and political arena of the institutions within which they operate, both visions, Eliot's and Whitman's, also represent any conscientious writing specialist's psychic nod to Blake: that is, the "contrary states of the soul" one might feel while creating an appropriate climate for computers and writing. Indeed, armed with a solid theoretical foundation for their pedagogy, such teacher-scholar-administrators must often simultaneously cope with not only the philosophical leanings of Blake, Whitman, and Eliot's "Prufrock," but also, alas, acquire the negotiating skills befitting the likes of scholar-politician Benjamin Disraeli.

Recent presentations at the Conference on College Composition and Communication and elsewhere would seem to indicate an advanced, sophisticated sensibility among most composition specialists regarding computers—hypertext and its relationship to literary study, for instance, being among the topics of note. Yet my experience as a consultant to a variety of universities and colleges in the United States and Canada would indicate the opposite: Many colleagues, for good reasons, are only just getting started. My purpose in this essay, then, is multifold, but primarily this: not only to suggest questions that the composition-English faculty might ask among themselves before they begin, but also to suggest alliances they must forge so that the project—and the laboratory environment—will be as successful as possible while, perhaps most importantly, remaining faithful to the goals of a solid, theory-based composition program.

WHAT ARE THE EXISTING LAB'S STRENGTHS? WEAKNESSES?

I first came to Governors State University in 1985 to direct the writing program. At that time, we had one IBM-equipped lab and one Apple II lab; there was little interaction, if any, between the humanities program (and writing in particular) and the computer center. At that time, the dean of the College of Arts and Sciences was a chemist-turned-computer-expert, and his advice to the computer center staff to change over from an early version of Wordstar to the up-and-coming Microsoft Word was heeded without question.

I had no trouble scheduling computer time for my writing classes, and in fact my participation in computer center life was viewed with only mild curiosity—and mostly enthusiasm—by the computer center staff, which to this day has been most helpful. However, my experience at GSU provides the grist for my first assumption, one I've found to be the case at most of the institutions I have visited:

> *Assume that the arrangement, design, and features of a multi-use computer center will predate any composition-computer effort.

I've written elsewhere about the faculty training program I had implemented at GSU to help interested colleagues begin to work with computers in the writing program (Holdstein, 1989). Much of this work, however, demanded that I work with what ordinarily might be perceived as less-than-desirable conditions to meet my own expectations for the process-oriented writing curriculum.

One complaint, for instance, might be this: The IBM laboratory has too few computers.

The solution? Emphasize the collaborative work so appropriate to both the process approach to the teaching of writing and the use of computers within that teaching process; both are enhanced significantly with the use of computers—both in teacher training and in the composition classroom itself. To my mind, technological shortcomings serve only to reemphasize for our colleagues and our students the importance of knowing how to write with or without the terminal and the fact that the writer—not the computer—is empowered with the skills and knowledge it takes to master the writing process.

WHAT ARE THE NEEDS OF THE STUDENTS AND WRITING PROGRAM AT MY PARTICULAR INSTITUTION?

The last three words of this question are the most significant to keep in mind: What works at the University of Illinois, for instance, might not be appropriate for Triton College, and vice versa. While it certainly can be helpful to observe our colleagues at other institutions and to learn about the hardware, software, and teaching methods they use, what works elsewhere might not work in a school with a different mission or, for instance, a different and highly diverse student body.

At a small, private college in the Midwest that I visited recently, the faculty were, for the most part, traditional: good, solid teachers of writing with little or no interest in technology. My task involved suggesting that they evaluate themselves—the strengths and weaknesses of the writing program; the strengths and weaknesses of their centralized computer facilities (there was no hope here for a department-run lab); the strengths and weaknesses in their alliances across the college—their links with the dean of their college, the head of the computing center, the computing staff, and so on.

Such self-analysis proved essential at this institution, as it does at others: The first task was rather a basic one, involving the negotiation by the chair of the Department of English for class-by-class computer time. (Up to this point, the center allowed no class use, only drop-in time.) Contrast this with an English department in an institution known for engineering and with extensive, well-developed computer facilities: Here, the self-analysis went outside of the department and writing program themselves to include university-retained architects and room planners, the provost's office, and the development office, all of whom would, it appeared, formed an alliance to establish computer facilities within the English department proper. Such an opportunity for faculty in English/Writing Studies to link with supporters throughout the university to control and create their own computer environment is certainly desirable—ideal, in fact—but quite unusual. For better or worse, the former scenario remains the most prevalent.

Yet even for the latter, more empowered faculty, the difficulties of speaking across technological and disciplinary boundaries became apparent over, of all things, several computer cables, placed by the designers for the convenience of the technology but to the detriment of teaching in that particular room. Rather than allowing the instructor to become a facilitator in the classroom, moving around the room as needed, for instance, the misplaced cable would restrict the instructor's movement among the students at the terminals, relegating him or her to an arbitrary "front" of the classroom when more collaborative, authority-relinquishing teaching methods would be most appropriate.

Poverty of imagination and design in computer classrooms, however, can often become tacitly *de facto* modes of support in other areas of concern to those teaching composition and their administrators: In my meetings with English department faculty, the chair, and the director of writing, we together noted that smaller classroom spaces with fewer computers could assist in restricting the size of composition sections. Sneaky? Not really, when, in this time of burgeoning enrollments and restricted budgets, beleaguered

administrators attempt to make ends meet by overenrolling sections of composition, thus eliminating the need for additional faculty for additional sections. Since the plan to implement computers within the curriculum was
wholly collaborative, uniting the perspectives of graduate students, the department chair, and others, this farsighted group of people learned anew
what they had known before: the value of multiple perspectives and political
knowledge, wide-ranging views that could become useful at any time in the
process. And in fact, during my time on campus as consultant, we together
became aware that by designing with fewer computers in a particular room,
we would of necessity limit the shortsighted attempt at one administrative
level outside of the English department to enlarge over the desirable limit the
number of students in computer-based classes in composition. In this, writing
specialists learned yet another important lesson that transcends institutions:
the misperception on the part of those who do not teach writing that the
computer somehow makes larger classes acceptable, this based on the misapprehension that it's the computer, and not the writer herself, that ultimately
"takes the sweat" out of writing. Thus, collaborative alliances—whether at
the small liberal arts college or the technologically endowed, larger institution—prove essential to any computers-and-writing effort.

BUT I DON'T WANT TO TEACH COMPUTING IN MY CLASSES. I WANT TO TEACH WRITING. CAN THE LAB ASSISTANTS TEACH MY STUDENTS THE SOFTWARE?

Composition specialists need to tread carefully here. On the one hand,
it is both pleasant and desirable to delegate—that is, to allow others to
take on tasks in the complex interrelationships that make up a successful
computers-and-composition effort. When the administrator of the computer
laboratory offers to allow his or her colleagues to "teach" your students the
software, that generosity and collegiality will seem both appropriate and a
relief, particularly when your job is to teach writing, not the technological
equivalent of secretarial skills.

On the other hand, most of the lab assistants are not writing specialists, nor, for that matter, can one assume that they are for the most part particularly interested in writing; can you trust their judgments in directing your
students when they guide them toward text-related issues at the computer?
"But," you might argue, "they're teaching the software, not writing." True,
but only up to a point. Ideally, let the computer lab handle the training, but
only if the writing program has had full input into the training of the lab
assistants themselves. What, for instance, is the writing instructor's position

on the use of spell checkers? I never allow my students—particularly writing-anxious ones—to use them right off, preferring instead to instill in them confidence as proofreaders and to make sure that they understand that the computer will not "do" it all for them—that the appropriate *they're* or *there* or *their*, for instance, is up to them, and that surface editing is not the same as deep revision.

Unless the lab itself is part of the English or humanities department, one cannot assume that the assistants in the center are at all interested in writing, but then again, one cannot always assume the appropriate philosophical leanings on the part of otherwise excellent English teachers. I recall a rather frightening experience at a high school in the Chicago area known for its computers-and-composition project. As an instructor led me and a group of my graduate students through an impressive lab after we had observed her fine class, we stopped to talk with the tutorial leader, another member of the English faculty. Her job is to assist remedial students, who, she pointed out, wrote much more text—and more freely—on the computer than they had done longhand. She went through their papers with us, but when asked how she would teach students to *revise*, she said (much to my horror), "Oh, Grammatik will take care of that for them." Certainly a surface-level (and often erroneous) style-checking program is not enough; nor should the fledgling writer be encouraged to see it as a crutch, as an end-all of proportions comparable to what I enjoy calling "biblical inerrancy" (Holdstein, 1990). Training, therefore—or, as I prefer to call it, "philosophical immersion"—doesn't necessarily begin and end with the laboratory assistants nor with the rudiments of the writing process and ways to execute a "block move." Department-wide colloquia to which other members of the computers-and-writing process are invited—the head of the computer lab, the lab assistants, writing faculty teaching with and without the computer—insure that the discussions continue, that the computer enhances rather than detracts from writing-as-process.

In addition to supplemental training of lab assistants by staff from the writing program, another possibility is a team-taught effort, where teaching assistants in composition, for instance, join assistants in the computer center; this works particularly well if sessions can be scheduled during new student week, so that instructors can spend their class time teaching writing and knowing full well that their students have mastered at least the fundamentals of whatever word processing program they will use at the institution.

At other schools, however, the orientation plan isn't feasible: First, some institutions simply don't have a formal new student week, and second, there isn't room in the plan—even where it exists—for anything else. However, it is a serious mistake to assume that most incoming students will have had experience with the computer: This proves particularly insensitive to students whose school districts were computer-poor, the misapprehension moreover restricting even further some students' access to technology and adequate instruction concerning it. Well, then, what to do?

Take the first few class periods to make your students comfortable with the software, and watch the collaborative process in action. First, integrate computer learning with writing-to-learn, encouraging students to write at the terminal about their experiences during that very class. Have the most proficient students assist the less proficient, serving as troubleshooters with both software and developing ideas for the essays. Since the better writers aren't necessarily the most familiar with computers, and vice versa, students learn that they each might have different types of strengths to share. In this, you, with your students as "co-facilitators," will have built the foundation for every collaborative effort thereafter—at and away from the terminal. Your own philosophy of teaching writing will come through in the way in which you foster your students' learning of software; as with teaching the writing process, your involvement is a matter of "flexible control," and it is imperative that your expertise as a writing specialist inform the computer-learning process.

HOW CAN I CONVINCE MY DEPARTMENT CHAIR AND MY COLLEAGUES TO SEE THAT THE COMPUTER IS USED THROUGHOUT THE WRITING CURRICULUM?

Don't even try. In my numerous travels I have advised against requiring on-line composition courses. There are as many effective teaching methods for composition as there are learning methods; similarly, there are as many individual approaches to the writing process. While computer use should be encouraged—if not as part of class, then at least outside of class, with appropriate "philosophical immersion" of students by the instructor—it should never be mandated at the expense of both students' and instructors' individuality and effectiveness.

WHAT SHOULD A WELL-DESIGNED ROOM LOOK LIKE?

As a recent essay in *Computers and Composition* indicates, "As early as 1980, Allan Collins and Dedre Gentner were theorizing about the potentials of 'WritingLand,' a computer-based reading and writing environment that

---

might assist students by suggesting strategies and structures to negotiate the several levels of cognitive activity in composing" (Kaler, 1991).

In fact, in a recent book, *Computer Writing Environments: Theory, Research, and Design* (1989), editors Britton and Glynn describe a number of goals for the ideal computerized writing environment, goals dealing primarily with the capabilities of the computer itself; to most instructors, however, "environment" connotes not only the capabilities of the machine at the core of the workstation itself, but the true environment, the room in which students will individually and collaboratively tackle the process of writing. In *WritingLands: Composing with Old and New Writing Tools* (1991), Jane Zeni discusses classroom environments themselves and the potentials for writing communities in those institutions with computer support. And yet it would be naive for faculty initiating computers-and-writing efforts to assume that one "perfect" environment exists or that their institution would have the commitment or resources—even if the institution basically supports computerized writing environments—to emulate the ideal WritingLand either theorized or in place elsewhere.

Tastes and circumstances indeed vary, and sometimes wildly, but several possibilities seem most appropriate for a pleasant, flexible environment with round tables and space at the terminal pod that allows for "regular" writing and editing of hard copy, one that provides space for notes and textbooks and notepads; that permits students to easily move to one another's terminals and the teacher to move freely among them; that allows students to look up easily (or to turn easily) to face the instructor or another student-colleague when group discussion seems appropriate or to see a projection screen when one particular text is under discussion.

Given these criteria (and of course there are others), a "horseshoe" format seems to work well; instructors I've spoken with are divided about whether or not students can face the wall or the inside of the circle with greater efficacy. A divided horseshoe format also works well (particularly for the placement of those recalcitrant cables)—that is, two horseshoes side by side, the open ends facing whiteboards and conference tables. (Such is the design of our IBM room at Governors State.)

WHAT IF THE ROOM ARRANGEMENT ISN'T TO MY LIKING? WHAT IF IT DOESN'T REFLECT MY PROCESS ORIENTATION AS A WRITER OR AS A TEACHER OF WRITING?

Small rooms cramped with computers on small desks—with no space for hard text, writing, or textbooks, for instance—can appear counterproductive. In this instance, it may simply be the case that not all sessions should meet in the lab, restricting time there, perhaps, to drafting assignments, for instance, with collaborative work completed in the traditional classroom with hard copy. However, even in the most apparently restricted circumstances, our students tend to make do, huddling together near a terminal for collaborative work, taking hard copy to the empty classroom next door for further discussion. Of course, the successful negotiator will have had one or two terminals taken out of the room for more extensive classroom interchange!

WHAT OTHER SUPPORT—AND ALLIANCES— WILL WE NEED?

If it has not already been thought of, consider alliances not only with the computer center staff, but with their representatives at higher levels of the administration—those making budgetary and software decisions, those who might not usually consider issues related to composition to be within their sphere of influence. (Interestingly enough, however, when some of these administrators need to make composition-related decisions, they don't often think to consult with English or composition program faculty.) Make sure that the vice-president for academic affairs, the director of information services—or their equivalents on your campus—know you and your interests. (Many faculty make this a team effort, wisely including their chair and the dean.) If you don't already do so, serve on research committees, internal granting committees, space resource committees.

Think as well about the hard-working staff in the development office and those who head the alumni association or university foundation offices. These valuable colleagues want you to succeed, not only for the glamour and recruitment value of computer-related efforts, but also because contributors to your institution want to see substantive philosophical underpinnings and programmatic benefits stemming from the efforts they support. It helps development staff do their jobs more effectively if they understand what it is that you do; they welcome suggestions for attracting contributions as well as ideas for ways in which they might assist you in doing the same. At Governors State, for instance, the alumni association recently instituted a faculty development grant series, created from some of the funds raised through an alumni phone-a-thon in which faculty and staff participate. Faculty apply to the alumni association committee as one might apply to any granting foundation, with funds available to support innovative teaching and research practice. As might be painfully evident, then, concerns about the lab are not enough: First, its design might well be a *fait accompli* long before composition faculty become involved in its use; second, initiating its use creates the proverbial ripple effect in resources, funds, room assignments, class sizes, and so on. Collaboration and negotiation—in places where most English faculty usually fear to tread—become the rule, something of a way of life.

Certainly such activity confounds the paradigm of the solitary scholar so prevalent in English studies, the notion that a successfully productive faculty member is the independent scholar. Composition studies has done a great deal to subvert this paradigm; collaborative learning and teaching—as evident, for instance, in the recent work of literary critics such as Gerald Graff—are the innovative legacies of those in composition, not literary or critical studies. Writing-and-computers' efforts demand all the more that we sensibly subvert the paradigm, with collaborative efforts not restricted merely to the composition classroom and our research, but extended to the ways in which we carry out the day-to-day rudiments of our mission. In extending the context for collaboration, we become less the alienated, Eliotlike "modern," chaste and isolated as the new-critical text itself, and more like the Whitmanesque "body electric," part of an essentially collaborative, productive chain. And how do we resolve, in this, these "contrary states" of our souls as we begin? For this change in self-concept—and, alas, in our need to learn the "art of the deal"—we must count on the passage of time and the increasing adoption by English studies in general of new paradigms of teaching, writing, and learning given birth by, nurtured, and shaped through composition studies.

REFERENCES

Britton, B. K., and S. M. Glynn, eds. 1989. *Computer Writing Environments: Theory, Research, and Design.* Hillsdale, N.J.: Erlbaum.

Collins, A., and D. Gentner. 1980. "A Framework for Cognitive Theory of Writing." In *Cognitive Processes in Writing* edited by L. W. Gregg and E. R. Steinberg, 51–71. Hillsdale, N.J.: Erlbaum.

Holdstein, D. 1989. "Preparing Teachers for Computers and Writing: Plans and Issues at Governors State University." In *Computers in English and the Language Arts,* edited by C. Selfe, D. Rodrigues, and W. Oates 131–40. Urbana, Ill.: National Council of Teachers of English.

Holdstein, D. 1990. "Theory, Research, and Practice in Computers and Composition: An Overview." Plenary address at the Conference on College Composition and Communication, Chicago.

Kaler, E. R. 1991. "Review of Computer Writing Environments." *Computers and Composition.* 8 (3 August):83–89.

Zeni, J. 1991. *Writinglands: Composing with Old and New Writing Tools.* Urbana, Ill.: National Council of Teachers of Education.

5

Administrative, Instructional, and User Decisions: Writing in an English Department's Macintosh Lab

Barbara M. Sitko

WASHINGTON STATE UNIVERSITY
WRITING PROGRAM

The writing program at Washington State University begins with an introductory writing course that students enter via a qualifying essay exam. This course focuses on the writing of six to eight papers, revising after peer group discussion and conferences with instructors, and folder assessment. The course is fully integrated with the Avery Microcomputer Lab, fifty Macintosh SEs networked to two Mac II file servers and two LaserWriter Plus printers. Classes meet in the computer lab once a week, and all students in introductory writing are automatically registered as network users. After successfully completing introductory writing, students have a choice of writing courses, depending on their interests and their majors,. but must complete at least two writing-intensive courses in their major field. In addition, soon after completing sixty credit hours, students must pass a written qualifying examination in the form of a portfolio assessment. The computer lab is available to all students through a one-credit pass-fail course designed to introduce them to more advanced uses of software and networks.

INTRODUCTION

Establishing an English department computer facility and maintaining it as a viable part of a writing program require decisions by many teachers, students, and university personnel in addition to lab administrators. While some decisions are temporary, others are relatively permanent, in that they affect not only those immediately involved in the design of the facility but also those who will be using the facility in the future. This essay discusses the decisions that Washington State University has made and is making about its Macintosh writing lab, the Avery Microcomputer Lab (AML). The AML was established to integrate computers with introductory writing courses in such a way as to make the facility available to as many students as possible. This close connection between the writing curriculum and the AML continues to influence the design and services of the facility. Thus, it is important to understand the purpose and structure of the writing program, in other words, the function of the facility, before considering issues of design. I will first briefly introduce the AML and describe the writing program. Then I will discuss two major categories of decisions, those concerning physical structure and those concerning the virtual structure of the computing environment. For each topic under these categories, I will first describe the arrangement of our facility and then discuss the advantages and disadvantages, including responses and recommendations of teachers and students from surveys and interviews conducted regularly at the end of each semester.

GENERAL DESCRIPTION OF THE AML
AND WRITING PROGRAM

In this section I will provide an overview of the facility and the program. Because a detailed description of the facility forms the content of the next part of this paper, the following description will be brief.

Avery Microcomputer Lab

The Avery Microcomputer Lab at Washington State University consists of fifty Macintosh SEs connected in a local-area network (LAN). Each grouping of twenty-five Macintosh workstations is connected to a Macintosh II file server and a LaserWriter Plus printer. The facility, established in the fall of 1988 by an equipment grant from Apple Computer, is located in two adjoining classrooms separated by a folding door (see figure 5.1). The rooms are used for instruction from 8:00 A.M. to 3:00 P.M. Each semester, 1,250 students meet once a week during their regularly scheduled class periods. The

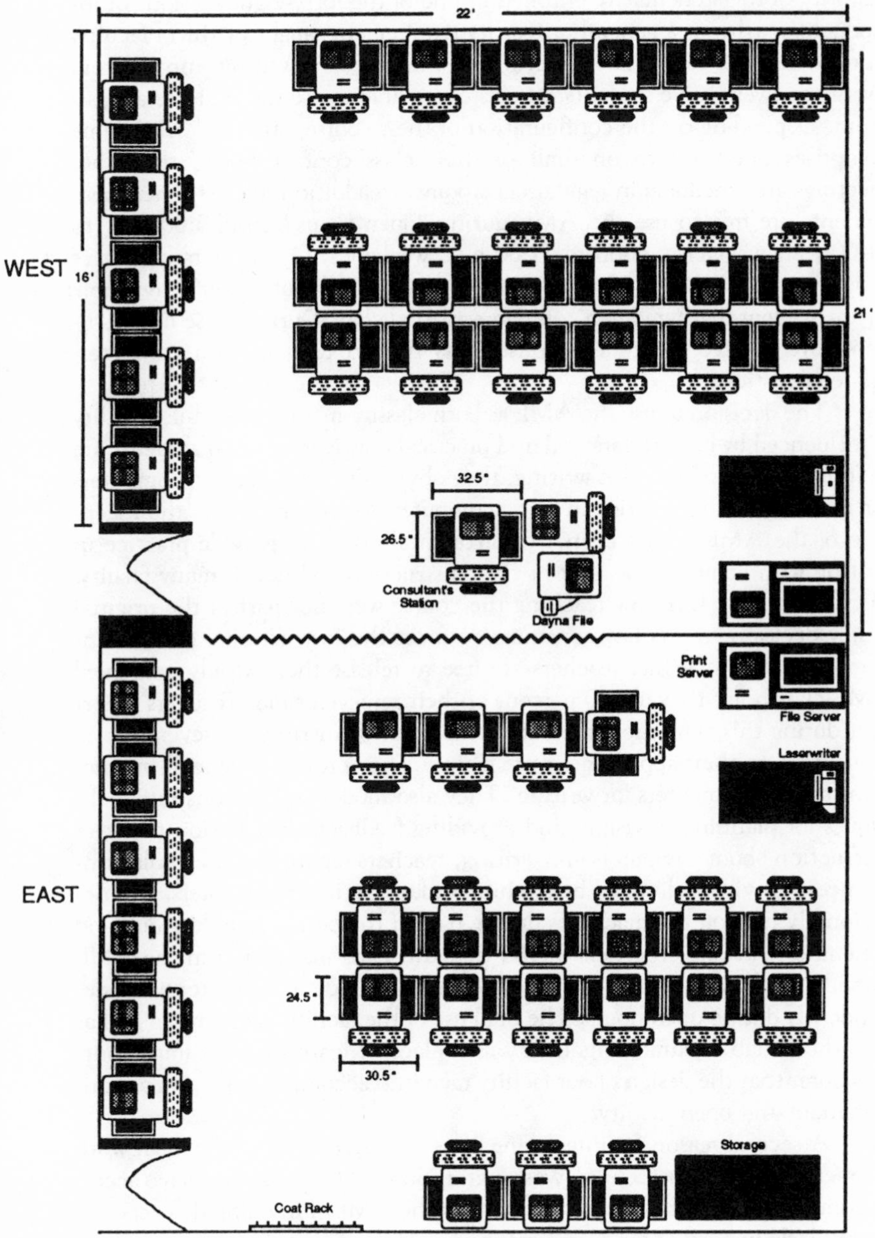

WEST 16'

22'

21'

32.5"

26.5"

Consultant's Station

Dayna File

Print Server

File Server

Laserwriter

EAST

24.5"

30.5"

Storage

Coat Rack

Fig. 5.1. Map of Avery Microcomputer Lab

majority of the students are enrolled in one of the forty-eight sections of introductory writing, a general university requirement taught by thirty faculty,
instructors, and TAs. Each section of introductory writing enrolls from
twenty to twenty-five students, so classes are able to use the AML as a classroom. Depending on the configuration of their course, students' AML time
comprises one-third to one-half of their class contact hours; the other
meetings are scheduled in regular classrooms. In addition to class time, these
students are free to use the AML during "open hours," from 3:00 P.M. to
11:00 P.M. weekdays, noon to 11:00 P.M. weekends. Open hours consist of
drop-in time when the AML is not reserved for class but rather is available
to any student registered in a computer-assisted class. During these hours students are assisted by student consultants trained to help with computer-
related questions.

The decision to use the AML as both classroom and general-use facility
is influenced by both theoretical and practical considerations. If students are
to integrate computers with writing, they obviously need access to computers
for instruction and practice in using computers for writing. From the inception of the AML, it has been a departmental policy to provide practice in
writing with computers as part of class instruction. Although many faculty,
instructors, and TAs now teaching the course were not part of the original
policy decision, the policy continues to meet the instructional goals of incoming teachers. While teachers are free to release their weekly scheduled
AML class hour, they use 80 percent of their reserved time. Teachers report
that during this time they integrate computers with writing in several ways,
depending on their approaches to teaching. They provide a general instruction in using computers for writing. They also model and demonstrate techniques for planning, revising, and providing feedback. In addition to direct
instruction about computers and writing, teachers report that they hold conferences, provide individual help while students write at computers, and occasionally turn off the machines during part of the period to hold group and
general discussions. Teachers intend that this class instruction in the AML
provide the basic instruction in techniques that students can later use independently during open hours. The dual use of the facility as classroom and as
open-hours lab maximizes its utility as a place of learning. It is important,
therefore, that the design of our facility take into account its function as both
classroom and open facility.

A second reason for integrating class instruction with individual work
is practical. Thirty percent of Washington State students do not have access
to computers other than those provided by the AML. Providing this access is
particularly important for a land-grant university whose mission is to provide
liberal and practical education to a wide population. Because 85 percent of
our students report previous experience with computers, including 65 per-

cent who have used them for writing before entering college, it is important that they have the opportunity to develop these computer skills in ways consistent with their educational goals.

The Introductory Writing Course

The introductory writing course at Washington State University is designed to help students become proficient at the kinds of writing they will be expected to produce in their college courses. The class focuses on the writing of six to eight papers, revising after peer group discussion and conferences with instructors, and portfolio assessment.

One aspect of the course that integrates well with computers is the curriculum design. All sections use a common set of readings, *Writing about the World* (McLeod et al., 1991). This collection of readings introduces students to a multicultural perspective on four topical areas: science and technology, government and politics, art and literature, and religion and philosophy. Because the text and course materials were developed as a five-year project involving the teaching staff of the introductory writing course, a large collection of electronic materials is available to new teachers. These materials include sample syllabi, assignments, student papers, and bibliographies, all stored on the network to which teachers have access. Teachers who piloted a rhetoric text designed specifically for the Macintosh, *Writing with the Macintosh Using Microsoft Word* (Duin and Gorak, 1991), have also stored materials on the network for common use.

A second aspect of the introductory writing course that integrates well with computer-assisted writing is the folder assessment. Students twice submit a folder of their writing for evaluation, once at midterm and again at the end of the semester. Included in the folder are a final clean copy of a finished piece of work, early drafts, a copy of the assignment, and a cover letter or memo explaining the author's purposes in writing and revising. Networked computers facilitate portfolio preparation by storing instructions, class assignments, sample memos, cover letters, and drafts for the individual student. The usefulness of the AML for folder preparation is attested to by usage numbers, which nearly double during folder deadline weeks.

The successful integration of the AML and introductory writing is attested to by teachers. Besides using 80 percent of the class hours scheduled in the AML, nearly all teachers who were interviewed at the end of a semester of teaching writing with computers reported that they would recommend instruction in the AML to a teacher who had not used a computer facility. The others qualified their recommendation only by the comfort level of the teacher. No teachers reported that they would discourage a colleague from teaching such a class. It is clear that teachers are heavily invested in the

AML, and that decisions about the physical design of the facility must be directly influenced by its function in the introductory writing curriculum.

Consultants

To meet the requirements of the design of the introductory writing course, the AML must function both as a classroom and as an unstructured writing environment. The presence of consultants in both classes and open hours blurs the distinction between these uses of the facility and emphasizes the primary function of the AML as a place for writing. At Washington State University, consultants are trained to be knowledgeable about technical matters such as how to maintain the network, run the software, and help with special concerns like virus detection, file recovery, and translation between DOS and Mac formats. Some consultants work directly with teachers during classes, making brief presentations of a new technique, such as sorting and formatting a list of works cited or retrieving a text from a peer response folder. Consultants often go over a proposed lesson with teachers, both to be familiar with the goals and procedures and to spot any potential difficulties. Because the consultants who work during class also assist during open hours, they have firsthand experience with the difficulties students are likely to encounter while following a procedure.

Consultants are specifically trained in how to guide students through problem solving. At weekly meetings, consultants identify the most common questions and discuss problem-solving techniques to deal with them. They confer, for example, on ways to find out how students are representing their problems, their goals, and their unsuccessful attempts at reaching those goals. They share methods for guiding students through correct solutions without taking control of the problem-solving process, either physically, by seizing the keyboard or mouse, or mentally, by simply talking through a procedure without discerning students' comprehension. For example, when students have opened documents from their own folders, they frequently have trouble saving the documents to a different place, such as a class folder or their own floppy disks. Consultants first ask where the student wants to place the document, then ask the student to scan the Save As dialogue box to locate any information that would help the student get closer to his or her goal. Consultants might ask the student to experiment by clicking on the Drive button, for example, and to observe what changes. Thus consultants try to direct students' attention to the information they need to make the decisions that will get them closer to their goals. Consultants track the questions most frequently asked during open hours. AML staff members then relay these questions to teachers during the biweekly staff meetings. In this way we try to maintain a close connection between class instruction and students' work during open hours.

Consultants also fulfill a practical need. Should a class not use its scheduled reserved time, the consultant on duty posts a notice releasing the AML for open hours. Opening the facility during released class time (20 percent of the total time scheduled) answers the request of many students to work during the day. For example, the arrangement suits the situation of students who find it difficult to schedule evenings at school because of child care or employment.

In addition to answering a practical need to maximize use of the facility, consultants are important because students do not learn computer skills all at once. Although after orientation students report feeling comfortable with the commands needed to produce a paper, they may not yet be comfortable with logging on to the network, saving to a disk and to a class folder, and such word processing commands as double spacing and justifying margins. Still later in the semester, students' goals change. They need to sort a list of works cited, use hanging indents, save and retrieve documents from peer response folders, and access documents from several levels within the network, such as general bulletin board materials from the root directory or collaborative work folders at the class-section level. It is evident that students learning to negotiate these paths need different kinds of help throughout the semester. And students learn at different rates, dependent on previous experience, practice, and awareness of their options. Consultants who are attentive and flexible can help with problem solving at the crucial point when students want to reach a new goal.

This introduction to the facility, the writing program, and the support staff of consultants was intended to show how many aspects of the writing curriculum intersect in the computer facility. It should be apparent that decisions about computer facilities are informed by theories of pedagogy whose sphere of influence stretches the boundaries of the traditional classroom.

PHYSICAL STRUCTURE OF THE AML

This part of the essay will delineate decisions relating to the physical structure of the AML. Specifically, I will discuss

1. equipment,
2. locating the facility in adjoining rooms,
3. room layout and furniture,
4. temperature control, and
5. security.

For each topic under these categories, I will first describe the arrangement of the facility and then discuss the advantages and disadvantages, including responses and recommendations of teachers and students from surveys regularly conducted at the end of each semester.

Equipment

The Avery Microcomputer Lab consists of the original grant from Apple Computer, two Macintosh II file servers, each connected to twenty-five Macintosh SEs and one LaserWriter Plus printer (see figure 5.1). In addition, we have purchased two Macintosh Plus computers as print servers. This decision was made when the use of the AML increased to the point that the "heavy traffic" of twenty-five machines operating simultaneously on the network made excessive demands on the Mac II file server. Although file servers must be "dedicated," meaning that they cannot run as a server and as a workstation at the same time, under conditions of light usage, file servers can also function as print servers. With heavy usage, however, the system may become unstable and even crash. Print servers "spool," or place the document in a temporary storage area, queuing up to go to the printer as soon as the previous print job has been completed. When a document is spooled, a user at an individual workstation can continue to work without waiting for the document to be printed. Thus, by managing the spooling and printing of documents, print servers increase the functionality of the printer. In the AML, for example, one printer can easily take care of the printing needs of twenty-five students, even at the end of a class period when jobs stack up in the print queue.

AppleTalk, a networking capability consisting of hardware and software configurations, is built into every Macintosh. To connect the computers, the AML decided on the most economical cables, Farallon PhoneNET connectors. The alternative, Ethernet connectors, would provide faster access but is much costlier in several ways: The cabling is costlier, and because Ethernet does not run on AppleTalk, additional cards would have been needed for each workstation. Ethernet provides nearly instantaneous response time. With PhoneNET connectors, typically a large application such as Word requires ninety seconds (yes, we timed it) to load. If a class of twenty-five students requests the application at the same moment, loading can take up to five minutes. However, students do not generally open the application at the same moment even during class. Rather, they log on and open documents individually during the ten-minute break between classes. Teachers have learned to post opening instructions on the boards rather than having the class wait for verbal directives to be executed by all students at the same time.

Completing the network is a Hayes interbridge. Bridges are physical devices used to connect two similar networks. Through a bridge, users can access file servers other than the one to which their workstation is primarily connected. In the AML, the Hayes bridge connects the two Macintosh II file servers.

A feature built into more recent Macintosh models is the ability to read DOS files. The Apple File Exchange application enables the user to read and translate files from DOS to Macintosh format, and vice versa. Other translators available from DataViz supplement this rudimentary exchange feature. The AML purchased a Macintosh SE/SuperDrive to run the Apple File Exchange, accommodating students who work on a PC or compatible computer. Approximately 30 percent of the registered students reported using this service during the first semester after it was purchased. Attached to this computer is a DaynaFile for file transfers between disks of different sizes, 5.25 inch and 3.5 inch.

Other equipment includes a Kodak DataShow projection pad mounted on an overhead projector and cart so that teachers in either classroom can use the projection capability. One workstation in each room houses the necessary video card. The AML is also equipped with a phone so that technical help is within reach.

Location: Adjoining Rooms

The physical space of the AML is an adaptation of two adjoining classrooms located on the ground floor of the English building. Because it involves space allocation, locating a computer facility is generally a university-wide decision. It is important for a department to be involved in this decision, because the space allocation may reduce the overall classroom space available to that department. At Washington State University, classes are scheduled for a regular classroom first; the computer classroom is provided in addition to their regularly reserved room. Thus when the AML was created, two classrooms were effectively removed from the pool of available rooms in the English building. This resulted in some introductory writing sections having to meet regularly in other buildings on campus.

Natural light in the classrooms is limited; each room has only one floor-to-ceiling glass panel. This window does not open, nor does it provide sufficient light for work. An advantage of the scarcity of natural light is the lack of screen glare. Additional light sources are overhead fluorescent lighting and incandescent lamps on a dimmer switch that controls brightness during overhead projection.

The two classrooms were modified somewhat to house the AML. Because one of the rooms had for several years been an Apple IIe lab, it had been wired for computers and was equipped with computer desks. At the time of the grant, all Apple IIe's in this classroom were replaced with Macintoshes. In addition, the wall separating the two classrooms was replaced with a folding door cut into two-thirds of the partition, and the second room was wired for computers.

The adjoining-rooms arrangement has some advantages for both class hours and open hours. Advantages during class hours include sharing material and human resources. Teachers share one DataShow projection pad, for example, located on a rolling cart and able to be attached to the computer equipped with a video card in each room. The second resource that can be shared easily via the folding door is the help of a consultant. One consultant can move between classrooms at those times when help is most needed, such as at the beginning of the hour when students are logging on or at the end when they are formatting a document.

Locating the equipment in adjoining rooms has benefits for open hours as well. The efficiency of the AML is doubled, in that one consultant strategically placed at a workstation near the center can check students in as well as be alert to students who need help.

Room Layout and Furniture

To make maximum use of the rather small classrooms available for conversion to a computer lab, the decision was made to place the computers around the perimeter of the room and in two center rows facing each other (see figure 5.1). The desks in the two classrooms, although similar in size, are constructed differently. The desks in the former Apple IIe classroom measure 26.5 inches by 32.5 inches, with a 16-inch-wide raised shelf; the desks in the other room measure 24.5 inches by 30.5 inches, with a single work surface. The desks do not match because at the time the AML was expanded in 1988, the larger desks were no longer available.

To compensate for the small work space, Curtis clips are available on each machine, attached with a Velcro strip to the top of the computer. These plastic arms with removable clips display hard copy next to the computer screen, minimizing eye movement and the need to readjust focus.

Desk chairs on coasters, adjustable for height, are used in both rooms. The linoleum tile floors are uncarpeted; no classrooms or offices in the building are carpeted.

As might be evident from figure 5.1, classroom size is the feature receiving the greatest number of negative comments by teachers and students surveyed. When the rooms are full, as during class, aisle space is limited, and teachers find movement around the classroom somewhat difficult. Students likewise have difficulty moving to and from the printer. The discrepancy between the two desk sizes also evokes comments. The flat desktop in one classroom makes spreading out papers and books cumbersome, whereas the raised shelf in the other creates a more spacious writing area. Given a choice, students prefer the larger work area. Many teachers also object to the room layout in rows of facing computers, because some students have their backs both to other students and to the teacher, unless they turn their desk chairs away from their computers. Other teachers, however, find the layout a more "natural" working environment than classrooms in which students automatically take seats in rows facing front.

Other features of this working environment also receive comments. Teachers and students like the ease with which the desk chairs move. Teachers find that the chairs facilitate group and class discussion in the AML. Students roll their chairs to confer during writing, perhaps more than if the room were arranged differently, such as in clusters. The Curtis clips receive a surprising number of explicit and positive comments.

Macintosh SEs are relatively small machines, and thus it is tempting to create small stations to house them. It is important to note, however, that although machines may not need much space, writers do. University students especially need both desk space and storage space for backpacks and jackets. Because many existing classrooms are built to hold twenty-five student desks, redesigning them to accommodate workstations for twenty-five students, as well as file servers and printers, may necessitate some trade-offs. If the trade-off to crowding means fewer student workstations, possibly even less than one per student, the decision would effectively disrupt the AML as a classroom, at least for introductory writing. Sharing computers may be an efficient use of machines and space for courses planned around collaborative writing groups; in this case the space might be designed for a variety of writing activities such as laying out documents and conferring about text. However, in classes where they are expected to submit documents individually, students need work space. Washington State students, for example, report average work sessions of from two to four hours per paper outside of class time. Although they may confer with another student or make a brief visit to the writing lab to meet with a tutor during this time, the majority of their AML time is spent writing at their workstations.

Temperature Control

Temperature control is surprisingly important, partly because of machine-generated heat, partly because of the heavy usage of the rooms. Controlling air temperature is important for the comfort of the users and for the stability of the network. The AML is full 80 percent of the time from 8:00 A.M. to 3:00 P.M. for instruction. During open hours, attendance hovers around 50 percent during the late afternoon and evening, and 80 percent during the late evening. The windows cannot be opened for air or temperature control. During warm weather we have found it necessary to use floor fans, in addition to air conditioning, for both circulation and heat control.

Security

Decisions about security are linked to decisions about furniture. At present, security systems that physically wire machines to furniture or to each other seem most practical. Motives of security also dictate that wires and power cords be located outside of traffic patterns. In the case of the AML, wires are attached to the back of the machines by being threaded through the cases and keyboards, then between the panels of the desks. Wires are placed under floor tiles to keep aisles clear. Although Macintoshes are lightweight and easily movable, security considerations often preclude taking advantage of these features in a room design. Movable carts or workstations might be an attractive alternative to fixed desks, in that they would save space and enable discussion groups to form easily, but they do not appear to be feasible where security and wiring are important considerations. Security must also be coordinated with the university personnel who are charged with responding to alarms.

In sum, if a computer facility is to function for both instruction and general use, the physical structure should reflect the influence of these two environments. Advantages in one environment might be disadvantages in the other. Study carrels, for example, create a private work space during open hours but would not work well during class or group discussion. A computer facility should strike a balance between ideal classroom and ideal open-lab environments in order to serve both needs.

THE VIRTUAL STRUCTURE OF THE AML

One of the great benefits of a computer network is that, by connecting workstations, it allows users to share applications, folders, and files. Even though a given student owns a folder (stores documents) on only one server, the network permits sharing documents with other servers and users. The networked computing environment includes decisions about such features as

1. links between file servers,
2. use of course sections as shared writing groups, and
3. software support.

Links between File Servers: Bridges

A bridge creates one large network out of smaller groupings of file servers and workstations. Although access to applications and files is somewhat slower across the bridge, because signals must travel farther, the device has many advantages. Chief among these is how a bridge expands the utility, and helps maintain the stability, of the network. Because of the bridge linking the two Mac II file servers in the AML, for instance, a student can sit at a workstation in either classroom and log on to his or her own file server. The bridge also makes both printers accessible to any user. A second bridge links faculty, instructors, and TAs to a graduate student research center located in the same building. Teachers can access their AML folders from this center. Thus, the bridges create virtual space different from the physical space of the AML.

During class time students normally sit in the area where their class materials are located. During open hours, however, bridges permit students to use the AML more efficiently. For example, if one classroom is crowded, students who would normally sit in that room, because their workstations are connected to that file server, may use a workstation in the less crowded room. Also, should a class release its reserved AML period, other students can use the workstations.

In addition to being a convenient solution to the problem of over-crowding, bridges have a valuable instructional use, namely, they permit conversation over time and across sections. Because our introductory writing students use a common set of texts and often research issues in similar ways, they have much in common with students in course sections other than their own. The bridge enables students to form peer response groups across sections. Topical interest bulletin boards on the network make it possible for students to exchange ideas with other authors.

Administratively, the bridge is useful in several ways. First, it saves the teacher time. Materials such as course syllabi, assignments, or writing exercises need be saved to only one place, a class folder held in common. Teachers also have available an instructional folder. Secondly, should a server or printer crash occur, the bridge permits emergency access to the applications stored on the other server. The bridge also permits students to send documents to the printer in the other classroom if their own printer has an exceptionally long queue.

One of the design principles of the AppleShare network is to present a "seamless" interface. Students are hardly aware of the technology supporting their work, including the link between classrooms—they know only that they can sit on either side during open hours and access their folders. Bridges that connect file servers in local-area networks enormously increase their usefulness without requiring intermediate commands that might confuse the user.

Use of Course Sections as Shared Writing (AppleShare) Groups

Networks make possible the sharing of writing across groups. In addition to using the peer response folder of their own class section, students can drop papers into general-access response folders where they can get feedback. This practice has several benefits. As I have indicated, students working on similar topics and interests can read and respond to papers that are stored on the network.

Teachers also can store papers from previous classes as examples or as a kind of "student reader." At the end of each semester, for example, I ask students to select one paper for a common folder accessible to future students in my introductory writing classes. The papers form a collection of readings for future students.

The network also enables students in a collaborative work group to write a paper together. Teachers report that they use two methods: (1) Students compose at a single computer, and (2) students compose parts of a document and store them in a commonly accessible folder. The access privileges available in AppleShare software permit students to store their work in a common folder. Other software is needed to provide simultaneous access to the same document. This and other software will be discussed in the following section.

Software Support

The decision about software is linked directly to the use of the AML by the English department. In our case, with 1,150 (93 percent) of the registered AML users enrolled in introductory writing, an easy-to-use word processing application is needed. Microsoft Word appears to suit the needs of most students. For those students using the AML to produce scientific or technical documents, we support a graphing application (CricketGraph) and a graphics application (SuperPaint). We also support a general-purpose database (Filemaker) and a typing practice application (Type). Virus protection is maintained with Disinfectant installed on each file server and on each boot disk. Disinfectant protects all machines from viruses.

Two other applications that directly support the writing process are being piloted by some teachers. Writer's Helper provides computer-generated prompts to invention and revision. Teachers may modify the prompts to fit a particular assignment or type of assignment. Aspects (simultaneous conference software) allows from two to sixteen users to view and edit the same document at the same time and is thus useful for collaborative writing. This software may also answer the needs of teachers who want to display an active document on all screens simultaneously so that they can demonstrate planning or revising a text.

Displaying a document visually is possible via the DataShow projection pad, which projects the monitor screen of the computer linked to it. AML staff use the DataShow extensively during orientation; consultants use it to demonstrate unfamiliar procedures; and many teachers use it to model planning and revising a text. Some teachers dislike the projection pad, however, because, given the room arrangement, visibility is somewhat limited.

As students and teachers become more familiar with the standard features of word processing, they begin to imagine other uses for the technology. Just as class discussion permits students to exchange ideas and texts with peers they might not meet on their own, the storage capability of the network permits students to get feedback from readers other than their classmates. Without electronic mail this procedure is a little cumbersome, requiring that participants agree on rules for moving documents and conventions for naming them. Students do not have a way of sending messages that would appear automatically when the receiver logs on. Dropping documents into a peer response folder, however, is a simple procedure requiring no special software.

An illustration from my own class plan might be helpful in seeing how the AML and instruction in introductory writing work together. The class meets twice weekly for seventy-five minutes, alternating between the regular classroom and the AML. As a general principle, I attempt to integrate the AML into all aspects of the writing process, simply designing the scheduled weekly AML period to match where students are in the process of working on a particular assignment. This curriculum plan permits me to introduce students to various uses of the computer in a spiral design, beginning with the basic commands needed to produce a document and gradually increasing complexity as needed.

For example, in the first paper students are asked to "link" or connect three text readings (McLeod et al., 1991) from a variety of cultures. The main point of the "link" is to explore some issue important to them. Previous to their first meeting in the AML they have scanned the readings to locate issues they find interesting. In their journals they comment on these readings, their reasons for selecting them, and the points they might later develop in a paper. During their first AML period they create a new document of their prewriting on different ways in which their combinations of readings can be connected. Gradually they formulate the issue and the purpose of their paper. Given the same set of readings, some students, for example, might focus on environmental issues, others on the relationship between cultural minorities and majority populations, and still others on feminist perspectives. During their next meeting in the AML, one week later, students select and enter journal entries, using multiple windows to begin to link them into a text. By the third meeting they have created a draft and are ready for some computer-assisted revision techniques. When they write their next paper, they practice using these techniques on their own. At the end of the second unit, they learn how to exchange papers electronically by making a duplicate of a class folder, retrieving a partner's paper, and using the footnote command to insert responses. In this sequence they move gradually from elementary word processing commands (entering and editing text) to desktop functions (duplicating and moving a document to a different folder and working with several documents at once).

Using the computer for this variety of activities over the course of one paper has several benefits. By saving these records of their developing texts, students are later able to trace their thought processes and to reflect on the interests, purposes, and decisions that have shaped their texts. A second benefit is derived from the extensive and original connections that students make among texts that at first appear disparate in time and culture. In addition to being elaborated in their written papers, the connections can be represented in electronic hypertext format. *Reading Links*, a HyperCard database created in the AML, stores the titles, authors, time periods, and cultures in a format that can be sorted to help students perceive the texts in new configurations. More important to the development of thought, however, *Reading Links* also provides opportunities for students to enter new links and explain the ways in which they see texts connected. This electronic conversation expands the boundaries of the classroom.

Four units like the one just described constitute the content of the introductory writing course. Using a combination of environments—regular classroom and computer facility—teachers can design instruction that incorporates orientation, practice, and increasing expertise with computer techniques.

CONCLUSION

The design of a computing facility to serve the needs of students enrolled in writing courses necessitates balancing the needs of all involved, if the design is to continue to meet future needs of the writing program.

The decision to give computer access to the maximum number of students led the English faculty of Washington State University to integrate computer-assisted instruction with introductory writing courses. This integration took the form of a combination of instruction in the Avery Micro-computer Lab and open hours availability. It is important that the AML serve both the instructional needs of teachers and students in classes and the learning needs of students writing outside of class. In our case, then, the AML has been structured to maintain this balance between class instruction and individual writing during open lab hours. Initially, both teachers and students have a choice of a regular or a computer-assisted writing section. Having made that choice, both teachers and students adjust their teaching and learning styles to integrate computers. For teachers, this integration may take the form of planning instruction differently than if the same lesson were held in a regular classroom (Bernhardt, Wojahn, and Edwards, 1990; Sitko, n.d.). For students, this integration may take the form of planning writing time differently to take advantage of the hours of the facility, the accessibility of peer responses, and the opportunity to revise a paper in time for a dead-line. Ideally, the design of a computer facility should support this human endeavor: the teaching and learning of writing.

REFERENCES

Bernhardt, S., P. Wojahn, and P. Edwards. 1990. "Teaching College Composition with Computers: A Timed Observation Study." *Written Communication* 7(3): 342–74.

Duin, A. H., and K. Gorak. 1991. *Writing with the Macintosh Using Microsoft Word.* Cambridge, Mass.: Course Technology, Inc.

McLeod, S., S. Bates, A. Hunt, J. Jarvis and S. Spear. 1991. *Writing about the World.* New York: Harcourt Brace Jovanovich.

Sitko, B. N.d. "Adapting Writing Instruction to a Microcomputer Classroom." Washington State University. In preparation.

6

Our Pal Penelope: Weaving and Unweaving Models of Theory, Practice, and Research for Designing and Operating Computer-supported Writing Facilities

Cynthia L. Selfe, Richard J. Selfe, and Johndan Johnson-Eilola

THE WRITING PROGRAM AT MICHIGAN TECHNOLOGICAL UNIVERSITY

The Humanities Department of Michigan Technological University has a long-standing reputation as a pioneer force in the profession's writing-across-the-curriculum effort. Beginning in 1977, this effort involved, among others, Art Young, Toby Fulwiler, Carol Berkenkotter, Randy Freisinger, Robert Jones, Bruce Petersen, and Cynthia Selfe. Growing out of these efforts pedagogically and intellectually has been Michigan Tech's computers-and-writing program. Begun in 1980 with a small cluster of machines, the program now involves faculty from a number of humanities disciplines; two fully equipped computer-supported writing facilities; courses that address such topics as electronic publication management, computer-supported video, computers and graphic production, hypertext practice and the-

ory, and computers in the humanities; and graduate students who spe-
cialize in areas such as teaching writing in computer-supported learning
environments, hypertext and hypermedia, computers and technical
communication, computers and postmodern theory, computers and
collaboration, computers and feminist theory, and computers and the
democratic project.

Almost a year ago, we wrote a proposal for this book in which we promised to discuss a model of designing and operating computer-supported writing facilities that worked for teachers and students of English composition.
At the moment, however, we're not very hot on models. We know they are
useful for describing phenomena within our field and that they can provide a
valuable framework for testing conceptions of how things happen in the
world of computers and composition; it's just that we have never been very
good at constructing them. Those models we have built or attempted to build
are about as stable as nitroglycerine. They constantly deconstruct and reconstruct themselves even as we attempt to fix them in words or images. Just
when we think we have identified a workable and stable model for designing, implementing, and operating computer-supported writing facilities, for
instance, we look again to find our thinking changed. This has happened
so many times, in fact, that we have reconciled ourselves to talking about
models in terms of narratives, rather than in terms of final products: For us,
they are representations fixed in time, but less than suggestive of the temporal dimension of discovery; photographs of a larger sequence, but ones
limited to showing discrete moments within that sequence; images of a product, not of the dynamic process of understanding that rests at the heart of
model building.

This essay is a story about the process of building models. Particularly,
it describes our attempts at Michigan Tech to identify and understand a
model for designing, implementing, and operating computer-supported writing facilities and, more importantly, where we went wrong in that process of
model building, being firm believers that those "where we went wrong" stories are always more interesting than the "where we went right" stories.

In 1989, we began holding a conversation with many of our computers-
and-composition-studies colleagues in a book called *Creating a Computer-
supported Writing Facility: A Blueprint for Action* (1989). In that book, we
described what we thought at the time was a productive model for shaping
the design, implementation, and operation of computer-supported writing facilities, based on some of the work we had done at our institution and on the

work we had seen done by many of our colleagues. We call this exchange a "conversation" because so many of our colleagues have written to us or talked to us about the ideas presented in that book or invited us to see facilities that speak eloquently about their own visions of lab/classroom design, and these comments have become part of our thinking and our talk about the design and operation of computer-supported writing environments. If Fred Kemp, the founder of Megabyte University, were to describe it, he might call this series of exchanges a "polylogue," an ongoing discussion among a group of colleagues about how such facilities should and could be structured.

But it has come to us lately that we may have been shortsighted in our contributions to this polylogue and, in at least one sense, downright wrong-headed in our thinking about this model of design. So, with this essay we would like to start a new conversation that may provide us as much fun and room for speculation as the old.[1]

We think we went wrong with our original model of lab/classroom design, implementation, and operation because we were afraid. Like many computers-and-composition specialists in the mid 1980s, when we were in the process of constructing that original model, we were afraid that computers-and-composition studies was becoming a practitioner's nightmare. In the journal articles and books we were reading, in the software we were seeing, in the conference presentations we went to, and in the labs we saw, computers-and-composition specialists were engaging in an enthusiastic, if myopic, kind of celebration: Each classroom teacher, each lab director, each software designer had his or her own successes with computers, and we told stories about these successes endlessly and with great excitement. In an article she wrote for *Computers and Composition* in 1986, Cynthia Selfe talked about her own personal compulsion to engage in this kind of sharing: "I . . . tell . . . [these] stories [because they] have a singularly soothing and powerful effect; they contain the comfort of shared experience and the germ of truth" (Selfe, 1987, 45).

Well, we were right about "the germ of truth," but like other computers-and-composition specialists at that time, we never seemed to get at that germ very well; we were still too new at the game of computer use, at least at Michigan Tech, and we had so little experience to go on that the only thing we could really do was to talk about what happened when computers were integrated into various classes and programs we had seen or participated in.

These success stories, however, were unconnected in one important way: They remained isolated within local circumstances and the individual efforts that produced them. Even as late as 1987, most computers-and-composition-studies people, except for a few distinguished pioneers, had done relatively little to tie the profession's thinking together by weaving the successes we had and the information we were collecting as individuals into a larger and more explanatory tapestry of theory. By necessity, then, most of us were teaching from the hip. We enthusiastically used the activities that worked for us and those that others told us to try; we immediately dropped those that fell flat, that lost their luster in our own computer-supported environments. But, disturbingly, we remained unsure of why we were doing what we were doing and why some things worked and some didn't. At this time, computers and composition studies had yet to map its experiences theoretically and, hence, had yet to become self-critical and gain perspective on its own direction.

In an attempt to address this situation, which computers-and-composition specialists were beginning to recognize and worry over and talk about at conferences in the mid eighties, we wrote a book describing a theory-based model of designing and operating computer-supported writing facilities. At that time, we saw this model as a sort of tapestry; one would start with the underlying theory, we reasoned, and this theory would give shape and substance to the thinking and the action that followed. Using the common intellectual warp and woof of composition theory, we described a model of computer-supported writers' environments that started with theory and that articulated theory from the design phase onward. (See figure 6.1.) We described how we thought our Department of Humanities had, from such a foundation, elaborated instructional goals and operational goals that shaped decisions about hardware, software, ambience, personnel, and programs in computer-supported writers' environments.

We can briefly discuss how we saw this model working.[2] In the 1970s and early 1980s, we had fashioned a sound writing-across-the-curriculum program, built primarily on the foundations of process-based composition theory and cognitive theory, and on the beginnings of social constructionism found in our field's early work on collaboration. From this theoretical base, we articulated instructional goals for our computer-based writing facility when we had the chance to design one. (See figure 6.2.) From these instructional goals, we articulated a closely related set of operational goals. (See figure 6.3.) Finally, using both of these documents, we designed a facility that supported plenty of peer-group work on clustered computers and one that encouraged process-based writing on an IBM network customized to provide separate virtual forums for private first drafts, later drafts that needed peer critiques, and final drafts that could be handed in as finished products. (See figure 6.4.)

But it wasn't too long before we began to recognize the flaws inherent in this model. Computer-supported writing facilities are not like tapestries at all; they are not woven once and completed. Rather, they are woven many

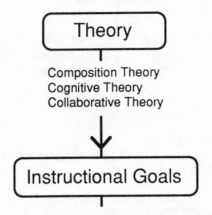

Composition Theory
Cognitive Theory
Collaborative Theory

What are we trying to teach?
What are our instructional objectives?

In what ways can operations support instruction?
How do operations relate to instruction?

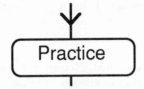

What are students telling us to pay attention to?
What are teachers telling us to pay attention to?
Where is theory inadequate in illuminating
practice?

Fig. 6.1. Theory-based model for designing and implementing computer-supported
writing facilities.

Goal #1   Encourage students to practice writing as often as possible and to improve their skill as writers.

Goal #2   Support the concept of writing for a variety of purposes, using a variety of writing strategies, aiming for a variety of audiences.

Goal #3   Promote a socially situated, process-based approach to writing.

Goal #4   Help students recognize that all writing takes place within—and is shaped by—social and political contexts.

Goal #5   Encourage collaborative exchanges among writers and teachers of writing: peer feedback, student-teacher conferences, student-tutor conferences.

Goal #6   Support effective process-based writing instruction for students and teachers who request it: writing-intensive classes, conferences, individual practice with writing.

Goal #7   Help writers learn to be critical readers of their own and others' writing.

Goal #8   Encourage writers to learn and share successful writing strategies.

Fig. 6.2. Instructional goals for Michigan Tech's Center for Computer-Assisted Language Instruction (CCLI).

times and continuously re-created. Nor are computers and composition specialists weavers who can realistically plan to finish a tapestry and hang it up on the wall to be admired. Rather, we are more like Penelope, who wove by day, then laboriously picked out her work at night, and then wove again the next day, not, as simply as Homer would have us believe, to fend off the suitors besieging the palace during Odysseus's absence, but rather, as a feminist reading of the myth might have it, because Penelope saw the story of her life changing, unfolding, before her eyes; because she knew that the narrative she had to tell was not complete; because she was yet to be satisfied with the vision she had created.

Goal #1	Purchase and maintain software and hardware that will support a socially situated, process-based approach to writing and the teaching of writing.
Goal #2	Provide CCLI access to any student enrolled in a writing-intensive class and to any instructor teaching such a class.
Goal #3	Make sure the CCLI is flexible enough to support writing communities of all sizes: individuals, small groups, whole classes, etc.
Goal #4	Make sure the CCLI is administered on a policy level by a writing faculty member and staffed on a daily basis by consultants who have expertise in both writing and the teaching of writing.
Goal #5	Provide hours that are flexible enough to accommodate individuals' writing habits and needs as well as groups' writing habits and needs.
Goal #6	Provide adequate technical support for maintaining, repairing, and modifying computer hardware and software so that writing faculty do not have to assume this role.
Goal #7	Ensure that CCLI policies encourage process-based writing ,writing as thinking, and writing as social action.
Goal #8	Provide a budget administered by a composition faculty member and sufficient to support staffing, scheduling, software/hardware purchases, and technical support.

Fig. 6.3. Operational goals for Michigan Tech's Center for Computer-Assisted Language Instruction (CCLI).

In our case, the model we had created had yet to represent an accurate vision of computer-supported writing facilities as dynamic environments. The model we had created was overly simplistic, reductionist, naive. We simply did not see how complex and dynamic a weave we were fashioning and refashioning in our computer-based writing facility every day. And we did not see the problems with our model, we suspect, because the original model we had created kept us from paying attention to certain kinds of evidence. The reanalysis of our model took some hard work on the part of some very bright faculty and students to alert us to the limitations we had built into our model, the flaws we had woven into our tapestry.

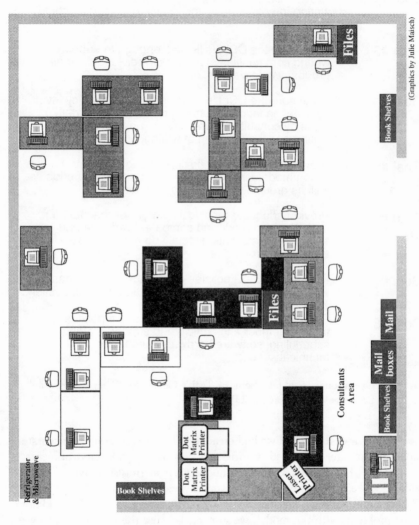

Fig. 6.4. Original center for computer-assisted language instruction. Founded 1985, IBM platform with text-based focus.

First of all, faculty began to unravel and then reweave the fabric we thought we had woven so tightly. These individuals taught us that the theoretical foundations that underpin a department's thinking involve constantly shifting perspectives, not only because the thinking of a profession changes, but also because the constituency of a particular faculty changes, continuously. Like most departments, our community was dynamic. Old colleagues left, and new colleagues joined us, bringing along their own particular visions of teaching and theory, few of which matched exactly our original conceptions when we were designing and planning the department's computer-supported writers' environment.

Marilyn Cooper joined our faculty, for example, and started picking at loose threads almost immediately upon her arrival in Houghton. She looked at the same IBM network we had designed to foster collaborative projects, but she saw different things, observing how students within the on-line conferences on this network resisted the discourses of other students, of faculty, of published texts as much as they accommodated their thinking to these sources. Students were using these forums, Cooper noted, to explore the nature of externally and internally persuasive discourses and the authority with which these discourses spoke. All of a sudden, our conception of electronic conferences shifted subtly but powerfully, and we began to see on-line conferences as spaces that had to be constructed to support both accommodation and resistance, both collaboration and individual effort (Cooper and Selfe, 1990). Students needed an environment in which they could benefit from conversation and guidance from others; but just as importantly, students needed an environment in which they each could learn to assert an individual identity within the community of writers and thinkers. Although we believe in the value of collaborative learning, we also believe, with John Trimbur (1989), that consensus is only one characteristic of collaborative learning:

> The consensus that we ask students to reach in the collaborative classroom will be based not so much on collective agreements as on collective explanations of how people differ, where their differences come from, and whether they can live and work together with these differences. (610)

Trimbur's consensus/dissensus and our roughly parallel accommodation/resistance are founded on a dynamic vision of society: that students should learn not only how to fit in, but also how to suggest change and drive change in society. Although Trimbur connects consensus/accommodation with "the new information society" (611), Cooper's unraveling of this viewpoint in terms of computer conferences allowed us to see this forum not only as a place in which students were free to agree and construct a group vision, but also as a place where social constraints to egalitarian discourse are removed or subdued: "If we can't eliminate the effect of racism, sexism, and classism in our traditional classroom we may be able to set aside smaller electronic spaces in which such problems can find expression and be debated" (Cooper and Selfe, 1990, 867).

But Cooper's observations were only the first sign that our theory-based model was unraveling, that we couldn't hope to identify a stable conception of a departmental theoretical base before making decisions about practice. Computer-supported writing facilities, in the words of Dawn Rodrigues and Raymond Rodrigues (1989), are "noisy, seemingly chaotic" environments that require teachers to rethink their teaching strategies (21); one cannot move from theory to pedagogy in one quick step. Theory and practice, we began to understand, were connected at a fundamental level in their own dynamic weave, one that had to be interpreted, seen, and understood hermeneutically.

The students also started pulling at the threads of our neatly articulated model, and there seemed to be more and more of these loose threads hanging around as time went on. Students showed us the limits of our early thinking and the danger of supposing that the relationship between theory and practice could be represented as a warp running in a single direction.

In our observations of students who wrote frequently in our computer-supported writers' environment, for instance, we began to notice consistent patterns of behavior that piqued our curiosity. These patterns were interesting not because they fit into our original conceptions of what went on when people write, but, rather, because they did not seem to be satisfactorily illuminated by those theoretical perspectives with which we had begun. On the three or four non-networked Macs we maintained in a corner of the lab/classroom, for example, we began to notice entire groups of students lurking outside the theoretically unified system we had set up so carefully on our central network. These students, despite the fact that the Macs were not networked, collaborated as much or more than did students who frequented our IBM network. They gave each other feedback about writing and made suggestions about each other's work as a matter of course. In addition, however, unlike other students enrolled in our writing-intensive program, these individuals tended to spend long hours manipulating not only text blocks but also images and design features as they constructed their texts; exploring the relationships of one idea to another, of one image to another; arranging ideas and the images of ideas in varying patterns of association.

What we saw then simply as a strange preoccupation with a new kind of computer that supported graphic images began to niggle. At first, we were both amused and mildly irritated at this "play."[3] We knew these students had plenty of work to do on "real" writing assignments, and yet we suspected also that it wasn't simply play that we were seeing. We were dealing with Midwesterners, to whom "play" was almost antithetical. These students played while they labored; labor, to them, was play.

One thing was clear, however: Our observation of practice was not mapping satisfactorily onto the composition theory framework we had originally constructed. That early framework, based on process-based theory and collaboration, helped us to understand the various processes students employed when they composed, but not why those students seemed so tied to the learning space they entered through the Mac screens. In this "space" (Bolter, 1991), using programs like Jay Bolter, Michael Joyce, and John Smith's Storyspace (1991), students worked on texts as if they were playing with Legos, building textual structures in a very physical, spatial way. (See figure 6.5.) This space in which writers worked and reworked their ideas by manipulating them in concrete forms was different from the virtual space in which other writers were constructing text-only documents.

Although we began to notice these differences more than five years ago, it was only recently that we began to understand how significant a concept students were communicating to us through their actions. We got help when we ran across an article by Sherry Turkle and Seymour Papert (1990) published in a recent issue of *Signs*. This piece deals with the learning styles of student programmers, and the dominant ideological/epistomological assumptions that shape the education of these individuals. More importantly, perhaps, this piece has helped us learn how important it is for us to pay attention to students as they practice meaning making.

In this piece, Turkle and Papert note that student programmers have traditionally been taught approaches to program construction that are formulated at fundamental levels in abstract, formal logic and are heavily dependent on representing such logical relationships abstractly, in the form of propositions within the rules of programming syntax. This "formal, propositional" way of "knowing" (129), according to the authors, has come to constitute a "canonical style" (133) of thinking and writing, a privileged way of relating ideas one to the other for those who enter the profession of computer science. More importantly, in Turkle and Papert's words, this abstract propositional representation has become "literally synonymous with knowledge" (129), so synonymous, so transparent a lens for programmers, in fact, that they can barely see it anymore, it is now equated with "formal" and "log-

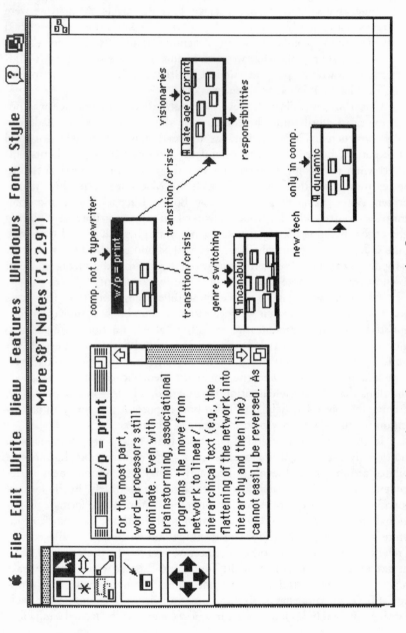

Fig. 6.5. Student's physical manipulation of concrete text images within Storyspace.

ical" thinking. And this way of representing knowledge has been given "a privileged status" (133) for programmers and others in scientific or techno-logical fields.

As an alternative way of coming to know the world, of learning, Turkle and Papert (1990) suggest an approach they call "bricolage" (135) in refer-ence to the work of Claude Levi-Strauss. *Bricolage*, as Turkel and Papert use it and as we will use it here, refers to the construction of meaning through the arrangement and rearrangement of concrete, well-known materials, rather than through an abstraction of thought in representations of formal propositional logic. Bricoleurs get to know a subject by interacting with it physically, by manipulating materials, or symbols, or icons in rich associative patterns, by arranging and rearranging them constantly until they fit to-gether in a satisfying or meaningful way. Bricoleurs reason "from within" (144) to come to an understanding of a problem rather than reasoning with the help of a traditionally validated pattern of logical representation.

We are convinced that this distinction, between individuals who com-pose by representing ideas in abstract, linear propositional representations (what composition teachers call "writing sentences") and individuals who compose by arranging and rearranging concrete symbols of text blocks, holds as true for writers as it does for Turkle and Papert's programmers. Those Mac-dedicated students we had observed in the process of making mean-ing for themselves were, and are, writing as bricoleurs, taking full advantage of the new spatiality of the "writing space" offered in computer environ-ments (Bolter, 1991). According to Bolter, the space available to computer users differs from the space of typed or printed environments, because the computer can encourage the concrete manipulations of symbols, icons that stand for text, rather than the representation of thought in abstract language structures.

While we have long realized that visual and verbal elements of the text both influenced how meaning was made from text (Fortune, 1989; Sullivan, 1991), we had not previously considered the two elements as overlapping to this extent.[4] Because our "writing" network of IBM computers supported pri-marily linear, abstract text production, we had emphasized this mode of writ-ing. Despite our intentions, students on the Macintosh computers were manipulating ideas within the writing space offered by Macintosh programs such as Storyspace in ways that they cannot do when working within the confines of the formal propositional structures we have privileged as a faculty.

Who might benefit from the space in which to write as a bricoleur? Well, as Turkle and Papert (1990) point out, strict adherence to proposi-tional logic is best expressed in terms of Western male gender norms. Those writers who have succeeded with the canonical approaches to writing that we had been teaching within our classes have learned to cope with these norms. However, many women and men may be even more adept at bricolage as a method of organizing and representing their thoughts and of coming to some insight about communication problems.

In the end, however, what we find most important about this story (we are, after all is said and done, still addicted to stories) is that our recognition of the phenomenon of bricolage grew not from theory, but from practice. It was only after daily observations of students working on the Macs using Storyspace, playing with HyperCard and Guide, that Turkle and Papert's (1990) discussion of epistomological pluralism made sense to us.[5] The student writers we had observed, in other words, had bothered us into a respectful understanding of other styles of thinking and representation, a perspective from which we can now see logic as "a powerful instrument of thought," but not as the "law of thought" (Turkle and Papert, 1990, 113; see also Turkle's 1984 ethnography of different computer-based learning styles).

This experience, in which our observations of students practicing writing changed our theoretical vision of the electronic environment we had created, was not an isolated incident. We have come to see that several of these loose threads led us to modifications of the writing theories and learning theories with which we had started.

Just last year, we had the opportunity to design another lab/classroom. When we did so, we saw ourselves making decisions in several new ways. We did, in fact, continue to work with theory, in part employing the same model we had five years ago. Of course, the department had changed; we were dealing with a different faculty, who had a much more diversified theoretical base: interests in visual representation and graphic discourses, in critical theory and cultural theory, in learning theory and cognitive theory, in feminist theory and theories of cognition. Our students had changed as well, even more so than is normal in academic situations. Our department now offered not only the bachelor's degree, but also the master's and doctorate. We found ourselves working with students from nearly every point on the spectrums of interest, ability, and academic area. Finally, our technology continued to shift. In supporting bricoleurs with hypertext programs such as Storyspace, we found that our traditional textual rhetorics had to be augmented by the rhetoric of new text forms such as hypertext, rhetorics that will continue to evolve as technology shifts (Slatin, 1990, 870), as the computer moves from a tool for writing print text to a medium in its own right (Oren, 1990).

The new facility had to be a place where these new epistomological weaves could be played out. But we also worked with the practices of writers and the practices of teachers more centrally in the design process. (See figure 6.6.) If our concrete experience told us that a certain design feature (hard-

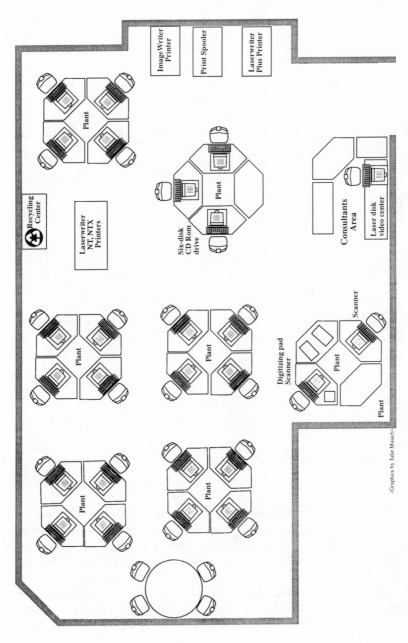

Fig. 6.6. New addition to the Center for Computer-Assisted Language Instruction. Established 1991, Macintosh platform with hypermedia focus.

(Graphics by Julie Masich)

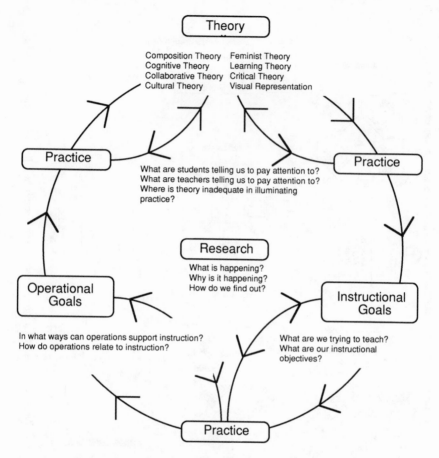

Fig. 6.7. Theory/practice interaction model for designing, implementing, and operating computer-supported writing facilities.

ware, software, furniture, media perspective) would work, we included it, without understanding why, hoping that we would come to a fuller understanding of the phenomenon at a later time, trusting that we could work at the complex knot produced by practice, observation, research, and theory.

Our new model, then, is less linear, more robust. (See figure 6.7.) We cannot say that it has resulted in a radically different writers' environment, however. The new lab/classroom is a Mac-based facility, rather than an IBM facility, and it is one that employs laserdisks and CD-ROMs and high-end multimedia programs to support the generation, revision, and publication of graphic and auditory images as well as text. These are technologies we did not have access to in 1985. But, like our other computer-supported writers' environment, it includes a network system that allows for the formation and operation of a variety of student-based writing communities and depends on a cadre of student consultants to keep it going.[6]

We are, however, convinced that the model is a more accurate one, one that allows a fuller and more complicated vision of how computer-supported writing facilities are designed and redesigned on a daily or weekly basis. We are, to our satisfaction, still picking at those loose threads: One of them is the role of research in the model represented in figure 6.7. We have yet to figure out exactly what research is and where it fits within this environment and how the environment is shaped by the results of research, just as we are still tying and untying the knots of theory and practice, still weaving and unweaving that tapestry that tells the stories of computer-supported writing facilities. Give us five more years. . . .

NOTES

1. For further analysis of this sometimes over-optimistic situation, see Hawisher and Selfe 1991; Handa 1990; Kaplan 1991; Barton, n.d.; Hughes 1989.

2. A more detailed history of our facility can be found in Selfe 1987.

3. For an extended (and contrasting) discussion of the issue of visual/ verbal play, see Marcia Peoples Halio's "Student Writing: Can the Machine Maim the Message?" (Halio, 1992a). Some of the features of the graphical interface that we now find so intriguing are, Halio contends, resulting in lower-quality writing. For a series of responses to Halio's article (including a counterresponse by Halio), see Slatin et al. 1990; Youra 1990; Kaplan and Moulthrop 1990.

4. For an early analysis in this vein, see John B. Smith and Catherine F. Smith 1984.

5. This situation seems characteristic of the "comfortable middle age" that Lillian Bridwell-Bowles sees in current computers-and-writing research; Bridwell-Bowles advises that we step back for a moment from empirical research to reobserve and rethink computers and writing.

6. The old and new coexist: Our IBM lab still supports on-line conferencing more fully than the Macintosh lab next to it. Given the finances, both networks could be made roughly equivalent in terms of support for composition, individual or collaborative, linear or bricolage.

REFERENCES

Barton, E. C. N.d. "Interpreting the Discourse(s) of Technology." In *Literacy and Computers*, edited by S. J. Hilligoss and C. L. Selfe. New York: MLA. In press.

Bolter, J. D. 1991. *Writing Space: The Computer, Hypertext, and the History of Writing.* Hillsdale, N.J.: Erlbaum.

Bolter, J. D., M. Joyce, and J. B. Smith. 1991. *Storyspace.* Macintosh computer program. Cambridge, Mass.: Eastgate Systems, Inc.

Bridwell-Bowles, Lillian. 1989. "Designing Research in Computer-assisted Writing." *Computers and Composition* 7(1): 81–91.

Cooper, M. M., and C. L. Selfe. 1990. "Computer Conferences and Learning: Authority, Resistance, and Internally Persuasive Discourse." *College English* 52(8): 847–69.

Fortune, R. 1989. "Visual and Verbal Thinking: Drawing and Word-Processing Software in Writing Instruction." In *Critical Perspectives on Computers and Composition*, edited by G. E. Hawisher and C.L. Selfe. New York: Teachers College Press.

Halio, Marcia Peoples. 1990a. "Student Writing: Can the Machine Maim the Message?" *Academic Computing* 4:16–19 16–19, 45.

Halio, Marcia Peoples. 1990b. "Maiming Re-Viewed." *Computers and Composition* 7(3): 103–7.

Handa, C. 1990. "Politics, Ideology, and the Strange, Slow Death of the Isolated Composer or Why We Need Community in the Writing Classroom." In *Computers and Community*, edited by C. Handa. Portsmouth, N.H.: Boynton/Cook.

Hawisher, G. E., and C. E. Selfe. 1991. "The Rhetoric of Technology and the Electronic Writing Class." *College Composition and Communication* 42(1): 55–65.

Hughes, Bradley T. 1989. "Balancing Enthusiasm with Skepticism: Training Teachers in Computer-aided Instruction." *Computers and Composition* 7(1): 65–80.

Kaplan, N. 1991. "Ideology, Technology, and the Future of Writing Instruction." In *Evolving Perspectives on Computers and Composition Studies*, edited by G. E. Hawisher and C. E. Selfe. Houghton, Mich.: Computers and Composition Press, and Urbana, Ill.: National Council of Teachers of English.

Kaplan, N., and S. Moulthrop. 1990. "Other Ways of Seeing." *Computers and Composition* 7(3): 89–102.

Oren, T. 1990. "Designing a New Medium." In *The Art of Human-Computer Interface Design*, edited by B. Laurel. Reading, Mass.: Addison-Wesley.

Rodrigues, D., and R. Rodrigues. 1989. "How Word Processing is Changing our Teaching: New Approaches, New Challenges." *Computers and Composition* 7(1): 13–26.

Selfe, C. L. 1987. "Creating a Computer-supported Writing Lab: Sharing Stories and Creating Vision." *Computers and Composition* 4(2): 44–65.

Selfe, C. L. (1989). Creating a Computer-Supported Writing Facility: A Blueprint for Action. Cynthia L. Selfe and Gail E. Hawisher (Eds.). Computers & Composition Press: Houghton, MI.

Slatin, J. 1990. "Reading Hypertext: Order and Coherence in a New Medium." *College English* 52(8): 870–83.

Slatin, J., et al. 1990. "Computer Teachers Respond to Halio." *Computers and Composition* 7(3): 73–79.

Smith, John B. and Catherine F. Smith. (1990). "Writing, Thinking, Computing." *Poetics* 19: 121–42.

Sullivan, P. (1991). Taking Control of the Page: Electronic Writing and Word Publishing. In G. E. Hawisher & C. L. Selfe (ED.), *Evolving Perspectives on Computers and Composition: Questions for the 1990s* (pp. 43–64). Houghton, Michigan and Urbana, Illinois: Computers and Composition Press and National Council of Teachers of English.

Sullivan, P. 1988. "Desktop Publishing: A Powerful Tool for Advanced Composition Courses." *College Composition and Communication* 39(3): 344–47.

Sullivan, P. (1991). Taking Control of the Page: Electronic Writing and Word Publishing. In G. E. Hawisher & C. L. Selfe (ED.), *Evolving Perspectives on Computers and Composition: Questions for the 1990s* (pp. 43–64). Houghton, Michigan and Urbana, Illinois: Computers and Composition Press and National Council of Teachers of English.

Trimbur, John. 1989. "Consensus and Difference in Collaborative Learning." *College English* 51(6): 602–16.

Turkle, S. 1984. *The Second Self: Computers and the Human Spirit*. New York: Simon & Schuster.

Turkle, S., and S. Papert. 1990. "Epistemological Pluralism: Styles and Voices within the Computer Culture." *Signs: Journal of Women in Culture and Society* 16(11): 128–57.

Youra, Steven. 1990. "Computers and Student Writing: Maiming the Macintosh (A Response)." *Computers and Composition* 7(3): 82–88.

7

Designing a Computer Classroom: Pedagogy, Nuts, and Bolts

Carolyn Handa

THE WRITING PROGRAM AT
AMERICAN RIVER COLLEGE

The English department's single computer classroom, installed during the spring semester of 1991, already serves approximately one thousand students per year. This classroom embodies the teaching philosophy of the department, which is to allow inventive combinations of teaching methodology, group dynamics, and instructional technology, while remaining focused on the students rather than the technology. The department plans on installing more computer classrooms in the near future and implementing the use of wide-area networks, interactive technology, hypertext, and collaborative teaching, both across the curriculum and across the country.

Teaching, of course, is holding open
the door and staying out of the way.

—Marie Ponsot

It took moving from a school with an established computer writing facility to another where a computer room was going to be installed to show me how much my approach to teaching in a computer classroom has shifted. Five years of conducting writing classes in computer classrooms have caused me to clarify my pedagogical stance. As a result, this stance now directs my priorities in room design, equipment, and focus. I think a computer classroom's design should reflect a student-centered pedagogy, the equipment should encourage student interaction, and the room's technology should help students to move out from the room to the world they will enter after graduation. But I didn't always think this way.

TEACHER-CENTERED ROOM DESIGN

The first computer classroom I worked in had no specific informing pedagogy. Those of us planning the room knew that we did not want students facing toward the front in regimented rows. But none of us had consciously voiced any desire for the room's design itself to emphasize pedagogy—for instance, to suggest to students that we think the teacher is there to guide the students, to help them to work together so they discover what they think, not what the teacher thinks. Not articulating our pedagogy, however, was actually tantamount to saying that we all agreed to an information transfusion approach (see Barker and Kemp, 1990, 6–8) to teaching in a computer classroom. The students ended up in four rows perpendicular to the front of the room, two facing each other in the center of the room, and two facing outward to the north and south walls. The teacher sat at the front of the room. (See figure 7.1.) The room initially had no networking apparatus, because we had not considered it important. At the time a network seemed like an extra. Later we did network the computers to a file server and the teacher's monitor, but no electronic conferencing or synchronous screen sharing were possible back then. We added a projection device, which, in the absence of any true networking, reinforced the position of teacher as expert only, not facilitator.

Without knowing why, I began feeling uncomfortable. During classes I teach in a standard classroom, I often break students into groups for brainstorming activities or peer editing. They share their ideas; they share their texts. I often send all the students to the board at the same time to put down their ideas for certain in-class activities, intentionally creating a near free-for-all. I move around the room as much as possible and often sit somewhere in the back to discuss what students have listed on the boards around the room. My tactics are nothing original, just my efforts at making the students comfortable with each other. Moving away from the front and sitting among the students also helps me to break down the teacher/student barrier erected by staying removed at the front of the room and to work on creating a sense

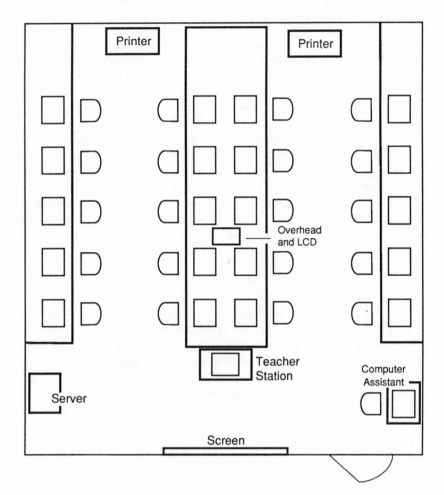

Fig. 7.1. Teacher-centered Classroom.

of community among the students. I try to work from students' ideas and get the students to do the same, to realize that what their peers have to offer is valuable. Gradually they begin to get the idea that they can talk to each other and that they need not direct remarks only to me. In a sense they feel freer once they have literally written all over the walls of their room.

What I didn't realize for quite a while was that the computer classroom's design effectively prohibited me from teaching in my customary way. I was installed at the front of the room. Students were immobilized in rows that, unlike rows in a standard classroom, could not be rearranged. My computer was hooked up to the liquid crystal display and the overhead, a connection that meant that only my computer screen could be displayed to the class. Although the students weren't actually looking straight at me, the room design and technology plus lack of a local-area network all reinforced my position as teacher and theirs as recipients of information only I possessed.

The room design fragmented my teaching approach. On the one hand, it lent itself to, and reinforced, hierarchical teaching methods. I found myself lecturing often and transferring exercises to disk so that I could project them on the overhead. But another part of me felt an inner agitation, something I could not express. I tried breaking students into groups clustered around a single computer screen. I tried moving around the room while students were writing, glancing over their shoulders and offering editorial comments and suggestions. But something still felt uncomfortable.

PEDAGOGY

I taught in this schizophrenic, vaguely dissatisfied state for a few more years until I happened to read Karen Burke LeFevre's *Invention as a Social Act* (1987) and Anne Ruggles Gere's *Writing Groups* (1987). These works helped me to articulate my approach to teaching and to realize how the room design of the classroom I had been working in was confining me. If anything, I was a social constructivist. Yet the pedagogical style that the computer room's design reinforced was hierarchical, one that centers on the teacher and what he knows, not the students. The teacher lectures. Students listen. Students respond to the teacher. Students nod agreeably. Paulo Freire describes such teachers in *The Politics of Education,* teachers who solve the problems of education through "the mechanical act of 'depositing' words, syllables, and letters into illiterates." Freire speaks of the connection between such a teacher and student as contrived and paternalistic. The educator becomes one who "fills" the student with words, with knowledge, and in the process a strange relationship emerges: The teacher assumes the role of a messiah, and the student recedes into the role of a lost man who must be saved by being filled with words (Freire, 1985, 7–8).

It is important to identify this approach, because the attitude underlying it is harmful to students: It excludes rather than includes them as participants in their own education. By being made receptacles of knowledge and not actively engaging in its construction, students taught in this kind of narrowly focused writing classroom have the power of their written expression neutralized (Barker and Kemp, 1990, 6–8).

Anne Ruggles Gere differentiates between two views of knowledge—
one imparted from on high by a designated knower, and the other socially
constructed—and two definitions of language. The fixed concept of knowledge "assumes that learning can only occur when a designated 'knower'
imparts wisdom to those less well informed. . . . From the fixed and hierarchical perspective, language is a medium, the vehicle through which knowledge is transmitted. As such it remains on the margins of knowledge." In the
social-constructivist view, on the other hand, knowledge is formed within a
group: "[This view] assumes that the interactions of collaboration can lead to
a new knowledge or learning . . . [and] places language at the center of
knowledge because it constitutes the means by which ideas can be developed
and explored" (Gere, 1987, 72–73).

Knowing now what my style is has helped me to understand how important a computer classroom's design is to conveying a pedagogical point of
view. As Cynthia Selfe (1989) has so clearly stated, teachers planning to
teach in a computer-assisted writing facility need to identify their instructional goals as much as possible beforehand, so that the facility can support
their program's teaching goals, the objectives of individual teachers, and the
activities of their student writers (22–26). Since my pedagogy was not clearly
articulated when I first entered a computer classroom, the room design I
helped to create reflected that fogginess.

STUDENT-CENTERED ROOM DESIGN

For the next classroom I was involved in planning, however, the committee planning the room openly stated its pedagogy before the room was
designed. Instructors wanted a student-centered classroom, wanted to deemphasize the instructor. This newer room, consequently, groups students in
pods, at hexagonal tables placed around the room in no special configuration. Students thus look at each other, not the walls and not just the teacher.
We moved the teacher's station as far as possible from an isolated spot at
the front of the room, although we still had to keep it near the front because
of the projection device attached to the teacher's monitor. (See figure 7.2.)
Embedded among the pieces of furniture scattered around the room, however, this teacher's station suggests to the students that the instructor is
more like another colleague in the room, instead of being the ultimate authority for whom they produce all their writing. The desk we chose to create
for the teacher has room for students to sit at it. This design resembles the
pods with editor's bays described by Carolyn Boiarsky (1990), and removes
the teacher from the style of classroom with the distant raised pedestal discussed by Thomas Barker and Fred Kemp. It helps the students approach the

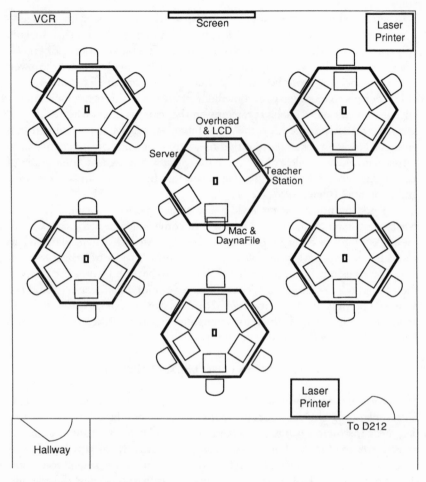

Fig. 7.2. Student-centered Classroom.

teacher as someone to collaborate with and who can offer suggestions for improvement. By enabling the students to see the teacher more as another writer, and by making the teacher one of the writers in the room instead of an education "banker" (Freire, 1970, 63), the design also encourages teachers to share the process of their writing, showing students that writing is messy, and inviting them to immerse themselves in this messy, creative process. In a teacher-centered computer classroom, rows of computers facing in one direction make the students feel regimented. Yet students are expected to tolerate the unattractive, rigid surroundings and produce their best, thought-ful writing. Barker and Kemp (1990) have argued that with a real-time net-work operating in a class, the rows-of-computers design has less serious consequences than such a design would have in a room without a network. We felt this point of view valid, but decided that ultimately the design also makes an important pedagogical statement and serves as a reminder to the teachers in the room as well as to those who visit it: The pods cause us to remember that the room is not teacher- centered, but student-centered. We are opening the door to knowledge and trying to remind ourselves to get out of the way. And those of us raised in the days of the hierarchical pedagogy need every reminder we can get to look to the students, not ourselves, for the power in the classroom.

This newer classroom is untraditional. Purposely untraditional. We hope it will discourage the type of traditional education described by Belenky et al. (1986):

> [In traditional education] the teacher himself takes few risks. True to the banking concept, he composes his thoughts in pri-vate. The students are permitted to see the product of his think-ing, but the process of gestation is hidden from view. The lecture appears as if by magic. The teacher asks his students to take risks he is unwilling—although presumably more able— to take him-self. He invites the students to find holes in his argument, but he has taken pains to make it airtight. He would regard as scandal-ous a suggestion that he make the argument more permeable. He has, after all, his "standards," the standards of his discipline, to uphold, and he is proud of the rigor of his interpretation. The students admire it, too. It would seem to them an act of vandal-ism to "rip into" an object that is, as Freire might say, so clearly the teacher's private property. (1986, 215)

Some other matters of room design worth serious consideration are sometimes dismissed pejoratively as "cosmetic," minor details merely show-ing "a woman's touch" and extraneous to the basic matter of "teaching writ-ing." But these matters, I argue, are necessary for creating an atmosphere that encourages students to be comfortable with writing and minimizes fears about reaching out to their fellow students to create a network of thinkers that will help them to learn. Our committee took great pains to examine carpet samples and to consider how comfortable the room would look. We chose the carpet, tabletop colors, and chair fabric so that they would com-plement each other; we also chose them because the classroom being renovated faces north and remains shaded from the sun. We wanted the room to appear warm and inviting. All of us had seen too many computer classrooms where no thought had been given to the overall appearance of the room—where, as a result, students working at computers are stuffed into unattractive rooms (often located in the building's basement) with no windows, or into rooms where the noise of the computers being worked on is deafening because no thought has been given to ways of absorbing or minimizing sound.

Since the hexagonal desks sit scattered around the room away from the walls, wiring presented a problem. We debated whether to run wiring for the room out from the walls or down from the ceiling. If the wiring came out from the walls to the pods, students and teachers would have a clear view to any point in the room, one unobstructed by electrical poles. However, since the room was already constructed, merely a classroom being renovated to accommodate the computers, we could not reconstruct the floor to run the wiring through it. To bring electricity to the pods we would need to run wiring from the walls through small tunnels. But we had to consider wheelchair access. While busy designing a furniture pattern to remind us to stay out of the way of the students' learning, we could very well have created a wiring barrier for students who already have too much else in their ways. Wiring tunnels would present a problem of access for students in wheelchairs, not to mention for those of us just walking around the room and not paying attention to the floor. In the end we decided to bring the wiring down from the ceiling so that the floor would be left clear. This choice would also allow us to rearrange the room sometime in the future if we wished, whereas the wiring tunnels would not.

Besides allowing students in wheelchairs mobility within the room, we needed to insure they could participate fully in computer classes. These students need desks at a different height from standard desks—and computer desks are even lower. We therefore requested one hexagonal table built at least thirty-two inches high so that students could wheel their chairs comfortably close to them.

Eventually we plan to place a few small tables around the room so that students can congregate there to discuss papers and edit by hand if they so choose. We all know we sometimes revise hard copy away from our monitors, and we felt that we should allow our students the freedom to move between different ways of revising.

We ordered two laser printers for this room. We installed one in the front of the room and one at the back, so that when students ended up printing at the same time, they would be moving to different parts of the room to pick up their papers. These printers are preferable to tractor-feed printers on three grounds. First of all, the laser printers are much faster. Several students needing to print at the same time don't have to wait long for copy. Second, laser printers are quiet. Even if several laser printers are running at the same time, their noise neither distracts class members trying to think nor interferes with groups trying to talk to each other. Finally, laser printers usually don't jam. With tractor-feed printers students continually tear paper off then forget to reset the printers for the next student in line. Teachers spend far too much valuable time getting the printers and the paper back on track.

As a sidenote: In our excitement over the more dramatic elements of room design, we almost overlooked some more practical considerations such as the room's lighting and temperature; we also nearly forgot to order lock-down kits and mouse pads. Our Computer Committee finally devoted a portion of one meeting to brainstorming and drawing up a checklist of practical design considerations and other minor, yet essential items. (See figure 7.3).

EQUIPMENT—HARDWARE

We chose Macintosh Classics for our classroom. The decision was partly financial: the Classic's price ($1,162 at the time) allowed us to outfit a room for a cost that would not exceed the $50,000 budget prescribed by our administration. But the decision was also prompted by concern for the student in the classroom. We could have gotten PCs for much less. But the Macintosh is a student-friendly machine that allows for a minimum learning curve and thus a minimum amount of frustration for the student. I have had many students remark in surprise how easy they found the Macintosh to use. Many said they had tried to use other computers but became so confused they never continued their efforts. With the Macs I have always spent a minimum amount of time teaching students what they needed to know in order to produce and print a paper. My instructions usually last no more than twenty minutes. After that, students know enough to experiment themselves and help each other.

The Classic is also a small machine, like its predecessors the Mac Plus and the Mac SE. The size enables students to see comfortably around the room without having their views obstructed by large, high monitors. The students dominate the scene, not the technology. Having taught briefly in a room of Mac IIs belonging primarily to the business department and shared by graphic arts classes, I must say that both the students and I found the size of the Mac IIs irritating. We found it difficult to see each other without considerable craning and moving around. Mac IIs *are* fast, no doubt about it, but they contain much more power and capability than individual stations need for most writing tasks. They may be fine for business and graphic arts. They are great as file servers. But they may not be quite the right machine to place

Part I: What to remember when transforming a regular classroom into a computer classroom:

———— Remove chalk boards

———— Repaint the room

———— Install white boards

———— Change locks on room; install tamperproof plates over locks (in some cases, fire regulations prevent using deadbolt locks on classroom doors)

———— Install static-resistant carpeting if possible

———— Consider whether the lighting in the room needs to be changed because of glare on the computer monitors

———— See whether the room can get its own temperature control, one independent of the other rooms in the building

Part II: What to remember to order after the computers and the software

———— Overhead projection device

———— Liquid crystal display

———— Lockdown kits

———— Surge suppressors

———— Mouse pads (for Macs)

Fig. 7.3 Checklist of Practical Design Considerations and Other Essential Items.

in front of students in a freshman writing class with an agenda that is primarily non-technological.

Our computers are networked to a file server with AppleShare for more than the usual purpose of sending material to the printers. The network and file server (another Classic, because of our budgetary constraints) are important because they allow the teacher's and students' machines to be connected, but more because they allow interactive software to be run. Machines connected only to a printer and not to each other or the teacher stay on the level of typewriters. The power of computers lies in their capability for electronically linking with each other. Computer classrooms that ignore this capability not only cut their students and teachers off from the possibility of using some of the more recently developed pedagogically sound interactive software available, but also make it difficult for teachers to use collaborative techniques and force these teachers into an authoritative, hierarchical style of teaching.

EQUIPMENT—SOFTWARE

Software should be kept as simple as possible given the pedagogical goals of the instructors. Since being at American River College and assuming more responsibility for decisions about computers and software than ever before, I have had the strange experience of dealing with representatives of the computer companies handling our accounts. These people think more is better. They want me to install more complex word processing software, spell-checking packages, thesaurus packages, and every conceivable kind of supposedly collaborative writing software.

I feel, though, that the software should not interfere with writing and that the many packages available on a computer should not confuse the student. Our job as writing teachers in computer classrooms is to teach writing, not computing or word processing. What we need is a low-end word processor for beginning and remedial classes, and possibly a more sophisticated word processor for the more advanced technical and creative writing classes. The classes could use an invention heuristic, electronic mail, and a local-area networking component that would allow students to communicate with their classmates in real time. If our budgets hold out, we also need a constructive hypertext package.

Before I arrived, my campus had been using Microsoft Works. This software made some sense, because it was operating in a classroom shared by the business, graphic arts, and English departments. For the English department's own classroom, however, this software makes less sense. It includes a spreadsheet and a drawing function that just distract students in writing classes. The software makes sense only because students learning to use it in our writing classes will find the same software in other open-access labs on campus. Simple word processors like QuickStart, part of the Daedalus Instructional System described below, or MacWrite II would make more sense. For a more sophisticated word processor, Microsoft Word would do just fine.

We have solved the problem of keeping the invention heuristic, electronic mail, and local-area network simple by deciding to use DIScourse, the Daedalus Group Inc.'s instructional system for the Macintosh. This system, developed by people who have been educators for years and have taught writing at all educational levels, offers in one package, simple applications that meet students' writing needs in each of the above-mentioned areas. One of the more exciting components of the software offered by the Daedalus Group is the InterChange application, a local-area networking function that allows students to share screens and conduct group discussions in real time. This function corresponds to the pedagogy behind the room. It offers the technological equivalent of students writing their ideas all over the walls of the classroom, and supports a student-centered, text-sharing pedagogy. The networking function allows students to talk as a group, on-screen; on InterChange's split screen the students can compose their individual comments in one box, then send their messages to the group screen when ready. InterChange also allows subconferences so a class can run different group conversations simultaneously. This function eliminates the problem of a group's gathering around a single screen and being hampered by the fact that only one student at a time can use the keyboard. This way each student can respond if and when he or she wants to. This software allows for the negotiation and collaboration that many students need in order to make learning personal, powerful, and meaningful in their lives.

A constructive hypertext system like Eastgate Systems Inc.'s Storyspace would also support, rather than detract from, the pedagogy informing this classroom. According to Michael Joyce (1988), a constructive hypertext, as opposed to a more static, presentational, audience-based exploratory hypertext, "requires a capability to act: to create, to change, and to recover particular encounters within the developing body of knowledge" (11). I do not intend to describe the differences between exploratory and constructive hypertexts here, because Joyce has already done so, brilliantly, and because my doing so would take me away from my main point in this essay, which is a pedagogy-informed computer room design. But I will say that this hypertext software, by encouraging interaction and collaboration, and by offering unprescribed investigatory paths, fits with a room designed to encourage students to participate in constructing the knowledge that will become theirs.

LONG-RANGE EFFECTS OF SOFTWARE
AND ROOM DESIGN

I cannot yet assess the effects of the room design and collaborative software we have chosen for our classroom, but the first results seem positive. Both encourage a camaraderie and bonding that occur much earlier than in other types of classrooms. In addition, more students participate in our on-line class discussions than in face-to-face discussions. However, those students who initially speak only during the on-line discussions do seem to end up, sooner or later, also speaking out in class. Somehow they seem encouraged to speak out in the class after they have gained acceptance on-line. Students invariably tell me they are having fun, that they enjoy coming to class, and that they look forward to coming to class. In a non-networked, noncollaborative classroom, students never seemed quite as enthusiastic. Something about this one works differently, and I would like to think the design and software contribute to that something.

Ultimately, a computer classroom's design and its software should not only encourage interaction between students but also end up causing them to expect such interaction. I would feel particularly gratified if students grown accustomed to such interaction started to rebel whenever they didn't get it. Indeed, something like this may be happening to a few instructors at my school who initially questioned the effectiveness of using computers to teach composition because they are so accustomed to controlling their classes and as a result can't quite see where computers would fit into their class plans. These instructors somewhat reluctantly signed up for one class session per week in the computer classroom, then had the unfortunate (for them) experience of having their students react so enthusiastically to the types of opportunities the room offered that they demanded more time in that classroom. In these situations, students have indeed begun to pressure their instructors to change their attitudes and approaches to teaching. Perhaps the room itself has begun subtly subverting hierarchical, authoritative teaching methods.

TECHNOLOGICAL FOCUS

Computer classrooms need no longer be constrained by the walls of the room, and indeed should not be. They cannot remain isolated. Planning for any computer facility at the end of the twentieth century should now automatically mean considering ways to link that room to a wide-area network, that is, one of the networks used internationally for educational and research information exchange between schools, colleges, and research organizations. We need to build our rooms to accommodate the changes taking place in computer technology and the changing face of the workplace as well as the entire business world.

Telecommunication in the workplace has grown increasingly common. More and more, employees spend some part of their forty-hour week at home communicating with their workplaces through modems; students who move from a computer classroom to an electronic workplace will have some advantage if they have learned how to communicate with each other from remote sites and feel comfortable completing major projects on their own without meeting daily with a teacher—or manager.

Telecommunications, ironically, rather than splitting people up and keeping them working at isolated monitors as we all feared at the dawn of the computer age, now seem to enable workers to maintain stronger ties with family and community, because more and more employees can do more of their work at home. This shift might well spell radical change in schools too. Certainly, the changes in society will need to be met by changes in pedagogy. Those teaching in computer rooms need to anticipate such changes by building classrooms that will accommodate the appropriate technology.

In a chapter entitled "Panoptic Power and the Social Text," Shoshana Zuboff (1988) describes the rise and fall of computer-conferencing technology in a large corporation during the 1970s. At its zenith the "information technology" in this company seemed to allow the creation of a "universal mind." "There were moments when it seemed [the conference participants] had achieved [pure thought]. Knowledge displayed itself as a collective resource; nonhierarchical bonds were strengthened; individuals were augmented by their participation in group life; work and play, productivity and learning seemed ever more inseparable" (Zuboff, 1988, 385–86). Elevated from the level of perfunctory messages and routine electronic mail to one of inquiry and dialogue, the new medium of electronic communication encouraged a give-and-take in ideas that generated creativity, learning, and new styles of communicative behavior. The medium broke down, however, when managers began gaining access to electronic conversations in order to control workers and used printed copies of conversations as evidence to damage those workers.

Electronic communication has already begun to cause us to question the ways in which our realities are constructed socially, and it will continue to make us ask even more questions in the future. Those involved in higher education need to be aware of this questioning. Our classrooms must allow not only us, but also our students, to hear it. If a discussion of electronic freedom versus control arises, we as humanists must participate in that dialogue, and our classrooms—doors open—should be sites that generate a rich, diverse polylogue, a collective voice meriting the attention of those in the next century.

"At the very apex of the pyramid of the educational hierarchy stands the professor, alone at his lectern, a silent, listening class before him. He is a mortal metaphor for much of what needs to be changed in American education. The strongest defense of the lecture format—that it works well for some students—is based on the assumption that our schools are serving white middle-class students. None of the measures of educational achievement support this view" (Nielsen, 1990/1991, 16). This essay has not so much been endorsing a particular room design. Rather, it is refuting the standard front-facing rows design, because one vehicle of change can be the computer classroom, but only if it does not replicate the above paradigm or the assumption supporting it. And with careful planning before it is installed, it need not. Hopefully our computer classrooms will be places that clearly encourage freedom of access to the knowledge that belongs to everyone, regardless of class or sex.

NOTES

Many thanks to Cathryn Amdahl, Mark Amdahl, and Mardena Creek for their perceptive comments on earlier drafts of this chapter and especially for their support as colleagues.

REFERENCES

Barker, Thomas T., and Fred O. Kemp. 1990. "Network Theory: A Postmodern Pedagogy for the Writing Classroom." In Computers and Community: Teaching Composition in the Twenty-first Century, edited by Carolyn Handa, (1–27). Portsmouth, N.H.: Boynton/Cook.

Belenky, Mary F., Blythe Clinchy, Nancy Goldberger, and Jill Tarule. 1986. Women's Ways of Knowing: The Development of Self, Voice, and Mind. New York: Basic Books.

Boiarsky, Carolyn. 1990. "Computers in the Classroom: The Instruction, the Mess, the Noise, the Writing." In Computers and Community: Teaching

Composition in the Twenty-first Century, edited by Carolyn Handa, 47–67. Portsmouth, N.H.: Boynton/Cook.

Freire, Paulo. 1970. *Pedagogy of the Oppressed.* Translated by Myra Bergman Ramos. New York: Seabury Press.

Freire, Paulo. 1985. *The Politics of Education: Culture, Power, and Liberation.* Translated by Donaldo Macedo. South Hadley, Mass.: Bergin & Garvey.

Gere, Anne Ruggles. 1987. *Writing Groups: History, Theory, and Implications.* Carbondale: Southern Illinois University Press.

Joyce, Michael. 1988. "Siren Shapes: Exploratory and Constructive Hypertexts." *Academic Computing* 3(4): 10–14, 37–42.

LeFevre, Karen Burke. 1987. *Invention as a Social Act.* Carbondale: Southern Illinois University Press.

Nielsen, Robert. 1990/1991. "Putting the Lecture in Its Place." *On Campus* 10 (4, December/January): 16.

Ponsot, Marie. 1988. "Not Academic." In *Audits of Meaning: A Feitschrift in Honor of Ann E. Berthoff,* edited by Louise Z. Smith. Portsmouth, N.H.: Boynton/Cook.

Selfe, Cynthia L. 1989. *Creating a Computer-supported Writing Facility: A Blueprint for Action.* Houghton, Mich., and West Lafayette, Ind.: Computers & Composition.

Zuboff, Shoshana. 1988. *In the Age of the Smart Machine: The Future of Work and Power.* New York: Basic Books.

8

COLLAB

Robert C. Green

THE WRITING PROGRAM AT HARRISBURG
AREA COMMUNITY COLLEGE

Harrisburg Area Community College is the largest undergraduate college in south-central Pennsylvania. Faced with a six-county service area that ranges from urban to remote rural environments, the writing program at the college is necessarily eclectic, making use of diverse methodologies that are selected by the individual full-time instructors. Part-time instructors are guided by a number of standardized suggested syllabi. To balance the diversity in methods, the writing faculty has drafted a series of shared objectives, chief among which are that students should learn the following: first, that writing is both a powerful instrument for, and a fundamental method of, inquiry, analysis, problem solving, and communication; and second, that writing is accomplished through a recursive process in which the writer discovers a need to communicate, envisions the audience, sets goals, produces notes and drafts, refines and clarifies feelings and ideas, develops ideas with appropriate detail, revises text to clarify the relations of the ideas to one another, and edits almost-finished text to meet audience expectations.

In 1987 some of us involved in the then-budding instructional use of computers at Harrisburg Area Community College (HACC) in Harrisburg, Pennsylvania, were asked by the college administration to solve a problem we had been fortunate enough to help create. Over the previous three years, increasing use of computers in our remedial and freshman-level writing courses had seriously overstressed the single computer laboratory/classroom available to English classes.

The HACC campus sported a number of computer laboratories and classrooms (mainframe and micro, almost exclusively MS-DOS), but our sections of English were generally restricted to use of a single computer classroom/laboratory with twenty-four Apple IIe computers (not networked). Arranged in a relatively traditional manner as a computer classroom, this facility was also being used by two sections of an Apple-based computer science course (primarily for liberal arts transfer students) and several sections of an introductory chemistry course, as well as by some graduate-level teacher-training sections in a state-funded program to raise the level of computer literacy among elementary and high school teachers in south-central Pennsylvania.

Once computer use by remedial and freshman-level writing courses took hold, that single facility clearly was overbooked. For its own inexplicable reasons, the administration resisted establishing a second, comparable Apple laboratory (even with the updated technology available at reasonable cost in the Apple IIgs). But they did finally make us an offer we couldn't refuse.

Since much of the pressure on the older laboratory had come as a result of recent increases in computer use by sections of composition, we in English were asked to design a classroom/laboratory that would be especially suitable for the kinds of new things we were trying to do in our writing courses. The kicker, of course, was in the form of some avuncular advice: "Times are hard, the budget is tight, and if you don't keep the costs down you won't get anything." Of course.

Properly motivated, we began our search for a solution. The limitation in funds meant that we could not hope for simply a second Apple laboratory, much less a second facility that had the hardware to allow us to network the additional computers. In addition, recent dramatic increases in overall enrollment at the college brought a firm "suggestion" from the administration that any extra room space we intended to use had to be easily convertible to normal (noncomputer) class use on a weekly, if not daily, basis. Clearly, we were being urged to look for a limited solution.

The basic concept for the limited but highly functional laboratory we finally decided on was suggested by our Campus-Wide Computer Planning

Committee, and most especially by two members of the committee, Professor Clifford Dillmann (a colleague in psychology) and Vice President of Academic Affairs Paul Hurley (a former English teacher with an affectionate regard for the computer as a tool in education).

Since we were interested in an approach to a writing process that emphasized a range of audience (peer) responses, we knew we wanted a room arrangement that avoided both the "eyes-front" lecture-hall configuration of the typical computer classroom and the "circled-wagons" effect of those computer laboratories that typically stress individual work in isolation or, at best, buddy work with the person next to you (on your left or on your right).

On the one hand, we wanted the space to support not pairings (since we wanted a healthy range of peer response), but groupings of four to six students. The groups were to be kept small to encourage some bonding and thus, one hopes, enhance the comfort level of students who might otherwise be nervous and overly defensive when others were looking at their work. On the other hand, we also wanted an arrangement that could easily make the space supportive of occasional audience work involving the entire class of twenty-four students as a single large peer group.

Budget limitations precluded a computer network, though a single network would not have been our solution anyway, since the hardware and software we were aware of did not support simultaneously ongoing multiple "conference calls" that could each involve just four to six students. The budget dictated also that we not simply buy twenty-four separate machines and try to position them creatively in a room to get the effect we were after. (In fact, that arrangement of machines had been tried in our already-established laboratory, where the machines were grouped in nodes of four so that students could "type and talk" together with some kind of small-group effect, but while that older lab space did have a warm feeling to it, students still resisted actual group work there.) The budget might have allowed purchase of one machine for every two students, but clearly that dreadful course of action would at best have promoted the buddy system of peer response.

The better solution was to buy fewer computers and to spend the remaining money on computer projection systems that could make each single computer a platform to support the type of space needed for effective peer response in the small group.

DESIGN OF THE CLASSROOM/LAB

The key new element in our solution was the PC-Viewer (sometimes called a "presenter," "datashow," or "electronic transparency"). This is a liquid crystal display, a flat plate that sits on top of a standard overhead projector. When the PC-Viewer is connected to a computer, it uses the overhead to project on a screen whatever appears on the computer monitor. In effect, the PC-Viewer becomes a dynamic overhead projector: Changes entered into text at the computer are reflected immediately in the projected image; no overlays, transparencies, or "foils" are needed. Most sophisticated computer users in education today are familiar with the PC-Viewer, but its uses in peer criticism in the small group seem to have been overlooked. We certainly had overlooked what the device could do for us.

A few of us on the computer planning committee had already used the PC-Viewer in our teaching. We had simply replaced our trusty standard overhead projector with the PC-Viewer during the initial weeks of the course when we demonstrated aspects of the software. I actually had used the viewer later in the course to present sample student work, but it had not occurred to me to try putting the device in student hands. Now it was clear that what we had in the PC-Viewer was a publishing tool students could themselves use in the small groups—if we managed to set up a series of computer stations that gave them effective computer-enhanced small-group space.

Once we had fixed on the PC-Viewer as the primary publishing device, determining the other components of a student/group station was not difficult. Each station needed an Apple IIe computer system, an overhead projector, a PC-Viewer, surge-protector plugs, a small projection screen, and a table to hold the equipment. Since the administration wanted the room to double as noncomputer classroom from time to time, the table had to be on wheels, and except for one chair for the person at the keyboard, seating would be movable student desks. (The administration wanted them in the room anyway.) Since many of our students do not have easy access to computers away from campus (and HACC is a commuter school), we also decided that each station should have its own printer so that hard-copy revisions would be available at the end of class sessions. (The printer sits by itself on a twenty-four-by-eighteen-inch audiovisual cart between the computer table and the projection screen. This leaves space for the overhead projector on the computer table and thus positions the overhead far enough away from the wall to give a good-size projected image on the screen.)

To encourage student interaction and brainstorming, we knew we needed a more group-oriented "notepad" at each group station than our software (and our single computer) would provide; the answer here was a dry-wipe board at each station. (Contrary to popular opinion around campus, we did not include dry-wipe boards in order to give our younger students a thrill when they uncap the markers.) Not only do dry-wipe boards avoid the problem of chalk dust around computers, they allow brief projection sessions of a small amount of text that can then be annotated with the markers—though any scrolling of the text produces bizarre results, of course. The glare on such boards, however, is such that longer projection sessions need to use a standard projection screen. We decided to mount the projection screen so that it pulls down over the dry-wipe board but covers only about two-thirds of the board, in case students wanted to make dry-wipe notations during a longer session involving the projection screen.

While designing a single student projection station was no problem, fitting a number of such stations into the same room gave us some difficulty. With a maximum of twenty-four students in a computer-based writing section, only four such stations would theoretically be needed if we set the size of each small group at six. Planning for a fifth station in the room struck us as wise, because of the flexibility it would give. In an intellectually active class, groups of five and even four can demand a great deal of time for quality peer response on all of the papers; in such a class, running four groups of six each may too frequently mean shorting some papers in order to get on with other necessary activities. (A fifteen-week semester that has to start with at least two weeks of computer training doesn't have a lot of free time in it.) The fifth station also meant that if a major piece of equipment failed, we would still have a decent chance of successful peer response in that part of the semester: Dropping from four stations to three with a full class would make successful group work iffy.

But the most significant potential benefit of the fifth station, we felt, was that when it was not needed by a student group, the extra station would make it easier for the instructor to shift the class back and forth between small-group and full-class work.

Using the fifth station for full-class response meant we had to find space for one extra-large projection screen somewhere in the room. We also had to worry about sightlines when placing the large screen, so that in shifting from small-group to full-group we wouldn't disenfranchise a small group awkwardly placed around a station in some far corner of the room. But the major problems with a fifth station were that it demanded more space than was comfortably available in the typical classroom and increased the draw on electrical power by 25 percent.

The concern about power draw turned out to be more than trivial once we did the math: Each of our student stations was expected to draw a maximum of about eight amps. The overhead projector was the major power user at each station. In a typical classroom wired with two twenty-amp circuits, the fifth station would have to have its overhead on one circuit and the rest of its equipment on the other. Even then, depending on what was going on in the room (and around it), there would be the potential for an overload as well as for power surges that could damage our electronics.

Space, however, was an even more important consideration, once we had decided on the fifth station. With five students per group, we anticipated a need for approximately ninety to one hundred square feet for each student station. To minimize distractions between groups, we felt there had to be a boundary of two or three feet of free space between one group and another. Given typical classroom dimensions (in the rooms "owned" by English at HACC, twenty feet across and thirty feet deep), it was clear that placing even four student stations in the standard classroom might involve some crowding at the boundaries. The fifth station would be impossible unless we found a larger room.

Worried about the political implications of trying to "grab a classroom" at a college where colleagues had already gotten quite defensive about available space, we toured the campus. Within a surprisingly short time, with the aid of Assistant Dean of Communication/Arts Michael Dockery (another former English teacher and avid believer in the power of computers in education), we found an oversized classroom that all reasonable people hated to teach in, primarily because its size, odd layout, and limited window space gave the instructor a feeling of holding forth in a subway tunnel or barn-size cave. Platonic allusions aside, we had found a space that we didn't have to battle for.

Situated above an art studio, the room is an awkward rectangle 40 feet across the front and twenty feet deep. Working with eight hundred square feet, we were able to fit easily into the room the five work stations, the thirty-some student desks (though our composition classes are limited to twenty-four students when we take a computer approach), and the necessary miscellany of additional classroom furniture (conference table and chairs, file cabinet, and the like). We added blackout screens for the windows and assorted incandescent lamps (from Goodwill), so that with the overhead fluorescent lights off, some groups could project while others worked with printed text. While electricians were in the building for a separate renovation, we were able to get an additional circuit installed for an apparently cheap price of about a thousand dollars. We plastered most of the available wall space in our room with screens (both dry-wipe and projection); procured five Apple IIe computers from the chemistry department (which was supposed to be upgrading to Macintosh); wheedled funds for five printers, five overhead projectors, and five PC-Viewers. We grouped the desks around five projection stations; and opened for business in a room that was both frightening and exhilarating. (See figure 8.1.).

We did succeed in keeping costs down. Even more important than cost, in our own minds we were succeeding because we had a facility that promised us new ways of using computers in improving our teaching of writing. The

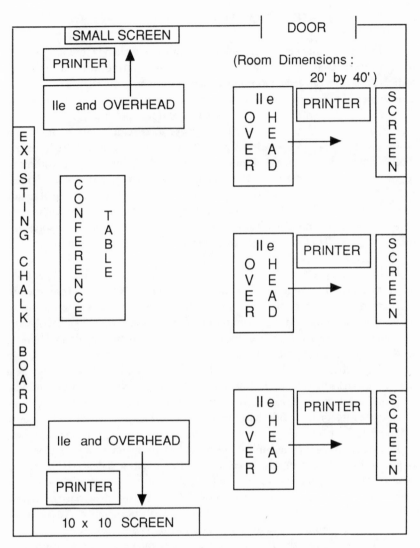

Fig. 8.1. COLLAB (Harrisburg Area Community College).

opportunity was exhilarating, in part because the instructional space felt so different. On the other hand, the very strangeness of the space also was intimidating; it was clear that we could not just use this place as if it were only another room, only another computer laboratory.

INSTRUCTIONAL USES OF THE SPACE

This electronic classroom, the Collaborative-Writing Computer Class-room/Laboratory (Collab), was designed for collaborative work, as its name indicates. The room feels more like a bazaar for word-acts than a classroom. One major difference, vis-à-vis regular classroom space, is that when the Collab is being used in group mode, it has no focal point.

To some extent, of course, diffusion of focus can occur in any room when small groups are operating separately, but the projection systems in the Collab raise the effect to a dominant impression there. Necessarily, when the room is working as it should, there is an appearance of chaos—sometimes just the illusion of chaos, sometimes the real thing—but even the real chaos most often seems to be productive. Students grow to like each other; they care about each other's work and grade. They actually talk about one another's writing. They become a real audience for writers who seem to want to communicate.

If I stand back and observe the whole room rather than float from group to group, I am reminded of the weekend farmer's markets that operate indoors in our section of the country: the image for me is one of winter weather (sunny but cold), a warm room, bright smiles, chat, laughter, nour-ishment in various forms; it's that wonderful Saturday morning. There is work, but it's a good place to be.

Typically, my students begin the course thinking that writing is a matter of marks on a page, rather than a way of tunneling into other minds. But that point of confusion between the concrete symbol and the less-than-obvious reality of the underlying process can be countered effectively only when we help this typical student grasp the fact that, except in special cases, good writing is not something done in isolation, no matter how alone we might be in the room in which we write. The Collab was designed to be the kind of place in which a student could really learn that principle, not just learn it in her head and for any kind of test that might close out the course but grasp it at such a level that it would stick with her even if she forgot all the terminology and techniques specified during the semester.

Though we use the room for some collaborative writing activities, its main work at present is collaborative criticism, a surprisingly effective ex-tension of peer criticism done in group mode. With the one oversized pro-jection screen, I'm able to take a full class through some reader-response activities for either model papers or their own essays, but the main function of the room is small-group reader response to the papers written out of class individually by the members of the small groups. The group members bring to class their own floppy disks on which they have current drafts of the essays done by each person in the group. When possible, all members of a small group, before coming to class, will have read all of the papers written by the people in the small group. (Various whips and carrots are used to guarantee that all of this out-of-class preparation is finished on time.) Group members reading one another's papers from their own disks prior to the group meeting are encouraged to type their responses and suggestions into the text on that disk and then pass that information back to the writer later during an in-class projection session (which includes elaborated oral comment), or through disk-to-disk copying, or in hard-copy.

A network would of course greatly facilitate this kind of interaction in every case except for response during a projection session, which I see as a method that probably has greater benefit than networking because of the psychological impact of face-to-face discussion and the inherent richness of the channel (oral/aural/visual elements as opposed to the pure text-visual channel that networking typically involves).

When the room is working well, it's a place of nourishment. When the room is working, its ambience seems to promote a comradeship that can support good writing. What forms is a sense of group identity that is rooted in the space. In fact, with floor lamps aglow, projectors running, text scrolling up the wall at five different points in the room, and students fully (and often quite vocally) involved with one another's work, these classes tend to attract some strange and wondering looks from outsiders (the students and colleagues passing in the hall). Viewed from that hallway, this scene looks, I suspect, somewhat like a party for the local cabal. The sense inside the room of being in a special place, and of belonging inside its mysteries, won't touch every student, of course. But for those who do sense it, however fleetingly, it's no mean thing to have a dim remembrance of something like magic having happened there. By the fifteenth week, for a number of students as well as for me, this isn't just Room A-215, it is a place with a past.

With a group motivated enough, and mature enough, to take some responsibility for their own learning, good things happen: Once a group has started to interact on a serious level about their attempts to communicate with one another (in writing and in speech), they actually seem to want nourishing advice from the professional; there weren't many of that type of student before, at least not in my traditional classroom. But if I'm not careful in this new space, I fall back into old habits and teach too much, too soon— lots of good advice that is most often valued at zilch. The students often tried before in that traditional classroom, but they were trying to please the teacher. Now, when the room is working, they seem to want to reach each other. A group that works well, bonds together firmly. They resist the periodic reforming of groups that I insist on, but they soon bond in the new groups, and eventually most of the class members seem to have formed a single confederation of people who want to communicate with one another.

MAJOR INSTRUCTIONAL PROBLEMS

Not long after our first semester started, the unanticipated began. Some minor matters first: Our initial problem had to do with student expectations about the technology. Though we stated prominently in the schedule booklet from which students register that those in the class would have to use specified hardware and software, some people came to the first meeting expecting to use whatever software they were familiar with on their favorite Apple or, worse, on whatever hardware they had at home or at work. Much of the exercise work in the course can be done on any machine, but drafts that have to be projected and passed to other students' disks need to be in a file readable by our software package.

Another problem we had not anticipated was the noise level in the Collab. Acoustically, the room turned out to be overpowering, especially when one or two groups found it necessary to print multiple copies of revisions while others were deeply involved in heated discussion (and while the somewhat-hoarse instructor despaired of getting everyone's attention, short of blowing a whistle or playing with the light switches). With its ten-foot ceiling, the room really is a cave, a cavern of hard surfaces, all vinyl tile and concrete block. Plans to carpet the floor raise questions about static electricity in a room of such often-active people. On the other hand, our other Apple laboratory, the one with twenty-four individual computers, has both carpeted floor and carpeted walls; the noise level there is significantly lower, and equipment failure in that lab is not noticeably higher than in our new electronic cave. (In the older lab, however, people tend to sit as if chained to their machines, rather than pop up and down or slide desks into various enclaves as they shift alliances.)

But the question of carpet may be truly academic; laying carpet in an eight-hundred-square-foot room costs more money than we are allotted at present. It may also be true that (for some strange cultural reason) the noise makes the group lab that much more attractive to students and it is only an old-guy instructor, used to decorum and control in the classroom, who finds himself bothered.

Such problems as these could be resolved without great difficulty, or at least tolerated at little cost to either sanity or the quality of the course. To the extent that a radically new space implies necessary adjustments in teaching method and curriculum, however, there turned out to be other, more challenging problems. The impact of such an environment on course content and teaching can be seen most clearly, perhaps, by noting how it differs from both the actual space of a traditional classroom and the virtual space provided by a computer network.

I myself am not always happy with what we can accomplish in the Collab. I've come to see that much of my dissatisfaction seems to arise from the larger context into which the Collab has to fit. None of us in the profession can expect to work consistently beyond the limits of the structures that surround us. In my own case, this wonderful space has the potential to become a source of frustration: While my students can learn a great deal more about writing, that learning takes more time, much more time. In a fifteen week semester, I often have to spend much of the first three weeks in the twenty-four-station older lab getting the students far enough beyond their frustrations with computer technology that the machines don't block them as writers. Generally, only 50 percent of the students in a day class have done sufficient prior work on computers to get going as writers within two weeks.

Time for productive use of the Collab is problematic in another way. The word processor is essentially a tool for revision. Revision (revisioning a piece of writing, not just editing it) is a creative act that sometimes demands much effort and time, especially time. Multiply the temporal demands of revision by the rich availability of audience response in our electronic farmers' market. (The broader range of thoughtful responses a writer receives, the more decisions that writer faces in revision; the more decisions, the more time needed for a revision process that produces not only a better paper, but also more learning in the writer.) Add to the growing total of minutes (or hours) needed for productive revision, the effects of the modeling factor—that is, the time needed if one is going to enhance the educational value of the revision process by encouraging one learning writer to observe how another student writer does, or does not, make successful use of audience response and new ideas in progressive revisions. Its suitability as a space for modeling is one of the real strengths of a laboratory like the Collab. But this strength has a cost associated with it: Minutes and hours so used have to be subtracted from the limited class time we have in a three-credit course.

But time spent does pay off. It is not unusual for a student who has been struggling with his own paper to tell me that the glimmer of a solution actually came while his group was working on someone else's paper. This student modeling of writer behavior in real time is one of the clear strong points of the room: We have progressive drafts, all easily brought up and projected; we have a multitude of progressive responses; in current time (during class), group members can propose What if . . . and Have you thought about. . . . Between class meetings, in addition to going ahead with their own work-in-progress, the students spend time critiquing drafts and revisions done by the other members of the small group, and that prior preparation helps make use of class time more efficient, but time in class passes quickly, too quickly. In a very real sense, this learning space is simply too good.

The result for me is that only three essay-length assignments will fit into a fifteen-week semester. Each essay is really a unit with extensive components. Typically the unit begins with a brainstorming assignment that requires each student to discover approximately twenty separate usable topics for the type of writing the unit covers. In the second stage of the unit, the student commits to at least two of her twenty topics for second-level brainstorming. Due to time constraints, most of this writing is done outside of class without group assistance. Next, the student makes a final commitment to one of the two topics and turns it into a draft that will be projected for thorough commentary by his group. This is the point at which group members have to make a serious commitment to analytic reading of one another's papers; each student comments thoroughly on each paper written by the other members of the small group. This stage can take a tremendous amount of time, as much as four or five class periods when the papers are substantial and the five people in the group have lots to say to each other. In most groups I'm stuck with a maximum of 150 minutes per week (class time) for peer interaction. This limit has significant implications for the time I can devote to the final stages of a unit assignment.

After group commentary (sometimes during it), this public draft is reworked and submitted as a grade draft. One of the primary in-class activities I would add to the course if we had the extra time would be further involvement of the small group at the revision stage after I have returned graded drafts. Writers satisfied with their work (and their grade) would be able to publish, and possibly therefore validate for themselves, their final work by taking it back to the group. Works still in progress would get further suggestions, and group members would have a final opportunity to tie down an understanding of what at least this one instructor means by the term *good writing*.

BENEFITS FOR THE STUDENT

Many of the benefits of the Collab accrue to the students using such a room, but no teacher will object to a situation in which students typically get some joy out of learning. Certainly, no English teacher will feel cheated that her students actually have fun communicating with one another about important matters.

One of the primary benefits for students is the ease with which they can respond to the writing (and to the counterresponses) of peers. The point here is the purely physical process of carrying on the conversation. Networking via computer rewards the typist, and while, with practice, everyone can get faster (and less obsessed with typos in conversational mode on a network), we need to recognize that interacting in real time through typed text is a good deal more frustrating than verbal interaction. For ease of ongoing interaction, oral language truly is primary. The written mode has benefits that voice mode lacks, but conversational ease is not one of them.

Closely related to ease is the matter of concurrency. The Collab environment provides a true concurrency of interaction among members of the group, something necessarily lacking on a network. I talk, you talk, she talks, we talk, you talk, they talk: We all are talking about your text scrolling up and down the projection screen; we sometimes talk at the same time, you talk louder, he tells a quick joke (which in this gang of students could too easily have been stillborn, or even aborted, in typing); good lord, this is more like a party than a class, but we are working intently to get you a better grade, because we like you; we have bonded, and you are going to start helping me with my paper as soon as we run out of steam on yours.

Even more important than ease of interaction and concurrency, the small-group projection system is a richer and more satisfying way of communicating, primarily because it allows a richer channel for audience feedback (voice and nonverbal elements, in addition to text, but even the text enriches—it glows and moves and stands inches high). This is the original broadband technology, face to face. In fact, the very richness is what gives the teacher a case of nerves: I'm not whipping the teams forward now; they smell the water, and they know where they want to be. I'm just along for the ride, and I don't always like the feeling, the unsettling loss of control. But I do know it's good to see people enjoying their own writing and that of their friends. (No wonder I'm so depressed by those occasional groups whose "members" insist on remaining completely isolated from one another, each person working so hard to build her own private intellectual ghetto, despite the opportunity the Collab experience offers. No wonder I wish I had spent the first forty years of my life studying group dynamics and small-group socialization.)

There are additional benefits for students, such as the personalized peer teaching and reinforcement of basic computer skills that—along with the local cheering section—help bring the technically slower student along in a nonthreatening way, but the multidimensioned, natural context for communication in the Collab provides the essential benefits. Use of the PC-Viewer in such a space promotes a level of synergy that tends to come through face-to-face real-time interaction, lacking on a network—unless the network, too, can be configured as part of a similar physical space.

BENEFITS FOR THE INSTRUCTOR

Not all of the benefits belong to the student, however. For a teacher still relatively new to the computer culture, the technology in the Collaborative-Writing Computer Classroom/Laboratory can be much less intimidating than a network, certainly so in a situation where the teacher has to depend mainly on himself for technical expertise. You start with the Apple IIe, a simple piece of software, and the overhead projector—then the PC-Viewer fits into its place on the overhead with just two plug-in wires. All the student work is on floppy disks. While the basic nature of this equipment can itself become a limitation once the teacher is beyond the beginning stage in technological literacy, and while the curricular and methodological issues involved in using the space effectively can be daunting later, getting started is no barrier as long as the teacher has achieved a level of comfort at producing his own work on a word processor.

With the Collab operating, the instructor finds a number of very nice features. A notorious problem with group work in the traditional classroom has to do with what is sometimes referred to as "time on task." Without the projection technology, it is difficult for the instructor to track what is happening in each group. In the Collab, I have the opportunity to float from group to group, watching what they are watching and listening to at least snippets of their conversations. The room is arranged so that the group members are in semicircles focused on the projection screens while I move freely behind them at whatever pace suits me.

I find that I can also enter any group more easily than I could when they were working from individual paper copies; I don't have to shuffle my copies of the various groups' papers, and I don't have to grab some student's copy and ask where they are on the page. When I am in a given group, I can refocus their attention easily and quickly on some aspect of the projected text by going either to the overhead or (despite the "rules" for effective overhead technique) to the projection screen. The dry-wipe boards at each projection station also let me (or the students themselves) give more emphasis to key points than can be done with just verbal comments. Theoretically, I could also take over the keyboard in a group and type into the student's projected text, but I've tried to keep sacred the principle that the author of the text "drives" (controls the keyboard). Leaving a group in order to float to other groups also seems to be easier in the Collab than in a traditional classroom, perhaps because the room is dim when we project—I just ease off into the shadows.

An additional benefit for the teacher springs from the nature of communication in the Collab. Combining voice, nonverbal, and textual elements, the channel is a very rich one. The students communicate with each other in many dimensions simultaneously, and that same multidimensionality is open to the instructor. As an instructor "teaching/preaching to" the group, I can, if necessary, talk to them (seated) while I stand. I can choose to talk while standing in front of them (in the projected light), in the middle of the group, or from behind them. I can change position for emphasis. I can sit with them for a moment (next to any member of the group), or I can crouch so that what I'm saying has at least some chance of seeming less threatening or directive. I can also test any communication the group is trying to claim for the text: With silence enforced on the author, I can point out specific passages in the projected text and ask individual group members specific questions about their understanding of a passage. In a group that is shy about hurting an author's feelings, I can play the "bad guy" role with questions to specific group members that elicit answers that show the author she didn't get her point across after all. And all this can happen at the speed of sound, not the speed of fingers typing.

But beyond all these benefits parceled out to either the instructor or the student, the most persuasive benefit of the Collab is that, relative to a network, it is truly a budget facility. For someone dealing with a cost-conscious administration whose typical attitude is that technology resources go first to science and business departments, this may be the single most important trait of such a facility: It is cheap. But we should recognize that for many of those administrators, demonstration of some success in using technology to improve the teaching of writing offers proof that more money for more technology in English is justified. Effective use of a Collab may be a way to get funds for networking, though a networked classroom facility that doesn't also make use of physical space to get people together in the good old-fashioned way may turn out to be a giant step backward.

Relative to traditional class space, even one with isolated computers in it, the Collab does present special challenges and problems as a space for teaching and learning, but I can think of no better way for a tired veteran of the English wars to put a little zing back into his professional life. And when renewed enthusiasm promises better teaching and more learning, who could ever say nay to that? The Collab isn't a do-it-all facility in its own right, but it might be a good instructional space for anyone who feels a need for a little more progress in her or his professional practice. And it certainly is a quality space for student learning.

9

The Evolving Computer Classroom for English Studies

Valerie M. Balester

THE WRITING PROGRAM AT TEXAS A&M UNIVERSITY

The writing program at Texas A&M University, where Dr. Balester currently teaches, includes courses in writing, such as freshman English, creative writing, and technical writing and editing, as well as courses in rhetorical theory and history. The computer classroom is located in the Writing Center and uses networking to support the general philosophy that writers learn best in a workshop environment where collaborative activities can take place. Current short-range plans are to double the size of the fifteen-computer classroom in order to increase the number of classes that can be taught there. The writing program at the University of Texas at Austin, where Dr. Balester made her primary observations, includes freshman-level and advanced-level writing courses and emphasizes a rhetorical, process approach. The computer classroom is not affiliated with a writing center; it is used heavily for teaching a variety of classes in English, from the freshman to the graduate level.

If the pedagogy employed in a computer classroom is to promote process writing, particularly a workshop or collaborative approach that encourages student participation or reader response to texts, networking software is essential. Equally essential is a classroom physically designed to maximize, not subvert, software's capabilities. My experience as a graduate teacher in the computer classroom at The University of Texas at Austin showed me that not all computer classroom setups are equally useful for supporting the process-oriented teaching I endorse. This essay describes two designs that have been used in Austin—the proscenium and the perimeter—and discusses how each influences pedagogy by affecting student and teacher roles. The proscenium design encourages the teacher to take an authoritative stance, while the perimeter design encourages students to participate as actively as the teacher and to take on some teacherly authority.

My first impression of the UT/Austin computer classroom, which opened in the summer of 1987, was positive. In one sense, the room looked radically different from an ordinary classroom: Replacing desks were rows of long tables holding monitors and printers, with masses of wires visible every few feet. Yet the difference, though exciting, was comfortably familiar. The room followed the plan of what Fred Kemp, then the director of the Computer Research Lab and an author of the Daedalus Instructional System, called the "proscenium" setup, with rows of workstations (PCs and printers) facing one direction, and a few exceptions ranged along a side wall (see figure 9.1). The same plan has been called the "traditional classroom grid" by Stephen Bernhardt (1989), who remarks aptly that it is a "default setting for many people" (98). As those of us teaching in this particular setting became more adept with using the computers as a pedagogical tool, we began to see new possibilities, and, in turn, the setting evolved to reflect them. In 1989, when Locke Carter, like Kemp an author of Daedalus software, took over the directorship of the computer classroom, he effected an evolution by rearranging the room into what he calls the "perimeter" plan (see figure 9.2). Bernhardt (1989, 101) also describes this plan, calling it both the "perimeter" and the "peripheral" plan. Although I did not teach in the perimeter classroom, reports from colleagues make it clear that the new arrangement has resulted in a significantly different teaching experience.

THE PROSCENIUM PLAN

Novelty was a factor in Kemp's decision to use the proscenium plan. The plan is deliberately modeled on a typical noncomputer classroom, the idea being that both teachers and students will find it easier to adjust to familiar rows facing front. Students' attention is directed either to their computer screens or to a focal point at the front of the room, where the teacher usually stands, within easy reach of the blackboard. Although the tables are not bolted down as in an old-style classroom, they might as well be, since the numerous wires and plugs prohibit their movement.

The teacher remains at the center, both physically and intellectually, the source from which emanates major authority. As figure 9.1 shows, there is no physical space in the proscenium classroom at Austin for a teacher's desk or even a lectern facing the students. In fact, there is nothing but a two-foot space in front of a blackboard that a teacher can call her own. Although nothing dictates that the teacher stand at this spot and use a computer to the immediate right or left (Workstation #12 or #13 in figure 9.1), this has usually been the case.

To compensate somewhat for the rigidity of the proscenium arrangement, classes sometimes met in a small student lounge in the same corridor. Since it was comfortably furnished with a carpet and easy chairs, it was conducive to relaxed discussions and was a good setting for small group meetings. On the other hand, we had to reserve it in advance, and we couldn't view drafts on the computer. If we wanted to work with hard-copy drafts, we lost some of the advantages of electronic text, in particular the ability to make immediate, clean revisions. As a result, we seldom used the lounge.

Occasionally during my classes, when students were hard at work on synchronous conferencing, I would retire to the back of the room (Workstation #1 or #2), and there I discovered new vistas: To see the screens of the students filling with electronic text was heartening, and occasional technological trouble was revealed as well. Even more important, I discovered that from the back of the room I could virtually disappear, that my influence was then to be felt only if I chose to participate in the dialogue occurring through the computer conference. I was reminded that an instructor should physically leave the classroom when students work collaboratively, to remove the sometimes oppressive and always intrusive presence of teacherly authority (Weiner, 1985). But when the conferences ended, I found that to be heard and seen I had to move back to the front of the room. Moving back to the front returned me to a position that reinforced my authoritarian role.

The proscenium classroom, by design, forces the teacher to take center stage by pushing him or her to the front. First, the focal point of the room is moved front by the immobility of the workstations and the positions of the computers. The difficulty of walking down narrow rows crowded with wires discourages excursions to individual workstations. All eyes are on the teacher—except when they are on the screens; the monitors are the major competitors for the students' interest, and this is exacerbated by the fact that from the front of the room the teacher cannot observe the students' monitors

COMPUTER CLASSROOM LAYOUT
(UT/Austin)

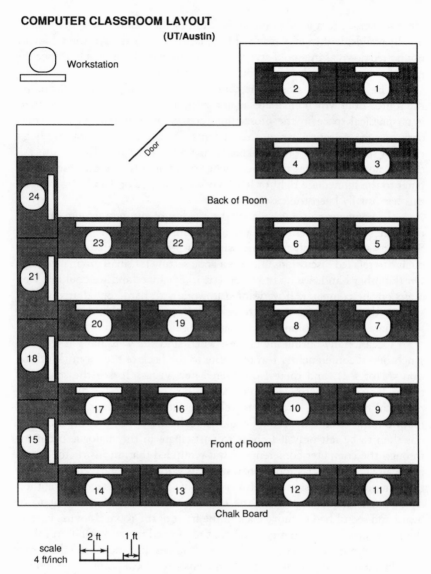

Fig. 9.1. The proscenium plan, 1987–89.

and thus does not know if students are following her when she is directing attention to something on the screen. The allure of the machine invites students to write out their thoughts or tinker a bit with a draft. Bernhardt (1989) points out not only these effects but also that when computers have large monitors (when they have, in computer jargon, large "footprints"), like the IBM PCs used at Austin, "students must crane their necks to see the teacher" (99). There are the keyboards, right at the students' fingertips, the monitors looming large. They have to look around them or over them to see the teacher at the front and to strain to hear her above the whir. Even when the teacher has gotten everyone's attention, ordered all typing to cease, all printers cut off, all monitors turned down to blackness, the machines whir between her and her listeners. Students' attention is thus being drawn away from the teacher, who must continually assert herself from the front of the room.

The teacher has a second incentive to remain at the front of the room, namely, to direct discussion. It is difficult for students to hear their peers, especially those with soft voices and those who sit behind them, and impossible to see them without making some effort. With the higher noise level in the room, the poor acoustics, and the long rows, movement and the visual/acoustic field are constricted. The teacher directs from the front, repeating questions and answers so that everyone hears. Eventually, I learned to coach students in speaking and listening, insisting they project their voices and face the majority of the class rather than me when speaking, and turn in their seats (or physically turn their chairs, though room to do so was limited) to face each other when listening; but the effort required me to act as director, constantly arranging events so that all could participate. Experience taught me to search for better ways. I eventually realized that electronic mail and synchronous conferencing could draw attention to all parts of the room via the monitor. The result was that one person, teacher or student, did not monopolize the floor. Still, it would have been far preferable to have both the computer and the physical layout of the room mediate group interaction.

Finally, the blackboard draws attention to the front of the room. As teachers become more accustomed to electronic text and place less emphasis on lecturing and more on writing or peer interaction, the blackboard becomes less useful. Certainly, there are always things to jot down, yet as lecturing decreases, so does the need to do so. However, electronic mail, synchronous conferencing, or network file-sharing do not entirely replace the blackboard. Better than a blackboard in a fully equipped computer classroom, no matter what its design, is an overhead projector hooked up to a computer projection panel. The advantage of this technology is that the contents of any computer screen can be magnified and projected for group viewing. And if a whiteboard is used for a projection screen, it can also double as a blackboard. A further advantage of a computer projection panel is that attention remains focused on a text, often to be manipulated in some way by the teacher or a student who has the floor, reinforcing the workshop atmosphere desirable especially in writing classes. In a literature or writing class, a projection panel can make it easy to discuss the transcript of a synchronous conference or a student-written text. Unfortunately, in the perimeter setup at Austin the only place to project the image was the front of the room; thus, the sense that the front was the teacher's exclusive stage was maintained, and students, although they may have been invited up front for performances, inhabited the pit.

In summary, the proscenium setup has proven most conducive to traditional structures of authority in the teacher/student relationship, in line with the "banking" concept of education described by Freire (1983): "In the banking concept of education, knowledge is a gift bestowed by those who consider themselves knowledgeable upon those whom they consider to know nothing" (58). Although the proscenium classroom is more comfortable for teachers new to the computer setting, it also encourages them to stick to old patterns—with the teacher as the central authority, often as lecturer. Yet networked computers are marvelous tools for a writing workshop atmosphere, one that decentralizes the teacher's authority. It is as if everyone had a large pad of paper and an overhead at his or her desk, so that they could write and share writing with ease. The "perimeter" setup to which the Austin classroom evolved in 1989 is far more conducive to a collaborative and workshop approach.

THE PERIMETER PLAN

When the layout for the proscenium classroom was designed, those of us teaching in the computer classroom were just beginning to formulate a theoretical and pedagogical base for our courses. Some of us were experimenting with collaborative learning and were committed to social-epistemic views of rhetoric. We found our software, the early version of the Daedalus Instructional System, particularly well-suited to this endeavor. The physical setup of the room, however, did not always foster the peer collaboration and diffusion of teacherly authority we sought. The perimeter classroom was designed to deliberately overcome some of the problems of the proscenium plan in this regard (Carter, 1990). In short, such factors as access to the front of the room and students' positions vis-à-vis one another are instrumental in defining roles played by teachers and students.

The perimeter plan, currently in use in the Austin classroom, is arranged with workstations (again, PCs and printers) along the walls and a central discussion table in the middle. A comparison of the two setups in figures 9.1 and 9.2 shows that the perimeter plan greatly reduces the amount of space for each workstation—every table holds two workstations instead of one, and there is one less workstation available; however, the greater overall

COMPUTER CLASSROOM LAYOUT

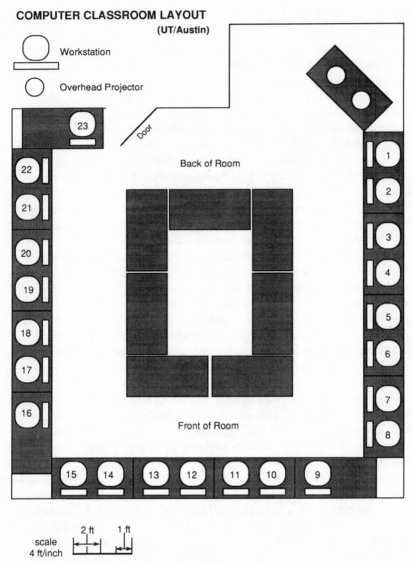

Fig. 9.2. The perimeter plan, 1989–present.

flexibility of the plan offsets the crowding. Students face a wall when working on the computers or face each other when they sit in the central discussion area. They may also turn their chairs around 180 degrees and face the center of the room, each other, or the teacher. There is no "front" to the room, no particular focal point for the teacher, although there is a center. Acoustics are less problematic, because the voice projects more easily, and perhaps because the computer, with its loud whir, is no longer directly between the user and anyone who has the floor.

Unlike the front, the center is a shared space—a theater-in-the round—where teachers and students find more room to move about freely, and even when someone has center stage, students can observe not only the central figure but each other. Predictably enough, teachers do seem to seek out a focal point by selecting computers in corners (for example, Workstations #1, #9, #16, and #23), but corners are nevertheless not as imposing as a front focal point and provide more possibilities for focus. For the teacher who prefers to circulate, to check in briefly with groups or individuals or simply to observe the screens, the ample walking space in the perimeter classroom provides a considerable advantage. Likewise, for those moments when the teacher wants the floor, the focal point can shift around the room rather than remain fixed at the front. Not only does such shifting keep student interest higher, but it also ensures a greater sense of participation by all sections of the room. It is simply harder to shrink into the middle rows.

The loss of a front to the perimeter classroom makes the wall-mounted blackboard that figured in the proscenium classroom inaccessible. A wheeled blackboard is a feasible substitute but difficult to position anywhere except in front of the door. Since a number of teachers in this setting want the ability to display a large image to the whole class, an ordinary overhead projector was installed in a corner (see figure 9.2). Yet, as with a wheeled blackboard, there is no good place to position a screen or projector except in front of the door. Locke Carter (1990) has suggested two alternatives: (1) Place a computer projection panel and overhead projector in the opening of the central square of tables, and project the image onto the front wall over the heads of students at Workstations #12 and #13; or (2) Eliminate a blackboard or computer projection panel, and instead put computers at the four corners of the central tables. They would be used only for demonstrations, and students could move their chairs to the center and cluster around them for viewing. Of the two alternatives, I think the first would be most flexible. Besides providing a central focal point, it allows for the manipulation of text without the use of special document-sharing software (such as Timbuktu). In addition, I would prefer leaving the central tables computer-free, to provide a more traditional writing/discussion area.

A collaborative classroom and a workshop atmosphere demand the ready creation of groups of various types; the perimeter classroom fulfills this requirement admirably. The most natural way to create groups of four or five

COMPUTER CLASSROOM LAYOUT
(UT/Austin)

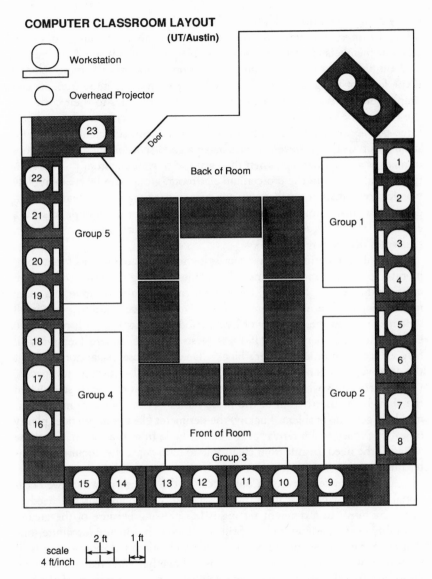

Fig. 9.3. The perimeter plan with collaborative groups.

is to take advantage of the room's square configuration. As Figure 9.3 demonstrates, natural groupings can be made around one computer; for example, students at Workstations #1 through #5 can move their chairs to Workstation #3. If the chairs had wheels, the matter would be even easier to arrange. Pairings, of course, are simple in any room. If random groups with different members are preferred over a stable group, it is a simple matter for students always sitting at the same workstations to log off and change places. If the focus of the group is to be moved away from computers, students can simply pull chairs together or can move the center tables to their corner of the room. The center discussion area can just barely accommodate twenty-three people for whole-class discussions, but it is not sufficiently ample for small-group work. However, it does make a good spot for one or two groups to meet at a time, perhaps when they want to move away from the workstations. And, just as in the proscenium classroom, groups can be created solely via electronic mail or synchronous conferencing, so that, as an example, students at Workstations #5, #9, #15, and #22 can form a group. In such a case, the wall the students face is not a barrier. All attention is focused on the words on the screen.

While the perimeter classroom is highly conducive to classroom community, it also can create a sense of singleness. Facing the wall, working on an individual piece of writing, the student can feel entirely alone in a room full of people. The atmosphere is conducive to concentration, yet not all writers can stand the intensity of long periods at a monitor with nothing to engage the view. Bernhardt (1989) suggests that the student facing a wall may suffer from a unique writer's block: "Does this close visual horizon limit the creative, idea-generating heuristic known to us all—staring into space?" (102). Particularly when invention or drafting is still at that early stage when the thought or the rhythm of the prose hasn't become all-consuming, this may be a genuine problem. Luckily, the perimeter classroom provides plenty of walking space and a retreat at the center table from the screen. For those who feel the need to shift from electronic to hard copy, the uncluttered center tables can be welcoming.

The perimeter classroom has access to the lounge to which we occasionally retired when we used the proscenium classroom, but the need to make the move to a different setting is less pressing because of the greater flexibility of the perimeter plan. Still, the lounge has its unique allure, one that cannot easily be duplicated in a wired and monitored room—that is, it takes one away from the classroom setting altogether and creates a more relaxed and friendly atmosphere quite conducive to conversation of the sort valued in a collaborative learning environment. Every classroom should have a spot like this, but computer classrooms, because of glare, noise, and bustle, need such a retreat even more. Some improvements to the Austin classroom could have been incorporated to improve the atmosphere, of course, and to bring it closer to this ideal. Every computer classroom, given the appropriate budget, should have raised floors or modesty panels to hide and protect wires, static-free carpet, sound-absorbing tiles, lighting to minimize glare, and access to an area with comfortable chairs. Plants, windows, and wheeled chairs would be added bonuses.

A few other changes might also be desirable. The rather crowded condition of the perimeter classroom, with two workstations per table, could be alleviated somewhat if each student did not have a printer. Noise level could also be significantly improved if laser printers (say four, one for each corner) were installed and printing jobs spooled to them. Furthermore, computers with the smallest possible footprint are advantageous for obvious reasons; PC2s, Mac Pluses, or Mac SEs are good choices.

ANOTHER OPTION: THE CLUSTER PLAN

Not every room will easily lend itself to either the perimeter or the proscenium design. Even so, the physical arrangement can and should account for its effect on teacher and student roles. For example, the classroom/writing center we are currently installing at Texas A&M is quite small (twenty feet by sixteen feet). Until we can acquire more space, we are limiting its use as a classroom to unusually small pilot sections. The room's dimensions make it unsuitable for the perimeter plan. Nor is the proscenium plan suitable, since, as I have indicated throughout this essay, it does not suit our pedagogical goals, which include collaborative learning and one-on-one tutoring. We have settled instead on a cluster plan, as shown in figure 9.4. (Bernhardt, 1989, 100; Boiarsky, 1990, 53). Our classroom is printerless, and thus quieter, because we are connected to a laser printer in a general-use computer lab located just downstairs from us. (Though this may sound inconvenient, it does save us from the considerable burden of printer maintenance responsibilities. Students work primarily from electronic text during class, but they could, if necessary, go downstairs for printouts.) Although the computers are close together, we provide a bookcase where students can leave the bulk of their possessions, making their work spaces less cluttered. Groups of five students can work together or be split into smaller groups, and a whiteboard at the front of the room also serves as a screen for a computer projection panel. A center table is available for working on paper drafts, for breaks from the computers, for small-group meetings, and so on. The projection panel is set on the center table when in use. Students can see each other and others in the room, since our classroom is equipped with Macintosh Classics, which have a relatively small footprint. Finally, there is a workstation (#1) for the teacher's computer, placed so as to be less central than a lectern up front might be.

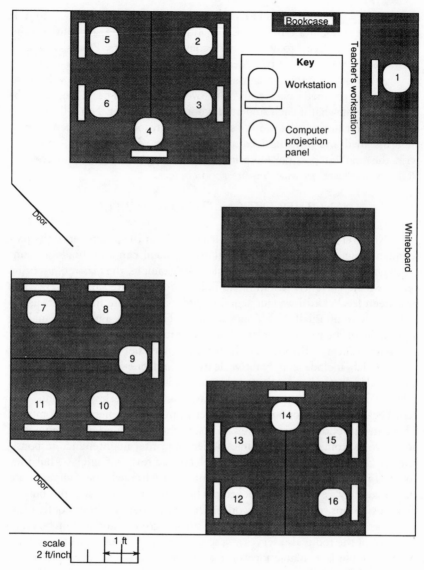

Fig. 9.4. The cluster plan, Texas A&M University, 1991. Designed by Mike Cherry.

Like the proscenium classroom, this arrangement may encourage the teacher to take center stage, because there is a focal point at the front of the room, at the whiteboard, and there is a separate and defined "teacher's work-station." The computer classroom is new to Texas A&M, and those of our teachers who still feel like a nontraditional classroom is alien territory may indeed wish to use the front space to establish authority and control. On the other hand, the use of clusters creates some space (though the small size of the room makes it a tight fit) for the teacher and students to circulate, and it encourages student interaction. In addition, the teacher committed to shifting authority to students can use the focal points of the room as much for student as for teacher interaction, and the empty center desk can and should be reserved for student rather than teacher use. The placement of the teacher's workstation off to the side is meant to encourage this approach. In the best-case scenario, the teacher will use her workstation for participating in electronic mail and synchronous conferences rather than as a lectern.

I have discussed how the perimeter classroom is more conducive than the proscenium to collaborative learning and workshop approaches to English instruction. I would like to emphasize two points as I conclude. First, without networking and the possibilities thus made available for file sharing, the potential for collaboration is greatly diminished and the advantage gained by the perimeter plan is negligible.

Second, no matter how the room is arranged, the influence and philosophy of the teacher will have the most profound effect on teacher and student roles. While the perimeter classroom can enhance and enable collaboration, it can also be used to conduct a class that promotes the banking concept of education. Likewise, while the proscenium classroom metaphorically promotes a highly authoritative role for the teacher, its physical limitations can be subverted, especially with the proper software. Ultimately, while it does have an effect, physical arrangement cannot make or break the sense of classroom community we wish to promote.

REFERENCES

Bernhardt, Stephen. 1989. "Designing a Microcomputer Classroom for Teaching Composition." *Computers and Composition* 7 (1 November): 95–110.

Boiarsky, Carolyn. 1990. "Computers in the Writing Classroom: The Instruction, the Mess, the Noise, the Writing." In *Computers and Community: Teaching Composition in the Twenty-first Century,* edited by Carolyn Handa, 47–67). Portsmouth, N.H.: Boynton/Cook.

Carter, Locke. 1990. Personal Interview with author. University of Texas at Austin, August.

Freire, Paulo. 1983. *Pedagogy of the Oppressed.* Translated by Myra Bergman Ramos. New York: Continuum.

Kemp, Fred. 1990. Email communication with author, 23 August.

Weiner, Harvey S. 1985. "Collaborative Learning in the Classroom: A Guide to Evaluation." *College English* 48:52–61.

10

Designing Computerized Writing Classrooms

Lisa Gerrard

WRITING PROGRAMS AT UCLA

UCLA Writing Programs is a subdivision of UCLA's English department. It offers a wide range of first-year, intermediate, and advanced courses, taught by approximately forty full-time lecturers and ninety graduate teaching assistants. The courses are typically conducted as workshops, with emphasis on reading and writing academic discourse, revision, collaborative work, and one-on-one conferencing. The program describes its underlying philosophy this way: "Writing must be taught as a vital process that aids the storing, structuring, discovering and re-visioning of information for self and others, a process central to our attempts to make sense of the world" (UCLA Writing Programs UCLA Writing Programs: An Overview, 1991, 6).

It stands to reason that computer classrooms should be designed for the kind of teaching that takes place in them. For UCLA's Writing Programs, a large program within the English department, the ideal computer classroom would have to accommodate a range of teaching practices. Our courses are taught by forty full-time faculty members with diverse academic backgrounds. Although not required to follow a single prescribed pedagogy, our faculty generally conduct their courses as workshops, with students writing multiple drafts of each paper, consulting with one another on revisions, and meeting frequently with their instructor for individual conferences. Beyond these similarities, individual practices can vary considerably.

It's not just that methods differ from one instructor to another; often composition instructors use widely differing methods in a single class meeting. Unlike courses in other disciplines, which are defined as lecture or discussion sections or laboratory sections, our composition classes typically move from one format to another, often during a two-hour class. Whatever the pedagogical bias of the instructor, during a class session students may write, read, discuss one another's work in pairs and in groups, confer individually with the instructor, make individual and panel presentations, watch the instructor demonstrate revising techniques, listen to guest speakers, watch films and videotapes, or listen to music.[1]

Such a range of activity is probably typical of composition instruction at other schools. And other instructors have undoubtedly found, as we have, that when computers are added to the course, this range is expanded. Students must also be able to write both on screen and on paper, and to collaborate both on- and off-line. With such diverse functions, the electronic writing classroom must be able to accommodate multiple and sometimes contradictory spatial requirements. The room must provide space for writing alone and in collaboration; for lectures, conversation in groups, and one-on-one consultations; for machinery and old-fashioned pen and pencil scribbling. It must be far more flexible than a traditional laboratory or lecture hall might be.

Of course, composition courses can and do proceed under less-than-perfect circumstances. But classroom space is not a trivial concern. The physical conditions of a composition classroom—computerized or not—tell students a great deal about what will go on there and what is expected of them. They have such an extraordinary impact on the success of a course that, whenever possible, I choose my teaching schedule by the room allotted to the course. I look for rooms with movable furniture. Writing workshops, with or without computers, are likely to be defeated by desks arranged in rows facing the blackboard, especially if each desk or chair is bolted to the floor.[2] Students sitting in rows of desks expect to hear a lecture. A hierarchical arrangement, with the instructor at the physical and metaphorical head of the class, makes the instructor the focus of attention and implies that she is the locus of knowledge and power. It tells students that she is the most important part of the course; that they should sit quietly facing her, take notes, speak when invited (one at a time), and remain in their seats until given permission to move.

This setup is useful when the instructor is making announcements, introducing a new writing technique, or otherwise offering information to the group as a whole. It is also useful for formal presentations by students, the instructor, or an invited speaker. But these activities typically occupy only a fraction of the time. In a writing workshop, where students talk to one another and to the instructor, discussing their ideas, sharing their drafts, offering and asking for help, rows of desks are more likely to inhibit than facilitate learning. Students need both the psychological and the physical freedom to move easily around the room, and they need to see their classmates' faces, not their backs. As they write in class, students should feel free to consult their instructor when the need arises. In a workshop, power and responsibility are distributed among all the participants rather than concentrated in the instructor. The student controls the writing, and the instructor responds as a knowledgeable reader; the instructor is an expert on writing, and the student an expert on his own text. Such a course demands a flexible classroom setup.

THE IDEAL COMPUTER CLASSROOM

The ideal computer classroom is more than a room with state-of-the-art equipment: It's an ideal writing space, a place for readers, writers, and editors to gather in groups and to work alone. Writing and writers—not computers—are the focus of the room. To enable work in small and large groups, computer desks and chairs are arranged in clusters, circles, or semicircles. Swivel chairs on casters allow writers to face any direction or move to any part of the room. Desks have compartments for personal belongings, so that the instructor and students can move around the room without tripping over clutter. The lighting is adjustable, so the room can be darkened for viewing films and using an overhead projector. The environment is personal, comfortable, and informal: The lighting is natural, not harsh; the floors are carpeted; the chairs are upholstered and adjustable. In short, this is a relaxed setting conducive to thinking. The lab provides enough computers for all students (maybe even an extra computer or two, in case one breaks down); a printer for every two students; a whiteboard (chalk dust from traditional blackboards can damage computers) with colored pens for formal presentations, informal messages, or graffiti.

The ideal classroom provides computer documentation; dictionaries, writing handbooks, and other reference books; and electronic databases for research. It's outfitted with tables for writing by hand, a projector connected to a computer for presentations, and a full range of hardware for instructors who want to teach through networked systems and for writers who want to share their work over electronic bulletin boards. Its software offers a variety of invention and revising aids as well as the special graphics, presentation, spreadsheet, and formatting software for journalism, business-writing, legal-writing, and script-writing courses. It has storage space for printer ribbons, disks, paper, and other computer paraphernalia, air conditioning to keep the machines (and people) from overheating on a hot day, carpeting to absorb noise, static protection mats, and electric surge protectors. It provides easy access to technicians in case of breakdowns, and, of course, it is secure against theft.

COMPUTERIZED CLASSROOMS AT UCLA

None of our three computerized classrooms resemble this description, but all are used enthusiastically by faculty and students in our writing program. The principal deterrent is lack of space—a serious problem everywhere on our campus. Don, the "space man" who allocates classrooms, has a hard enough time finding a place for our writing classes, let alone rooms suited for computers. Given this space crunch, all our computerized classrooms double or triple as other things. The WANDAH lab is half a room. The space is divided down the middle with a movable partition: On one side, which alternately functions as a classroom and a walk-in lab, are three rows of computers; on the other side is a tutoring center. The Dykstra lab, located in a student residence hall, alternates as a classroom, private lab, and public space for dormitory residents. The Haines lab doubles as an electronic classroom/walk-in lab and as a storage area for large boxes of computer equipment.

THE WANDAH LAB

The WANDAH lab is our oldest, most old-fashioned, and least-used lab. Its hardware and software have not been updated since the lab's beginning, in 1984: twenty IBM PCs (double floppy drives, 256K RAM, no hard drives), nine dot matrix Epson FX 80 printers, a typing program, and WANDAH—a combination word processing, prewriting, and revising program that we developed here.[3] Switch boxes connect two or three computers to a single printer, and students take turns printing their drafts.

The lab has carpeting, a whiteboard, bookcases, a dictionary, and a portable fan, but no other amenities—no storage space, no overhead projector, no choice of hardware or software. The room is crowded, but not un-reasonably uncomfortable. The overhead fluorescent lights provide adequate, though harsh, lighting, and the cables that run underneath the computer tables are generally safe from foot traffic, though occasionally someone kicks a wire and disconnects a machine. The lab's users cannot control its temperature; the entire building is controlled by a single thermostat, which turns the heat on in late November and off a few months later, regardless of the weather. There is no cooling system, other than the fan, and during heat waves the machines have been known to shut down.

The lab is located on the third story of a building with high windows, thus limiting access to thieves. A lock guard is placed on the door lock for extra protection when the door is locked, and the computers and printers are bolted to their tables. Student monitors oversee the lab during walk-in hours; they check each user in, exchanging student identity cards for WANDAH disks.

The WANDAH lab was originally meant to be both a classroom and a walk-in facility, but only rarely do our faculty teach in it anymore. Instructors can reserve class time in the lab, but when they do, they use it only for a meeting or two, primarily to introduce students to the software. The room's physical setup limits the kind of teaching they can do there. The computers and printers are lined up in three long, crowded rows (see figure 10.1), al-lowing students to work alone and in pairs, but discouraging group work.[4] The setup is awkward for presentations: The whiteboard is tucked in a corner of the front wall, behind a bookcase, where it is difficult for the presenter to reach and the audience to see. The straightback chairs are not adjustable and don't roll or swivel, and there are no tables, apart from the long ones under the computers. Nor is there a foot of space for additional furniture or to move the equipment already there. The only place a speaker (a guest, a student doing an oral presentation, or the instructor) can stand is at the far end of the room, where she needs to shout to be heard at the other end. But with tutors working quietly three feet away, any oral presentation is impossible. The only way to teach in this lab is one-on-one, but this, too, is cumber-some. Students are crammed tightly together in their rows, so that in work-ing individually with them, the instructor stumbles over backpacks, books, jackets, motorcycle helmets, skateboards, portable sound systems, and the students adjacent to the one she is helping.

The reason for this awkward setup lies in the WANDAH lab's history, specifically in the history of WANDAH itself. Though a writing tool for stu-dent writers, WANDAH originated not in Writing Programs, but in the psy-chology department. It began as a study of how word processing affected the writing process, but quickly evolved, under a grant from the EXXON Foun-

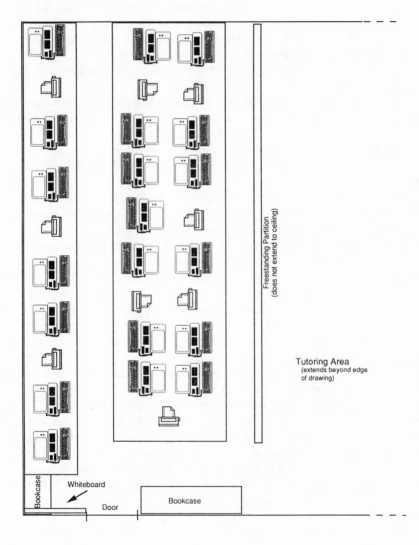

Bookcase

Whiteboard

Door

Bookcase

Freestanding Partition
(does not extend to ceiling)

Tutoring Area
(extends beyond edge
of drawing)

Fig. 10.1. WANDAH lab (not according to scale).

dation, into a project to develop software. Although two members of Writing Programs were part of the development team, Writing Programs was not involved in the project administratively and was pressed into service only when it came time to test WANDAH.

Thus, unlike many writing departments, we didn't begin with an idea for a lab and then plan the room and the software according to the idea. We began with the software. As the logical testing ground for a computerized writing tool, Writing Programs had to come up with a writing lab fast, before we could think about what we wanted. Unlike many schools, whose first lab is a writing center gone electronic, we didn't have a writing center or any other obvious space for this facility. As a result, the WANDAH lab migrated from one temporary site to another: In the first year, it was ten computers in a room in the library, shared with the tutoring center; in the second year, it was twenty computers on the back wall of the media lab, behind the cassette players; in the third year, it settled into its current location, in the building that houses Writing Programs.

Though the WANDAH lab has remained in the same place for four years, it has been the subject of little long-range planning, for several reasons. First, the current site is still regarded as temporary: Several other university organizations have claims on the room. Second, from the outset the university did not want to commit resources to a project it didn't know would work. Before expanding and refurbishing the lab, it wanted tangible evidence that WANDAH improved students' writing—evidence that WANDAH's developers believed could not be produced, given the many variables that go into a student's writing performance and the difficulty of creating a valid control group. The empirical assessment that was performed (citing students' improved attitude toward writing, increased time spent on their papers, increased willingness to revise, and development of a flexible writing strategy) did not impress the university. Though it allowed us to keep the ten computers it had allocated to the lab (Writing Programs had bought the other ten), it would not expand or upgrade the lab.

In spite of its limitations, the WANDAH lab has served us well. It has provided many instructors and even more students with their first encounter with computer-based writing; though most of them have gone on to newer software packages, quite a few still return to WANDAH. The lab gave us a chance to discover how best to operate a facility and how to teach with computers—information we have used in our other labs. We learned simple things, such as how computers overheat and shut down in a heat wave. (None of our labs is air conditioned, though at times—even in December— the temperature can exceed 90°F). We learned unexpected things, such as how inefficient it is to hire writing tutors as lab monitors: Though we hoped they could troubleshoot both software and writing problems, students rarely asked for help with their writing, and the tutors' expertise was largely wasted. We discovered prime-time use (10:00 A.M. to 3:00 P.M., except during finals week, when the lab is always busy) and optimum lab hours (usually 8:00 A.M. to 10:00 P.M., Monday through Friday, and 10:00 A.M. to 6:00 P.M., Saturday and Sunday). We found that locating the lab near Writing Programs made it easy for students to find their instructors for quick consultations on their writing. We saw how the computer bred cooperation: Students socialized in the lab, offering advice on the software and on their papers, and sharing books, disks, and experiences.

We also found that students got attached to the computer; once they saw how much easier it made the writing task, they wanted to use it for all their courses, not just composition. In the early years, we restricted the WANDAH lab to students enrolled in our Freshman Preparatory Program—a sequence of intensive writing courses for high-risk first-year students. The rationale for this limitation was partly administrative—the lab simply couldn't accommodate the entire student population, and the preparatory program was about the right size; and it was partly pedagogical—we wanted to provide as enriching a program as possible for students in this program, most of whom did not have a computer at home. This was one of our most successful decisions: Students in this program did extremely well with WANDAH and were delighted at the opportunity to use computers. It was the first time for most of them.

Students in the Freshman Preparatory Program praised WANDAH to their friends, who understandably wanted access for themselves and often slipped into the lab surreptitiously. We usually looked the other way, not wanting to obstruct any student's effort to write, though during finals week the lab became so busy that the wait for a computer routinely exceeded an hour. Our students became so attached to WANDAH that they wanted to continue using it after they had completed the writing program. Although we had not intended ex–Preparatory Program students to continue using the lab, it seemed unfair to train them in the system, encourage them to use it, and then take WANDAH away from them a few months later. Again, we seldom enforced our exclusionary policy. If students wanted to write with computers, we were not about to discourage them.

The WANDAH lab has been an invaluable resource not just for our students but for us. In its first few years of intensive service, it functioned as a testing ground for the software, new curricula, and the workability of the lab itself. In addition to trying out different arrangements for hours and lab monitors, we experimented with course materials geared to WANDAH, with classes taught in or in concert with the lab, and with new pedagogies.

In all, the lab provided a learning experience for the institution, its faculty, and its students.

The WANDAH lab is dated now: More powerful hardware and software are available on campus and off, and more and more students have their own systems—equipment that is not always compatible with WANDAH or with the IBM PC. Our instructors seldom schedule classes in the lab any more, so it primarily serves walk-in use, primarily for graduates of WANDAH's early years and students taking first-year composition in the Dykstra lab.

THE DYKSTRA LAB

In 1987–88, the Office of Residential Life, which administers student residence halls, decided to set up a computer lab in one of these residences, Dykstra Hall. Although it was principally a walk-in facility for students living in the residence halls, it also became a computerized writing classroom for several hours a day. Each term, one or two Writing Programs faculty members teach in Dykstra. Originally they used WANDAH, but now the lab offers WordPerfect, and most instructors use that. The lab originally had sixteen IBM PCs (256K RAM, double floppy drives, no hard drives), but the computers have since been upgraded to accommodate WordPerfect. It also provides eight IBM Proprinters, one modem with a hookup to the library's on-line catalogue, and a small assortment of reference books.

The Dykstra lab is jointly run by the Office of Residential Life, which owns the room, and Writing Programs, which owns the computers. Any student living in the residence halls or enrolled in a Dykstra lab writing course is eligible to use the lab during walk-in hours, which usually extend to 11:30 P.M. This is a boon to Dykstra residents who study late, because it saves them a walk across campus to the WANDAH lab—a walk that, in a large urban university, is not always safe at night. According to surveys they filled out, the overwhelming majority of students taking the Dykstra course enjoy working with the computers in class and appreciate taking class near their living space.

The faculty, however, have mixed feelings about this arrangement: They enjoy teaching with computers, but they find this particular setup inhibiting. The computers are arranged in rows facing a single direction, so that the students cannot see the people sitting in front of or behind them. (See figure 10.2.). The machines form a physical barrier that divides up the class, discouraging collaboration with anyone except immediate neighbors. The instructor is stationed at the front of the room and, looking over the monitors, sees only the tops of students' heads. The computer tables are close

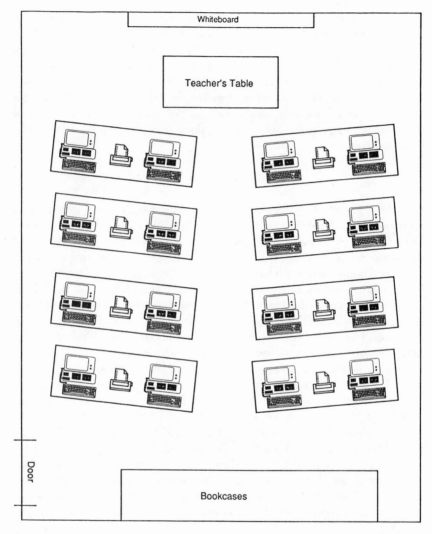

Fig. 10.2. Dykstra lab (not according to scale).

together, so that, as in the WANDAH lab, it is difficult for the instructor to circulate among the students. If groups of students want to work away from the computers, they can move the chairs, but there's scarcely any place to put them.

Joint ownership of the lab has created some logistical problems. The residence hall is responsible for security, so to enter the lab, instructors must stop at the front desk, sign in, and exchange their IDs for a key. When they leave, they sign out and return the key. This is a reasonable enough procedure, but it often requires instructors to wait in long lines at the front desk before and after class. Given the high turnover in student employees, sometimes the person working at the front desk knows nothing about the writing class and refuses to surrender the key. Writing Programs also has no control over the hiring of lab monitors for walk-in hours. If the residence hall is unable to hire lab monitors until several weeks into the term, the lab remains locked during walk-in hours, and students cannot work there outside of class.

In spite of these drawbacks, the instructors who teach in Dykstra, like those who use the WANDAH lab, continue to praise the experience, largely because of the advantages of teaching with computers: Students write a lot, revise easily, and, if they use WANDAH, enjoy the prewriting and revising features built into the software. At the same time, however, many of them are discouraged by the lab's difficulties and are turning toward the Haines lab.

THE HAINES LAB

In 1986, the university established the Humanities Computing Facility to coordinate computing efforts in the Humanities departments. This facility collects and reviews software, helps faculty members develop instructional software, provides technical support to departments and individuals, and directs two student computer labs, one of which—the Haines lab—is also a classroom. The Haines lab operates as a classroom whenever instructors reserve it for teaching; the rest of the time it is available to students on a walk-in basis. It offers twenty-one Macintosh SE computers with double floppy drives, four Apple Imagewriter printers, Microsoft Word 3.0 for the Macintosh, MacWrite, MacDraw, and MacPaint. The computers are connected to a sixty-megabyte AppleShare file server (Caspian), and the instructor's computer is connected to a Kodak DataShow HR projector for projecting images and text from her computer monitor to a large screen at the front of the classroom. While the Dykstra and WANDAH labs are free to students, the Haines lab requires a $15 fee per quarter for any student using the lab during walk-in hours. (This fee includes use of the Humanities Computing Facility's other lab, a walk-in facility containing both IBMs and Macintoshes and located in the undergraduate library).

The Haines lab is the most popular of our computer classrooms. Its location, Haines Hall, is convenient—in a building opposite the one housing Writing Programs and the Humanities Computing Facility and close to the other humanities departments. Security is reliable and unobtrusive. The room is located on the second floor, and the computers are locked to heavy metal cables. A powerful electronic alarm system sounds an alarm in the campus police station if an unauthorized person enters after hours. The system operates by means of several motion and glass-breaking detectors that are so sensitive that a gust of wind can set off the alarm.

Unlike the other two computer classrooms, which primarily serve students enrolled in composition courses, Haines is available to all humanities courses and thus must address different pedagogies. The literature and foreign language courses that use the lab don't necessarily operate as workshops, the way our writing courses do. Thus, the lab is set up to favor individual work or a lecture/demonstration-based pedagogy. The students' work stations are arranged in four parallel rows—five computers to a row—facing the front of the room. (See figure 10.3.) Off to the side is the teacher's computer, which is attached to the projection equipment.

Four activities work most successfully here: (1) Solitary revision, with the instructor circulating among students as they write and offering help when invited: The Haines lab is larger than the other labs, so the instructor can move relatively easily from student to student. (2) Collaborative editing and writing in pairs: The extra space and the movable swivel chairs allow two students to sit in front of a single computer. (3) Demonstrations for the whole group on the large screen: The projector allows the large screen in front of the class to operate as an extremely flexible blackboard. The instructor or students can demonstrate revising techniques by projecting a text from the instructor's workstation to the large screen. As the writer manipulates the text on the computer, the changes appear for everyone to see. The projector has many uses—anything we do on the computer can be shown to the whole class at once—so it is one of the most powerful features of the Haines lab and one of the most frequently used. (4) File transfer through the file server, which creates all kinds of teaching possibilities: The file server allows the instructor and students to transmit materials to each other electronically. Students can store their papers on-line for their classmates to critique, and the instructor can make other texts available for students to copy onto their disks and work with—for instance, passages to imitate, analyze, revise, or incorporate into their own writing. The file server also provides an additional means of collaboration among students. By copying each other's drafts to and from the file server, students make their work available for others' comments. This is far more limiting than an on-line conference system would be, but less clumsy than gathering groups of students around a single computer.

From an instructor's perspective, the Haines lab has several drawbacks. The row arrangement makes group work and full-class discussions difficult, and space, though less of a problem than in the other labs, is still limited. There's no room for a seminar table or small (hand)writing tables, nor is

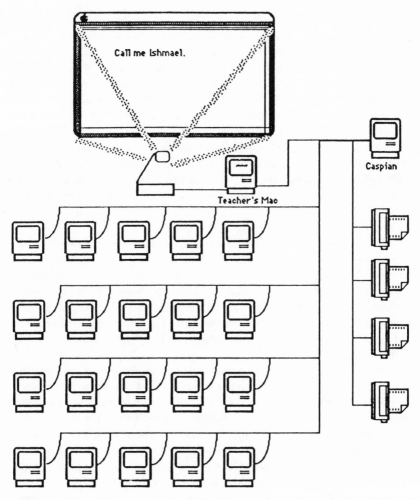

Call me Ishmael.

Caspian

Teacher's Mac

Fig. 10.3. The Haines Macintosh classroom (not according to scale).

there space to move chairs away from the computers. The computers present a physical barrier between one row and another, as they do in Dykstra, though in Haines the students and instructor have less difficulty seeing each other over the monitors, because Macintosh SEs are smaller than IBM PCs. The room is comfortably lit for individual computer work, but is too bright for effective use of the Kodak DataShow. The venetian blinds on the windows do not shut out enough light, so that the image on the screen appears faint most times of the day. Finally, the room is cluttered with equipment. As the Humanities Computing Facility's offices grow increasingly crowded, they find themselves storing large boxes of machinery and supplies in the Haines lab. So there's less and less floor space, and, with the increased clutter, the room is becoming a distracting place to write and teach.

In the last year, little has been done to improve the Haines lab, because its location—like those of the WANDAH and Dykstra labs—is regarded as temporary. Next year, the Haines lab will move to the building that houses both the Humanities Computing Facility and Writing Programs. The WAN-DAH lab is scheduled to move next door to it, a convenience for Writing Programs, the Humanities Computing Facility, students, and writing faculty. Although space will continue to be limited, the move will give us an opportunity to arrange the furniture in ways that support the workshops we run. It will also give us a chance to consult the instructors and students who use the lab and find out what is important to them.

In the past, our labs have been set up hastily, in temporary locations, on a limited budget, and with little recourse to students' and instructors' preferences. Although few budgets can serve everyone's choices for furniture, hardware, and software, they can certainly accommodate the inexpensive decisions that are equally important to a lab's success—decisions about hours of operation, furniture layout, and allotting classroom and walk-in hours, and features like bulletin boards, whiteboards, plants, lockers, fans, and bookcases.

Although it is not always convenient to consult students and faculty—especially on a large campus with many computer users—these daily users are the people most likely to know how to make the electronic classroom a stimulating place to write and learn. Administrators, instructors, and students often have different concerns and thus pay attention to different features of the lab. The ideal computer classroom should satisfy all of their concerns. In addition to providing a friendly place to work, it must protect the equipment from theft or damage, it should complement other computer services on campus, and, of course, it should be manageable financially. Ideally, then, a computer facility would be planned cooperatively by administrators, faculty, and students representing all groups using the computer facility. Ultimately, the ideal computer classroom works for everyone who has a stake in its success—those who manage and pay for it, those who teach in it, and those who spend hours of their lives in it.

NOTES

1. As Richard Fulkerson (1990) has discussed, a workshop approach can support any of the major composition philosophies and the pedagogies

that go with them: expressive, which emphasizes the writer; rhetorical, which focuses on the reader; mimetic, which is concerned principally with external facts and logic; or formalist, which emphasizes formal features and correctness.

2. To make rooms easy to clean and to discourage theft (which has left many a classroom bereft of chairs), UCLA has been replacing its seminar tables and movable chairs with desk/chairs (the ones with an arm that becomes a writing surface) nailed to the floor in rows.

3. Commercially, WANDAH is known as *HBJ Writer* (Harcourt Brace Jovanovich, 1986). It was developed at UCLA by the Word Processor Writing Project: Ruth Von Blum, Michael E. Cohen, Lisa Gerrard, Andrew Magpantay, Susan Cheng, Morton Friedman, and Earl Rand.

4. I am grateful to UCLA's Humanities Computing Facility for providing the diagrams of the WANDAH, Dykstra, and Haines classroom/labs.

REFERENCES

Fulkerson, R. 1990. "Composition Theory in the Eighties: Axiological Consensus and Paradigmatic Diversity." *College Composition and Communication* 41 (December): 409–29.

Popham, S. 1989. "Using WANDAH for English 3 in Dykstra." UCLA Writing Programs.

Shapiro, H. 1989. "The Dykstra Computer Classroom: Using Computer-assisted instruction (WANDAH) in a Special Section of English 3." UCLA Writing Programs.

UCLA Writing Programs. 1991. *UCLA Writing Programs: An Overview.*

11

The Teacher-designed Computer Writing Classroom

Karen Nilson D'Agostino

THE WRITING PROGRAM AT BROOKDALE COMMUNITY COLLEGE

*The writing program at Brookdale Community College is pro-
cess oriented and based on the approach to teaching writing shaped by
the work of Janet Emig, James Britton, Donald Murray, Peter Elbow,
and Nancy Sommers. Journal writing, conferences, peer response
groups, writers' workshops, and revision are an integral part of all
composition instruction. Writing portfolios, which are evaluated holis-
tically, are used for assessment.*

This essay will describe the evolution, layout, and basic operation of
the computer writing classrooms at Brookdale Community College, which
were designed by two composition teachers, myself and my colleague Sandra
Varone, to complement our writing curriculum. When Sandy and I started
experimenting with computers in the mideighties, we never dreamed that we
would find ourselves designing classrooms and redesigning our pedagogy because of these machines. But computers have changed our teaching in ways

we never could have imagined. We are about to build our third computer classroom, and we are actively involved in researching and working through new ways of teaching with technology. This essay provides a description of the computer classrooms we have designed, which provide teaching and learning environments that serve to encourage writing, revision, collaboration, and teacher-student interaction and inspire classroom research.

HOW WE STARTED

In the spring of 1986 Sandy and I began discussing the possibilities for creating a pilot project to integrate computers into our basic writing instruction. We both were experienced in using word processing programs on PCs (Sandy had a Mac and I had an Apple IIe), and we recognized that writing with computers had a positive impact on our own work. We found ourselves more willing to work through several drafts and revise extensively, and writing seemed to become more of the multidimensional process that we had been describing to our students.

At this time our department's computer resources were meager: Two Apple IIe computers with a shared printer were located in our writing lab. I took the first step with an entire class by encouraging students in my Fundamentals of Writing (ENG 095) class to use these computers. When time permitted, I brought my entire class to the lab, where they took turns entering their drafts at one of the two computers. My motives were simple: Students could revise or add to their texts easily, the problems of reading and proofreading bad handwriting would be eliminated, and students could use a spell check to help them identify errors. I was gratified by the willingness of these students to try something new in transcribing their texts on the computer, especially because they had to queue up and wait for a turn at the computer.

As I watched them work, I soon found myself intrigued by the processes I observed. My students rarely copied or transcribed their handwritten texts onto the computer without making some changes in their writing. Most of the changes, were minor—students substituted a "better" word or shifted the sentence construction. However, the important aspect of these changes was that the students made them on their own initiative, without my input or suggestion.

Teaching with two computers in a busy lab was far from ideal, but the impact seemed promising enough to warrant further exploration. It was quite apparent that if we wanted our students to use computers, we would need a computer classroom. However, personal computers were still very new products, and there was some skepticism within the department regarding their function in a writing classroom. But the more-critical element was funding, and we simply did not have the funds to build a computer classroom that year.

TEACHING IN THE BUSINESS LAB

A new business lab had just been built and was still being used just minimally, so we received permission from our dean to schedule class time for two composition classes there. The business computer lab was designed as a traditional teacher- centered classroom, with a whiteboard and teacher's desk located in the front of the room, facing four rows of tables with computers bolted securely to their surfaces. Each monitor was mounted on top of its CPU, and each row of computers shared one printer, with manual printer switchboxes between computers to provide printer access. We were so pleased to have the opportunity to teach with computers that the room design was unimportant to us.

We knew that to teach with computers it was imperative to know our word processing program thoroughly before we began (Rodrigues and Rodrigues, 1986), so we spent most of the summer preparing to teach by writing with the word processing program PFS:Write and learning the operations of the MS-DOS IBM-compatible computers in the business lab. We wrote a brief computer manual that explained the basic word processing functions that students would be using, and by the time September arrived, we felt well prepared to teach with computers. Yet we were also aware that we had to expect the unexpected, so we set aside time in our schedules to confer with each other as we undertook this new endeavor.

The students in our first two computer-integrated writing classes were selected at random. They were enrolled in the basic writing course based on their unsatisfactory performance on the sentence skill portion of the New Jersey Test of Basic Skills. Instructor names were not listed in the class schedules, so students had no indication of who their instructor would be or that their writing course would include computers. Indeed, the only option in course selection was the class meeting time, so we selected one morning class and one afternoon class.

At our initial class meeting, we provided a brief computer orientation for our students and assured them that they needed no prior computer experience and that typing skills were not required to work successfully with the word processor. Although most of our students had no previous computer experience, generally they seemed receptive to the idea of writing with them. And even though it was always an option, none of the students asked to transfer to a noncomputer class.

Working the computer into the curriculum gradually, we provided basic word processing instruction in the context of our writing assignments. The students seemed to respond positively to using the computers to compose, although a few were more comfortable with composing with pen and paper first and then transcribing their text to the screen. We encouraged them to use whatever combination of these strategies they felt most comfortable with. My class met for the three-hour class session (once a week) in the computer lab, while Sandy chose to meet in a conventional classroom and moved to the computer lab when students wrote. Within the first few weeks of teaching in this environment, we learned the importance of classroom design.

We found that it was difficult, if not impossible, to involve the entire class in a discussion in this lab, where computers sat directly between the teacher and the students. Indeed, our view of our students from the front of the room was obstructed by the computers. We also learned that once our students turned their computers on, they paid us little heed, and during class discussions there was always the sound of a keyboard clicking somewhere in the room. Initially, this was somewhat disconcerting, but it helped us to realize that we could not simply transfer pedagogy from the traditional classroom to the computer classroom.

Students responded differently here, and there was a genuine enthusiasm about writing with computers. Our basic writers, who had always been reluctant to start writing, were becoming increasingly reluctant to stop. We recognized that it was critical that we adapt our teaching and eventually adapt our classrooms as well.

In addition to teaching in the computer classroom, we also had to take responsibility for resolving the minor computer problems as they arose. We often had to format disks, recover lost files, and fix printers. Indeed, the shared printers in this classroom were often the biggest problem. As our students attempted to print their papers at the end of class, they had to turn a manual printer switch and take turns printing. The wait to print papers at the end of class was considerable, and if even one printer jammed, the printing quickly became bottlenecked.

After two semesters of teaching in the business lab, we recognized that our teaching was changing: Our instructional emphasis was shifting from invention to revision, and there was more one-to-one instruction in the computer classes. We knew that when the time came to design our own computer classroom we would develop a room that would complement our teaching. However, teaching in this less-than-ideal environment was critical in shaping many of our classroom decisions. Some of the difficulties in teaching in a computer environment had become apparent: how easily students are distracted by computers, how important it is for teachers to have access to each student as he or she writes, and how shared printers can create bottlenecks at the end of class. Despite these problems, we also recognized that our teaching was changed in the computer classroom and that there were more possibilities for instruction than we had begun to imagine.

DESIGNING OUR OWN CLASSROOM

In the spring of 1987, we received budget approval from the college to build a computer writing classroom. We envisioned a classroom where we would integrate computers into our teaching, not a lab that would be supplemental to our program. At that time Brookdale had open-space classrooms, which lacked walls and doors and were separated only by six-foot-tall, movable partitions. Therefore, we had to consider location, security, and classroom design, as well as hardware and software, as part of our planning of this computer writing classroom. One of our primary concerns was to find or create an enclosed room for our computer classroom, so we could secure the computers effectively and minimize any negative impact of noise. After meeting with our division chair and colleagues, we negotiated the use of a large circular room that stood adjacent to our existing writing lab. This room had wall around three quarters of its periphery, so to enclose the room completely we only had to have a wall built along the open one-quarter of the room, in effect completing the circle. This construction was relatively simple and was handled by the college's building and maintenance staff.

Our next step, and undoubtedly the most critical step in our planning, was the layout of computers, tables, and chairs. Our objective in designing the classroom layout was to provide teacher access to students and student-to-student access for collaboration. Like Selfe (1987) we felt it was critical for our program to have writing and not computers as the center of instruction.

First, we felt that it was essential that the classroom be arranged so that teachers could have access to our students as they worked: to answer questions, solve computer problems, and provide individual instruction. We had learned in the business lab that students had frequent questions about technology and their writing that required individual responses. When the student with the question was seated in the middle of one of the rows of computers in the business lab, we had to squeeze past the other students in the row, often disrupting them and occasionally brushing papers and books to the floor. Once we reached the student, there was little room to work and no privacy for discussion of the writing. Thus, we felt it was critical that the room be designed so we could have informal conferences with students at the computers without interrupting the neighboring students.

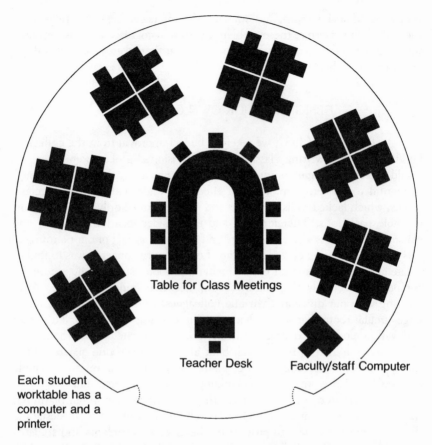

Table for Class Meetings

Teacher Desk   Faculty/staff Computer

Each student
worktable has a
computer and a
printer.

Fig. 11.1. 1987 Classroom

Second, we wanted the room to work for students: We wanted a room where those who desired privacy could work with minimal interruptions, and yet, when they desired, they could collaborate with their peers. We had seen the computer writing classroom at Montclair State College, New Jersey, where the computers had been clustered into groups of four, and we felt that a similar approach would serve as an excellent alternative to rows. Working with a "to-scale" drawing of the room and construction paper cutouts of the computer desks, Sandy and I arranged the clusters of desks around the periphery of the room. We agreed to keep a large U-shaped table that was already in the front-center portion of the room to use for class discussions and interactions. (See figure 11.1.) Our only other concerns with the physical layout were to accommodate the existing floor-to-ceiling air vents located around the periphery of the room and to insure that our design provided adequate wheelchair access.

Furniture

Choosing the right classroom furniture was also important. Knowing that students need space to prop up notebooks and spread out printed drafts of their papers, we requested that the college purchase thirty-by-forty-eight-inch computer desks for the new classroom. Each computer table would contain one computer and printer, and acoustic printer covers would minimize noise. We chose chairs with wheels, so students could slide over to the next computer easily when they wanted to confer with one another, or we could easily pull up a chair to sit with students as they wrote.

The classroom did not have adequate existing electrical outlets, so the administrator who supervised electrical work in computer labs had an electrical circuit installed for all of the computers in the classroom, with the power routed through a separate circuit-breaker box. Each computer was plugged directly into the electrical outlet, without surge suppressors. One drawback to this single-circuit design has been that a loss of power in the room, even momentarily, turns off all of the computers, and, of course, anything not saved to disks is lost. However, during the past six years we have experienced only a minimal number of power failures and have had no apparent problems with power surges. A more frequent electrical problem was caused by the original location of outlets. No one at our college had designed such an unconventional computer lab before, so there was some awkwardness in the interpretation of the classroom design when the wiring was laid out. The electricity was run through channels on the surface of the floor, and some outlets were too close to the front of the tables. When moving their chairs, students would inadvertently kick the plugs and disconnect their computers. Recently this problem was eliminated when the outlets were moved farther under the desks.

Hardware and Software

While we were planning our lab, IBM introduced its PS/2 model computers, which were recommended by our Academic Computing Office. After one visit to the computer store and a few minutes examining the color monitors and working with the enhanced keyboards, we were convinced that these computers would be ideal for our needs. The monitors provided sharp screen resolution, and the enhanced keyboard allowed our students to operate the Page Up, Page Down, Home, End, and arrow keys, all of which were integral to our word processing program, without having to worry about the Num Loc function, which affected those keys on the older IBM keyboards. We purchased twenty-five of these then "state-of-the-art" computers: IBM PS/2 model 30/286 with twenty-megabyte hard drives. Hard drives were still relatively new and were especially appealing, as they saved us countless hours of program disk distribution and collection. Now I would consider them essential. Twenty-four of the computers were designated for student use, and the twenty-fifth system was designated as a faculty system.

An important part of our hardware request was that the college purchase one printer for each computer. We felt this was important, because we often asked students to print a draft to examine and discuss, something that can be done quickly when students have immediate access to a printer. Fortunately, our college supported our recommendation, and we were able to purchase twenty-four IBM Proprinters (dot matrix) for the student systems and one IBM Quietwriter (letter quality) for the faculty system. The college also purchased acoustic covers for the dot matrix printers to minimize noise.

As noted earlier, we had used PFS:Write, a simple word processing program, while teaching in the business lab and were quite satisfied with it, but it was no longer available, thus we were required upgrade to its replacement, PFS:Professional Write. We continued to teach with this program for six years, just recently upgrading to the latest (2.2) release. We find that it still meets our needs as a simple word processing program that students can operate successfully in the context of their first writing assignment. This program has pull-down menus, so commands are easy to find, and has sufficient on-line help, so that students rarely need to refer to computer manuals. Yet the functions are sophisticated enough to format text and meet the more complex needs of our advanced composition students. Furthermore, PFS: Professional Write is used throughout the college, so students can access it in all of our central computing labs, as well as most other computers on campus.

The college purchased and installed our word processing software, along with a wonderful "instant access menu" that enabled us to make the computers "transparent" to our writing instruction. This program, stored on the hard drive, provides a customized menu of program choices when the computer is turned on. Our menu is set up so students can access PFS:Professional Write in two keystrokes. We examined commercially available writing software, but we found that overall they had little to add to our curriculum. Most of the more promising functions of these programs could be duplicated by the manipulation of text with the word processing program. (For further discussion of these strategies, see D'Agostino and Varone, 1991). Thus, we chose not to include any "instructional" software, aside from a typing tutor program which students can use voluntarily during lab hours.

Security Systems

Because we had converted an existing classroom, there was no need to install lighting or carpeting, but security was an important consideration. A three-part security system was installed. It included an infrared motion detector, door alarms, and an alarm system, which was threaded through the case of each computer component. While the system worked quite well to prevent theft, connecting each individual computer component to the alarm system required us to disarm the entire system each time one computer needed repair, which created some unexpected problems with repair and maintenance. We had several hardware problems during our first year of operation, and fortunately our computers came with a one-year warranty. However, the warranty specified that necessary repairs be made at a computer store, off campus. Thus, during our first year, whenever a computer component (i.e., a monitor or CPU) needed repair, it was removed from the classroom. The wiring that connected the parts of the computers was so complex that it prevented us from connecting the remaining parts to create workable computers from them. Therefore, repairs on a monitor from one workstation and a CPU from another left us with two fewer computers. There were a few weeks when we had as many as eight parts of eight different computers out for repair at one time. This created a real challenge in the classroom, where each student usually worked individually at a computer, so we had to send our "extra" students to our writing lab or to our faculty systems, located in our office area, to write. This problem was finally resolved the next year when our computers were included in a collegewide, on-site maintenance contract. Last summer the alarm system that wired the computers in place was replaced with a simpler, yet equally effective, security system that cables each computer part individually to the desk.

TEACHING IN THE TEACHER-DESIGNED CLASSROOM

In September of 1987, Sandy and I began teaching in the computer classroom of our own design. Here, we found ourselves intrigued by the impact of technology on student writing and the impact of computer integration on our teaching. In our classes in the business lab we had examined student attitudes toward writing as part of a study of the impact of computers and found that students in our computer classes wrote substantially (40 percent) longer papers than students in our noncomputer classes. We attributed this to the motivational factor of the computer, our increased emphasis on revision, and student willingness to expand and revise a piece of writing beyond the first draft. Instead of the more reluctant "Why?" that had once greeted our requests for revision in our noncomputer classes, we found that our students in our computer classes responded to our requests to develop and revise papers with questions such as "Where?" and "What should I say?"

As we continued to teach in our computer writing classroom, we found that the design worked well and provided us with access to students as they wrote. Students who encountered problems with the computers usually asked for help, and we maintained a "hands-off" policy, talking them through computer problems rather than seizing control of the keyboards and solving the problems ourselves. We feel this approach is critical if students are to manage their text as well as the computers and gain confidence as writers. We have learned how to recognize when students need help, and when we need to leave them alone to compose. Often the more reticent students wait until we are nearby before asking a question, so circulating among students is an important part of our approach to teaching, which is facilitated by the design of our classroom. We always try to take the opportunity to talk with students about their text, as well as the computer problem at hand.

CLASSROOM AS LAB

When not used as a classroom, our computer room is used as an "open lab" for writing students. Since we emphasize writing, not computers, we feel that it is critical that writing tutors staff the lab hours. Our professional writing tutors have been very involved with the success of this endeavor. We provided their initial word processing instruction as well as sufficient training in DOS operations, so they can format disks and create directories. Many of them have become quite proficient in teaching with and managing computers.

Early on we scheduled fifteen to twenty open lab hours each week, so students could use the computers for writing, but increasing demands for computer classes have limited our open-lab hours to approximately ten hours per week. Basic writing students also have access to twelve computers in our writing lab, which was purchased in 1990 with grant funds. First-year and advanced composition students use the college's central computing lab for their work.

Many of our colleagues within the department have begun to teach a class or two in computer classrooms. Increasing faculty interest has inspired the college to build two additional computer writing classrooms, one in 1991 and another this year (1992.) In this second and third generation of classrooms, we made some minor changes to our overall design, yet maintained the basic principles of clustered computer work areas and a separate table for group work.

SECOND- AND THIRD-GENERATION CLASSROOMS

The construction of our 1991 classroom coincided with extensive building renovation, so we were able to design the room as a part of that process. In this classroom, we decided to put the clusters of computers at one end of the classroom and the table at another. (See figure 11.2.) This is an improvement on our 1987 classroom design, as it increases the proximity of the clusters, thus decreasing the amount of walking the teacher has to do in conferring with students as they write. This also reflects our increased emphasis on individual instruction at the computer, and most instructors who teach in this room remark that they find themselves spending less and less time at the "big table."

The 1991 room has twenty IBM PS/2 386 computers and an equal number of dot matrix printers and is used exclusively for basic writing classes, which meet for the entire class period in the computer classroom. Additionally, we purchased a Hewlett Packard Scan Jet Plus to scan text files. This is especially useful when students have a hard copy of a paper and they cannot retrieve a file from a disk. Students who use dedicated word processors or noncompatible computers for their writing can have their texts scanned and put into a PFS:Professional Write file and made accessible for revision in class.

In building our second classroom, we learned that the construction of each computer classroom presents a unique set of problems; however, our experience in building the first classroom made it much easier to identify potential problems and resolve them quickly. Nevertheless, even minor setbacks always manage to feel like major setbacks when they occur.

One such setback occurred during the building renovation last summer. Our 1987 (circular) classroom was totally disassembled at the end of a week, without notice and in the middle of a summer semester. This left four composition classes without computers halfway through the term. Our Academic Computing Office arranged for the instructors to teach in another computer classroom; ironically it was the same business computer lab where Sandy and I had started five years earlier. Although the hardware had been upgraded since our first classes, the room configuration was essentially unchanged. And while they appreciated having access to any lab, our writing faculty remarked how difficult it was to teach composition in the business lab, where access to students was limited by the classroom configuration.

Another minor problem that is more typical of computer classroom construction arose when the printers were delivered late for the 1991 classroom. The semester had already begun, and classes were in session when the printers arrived, and only one computer technician was available to install

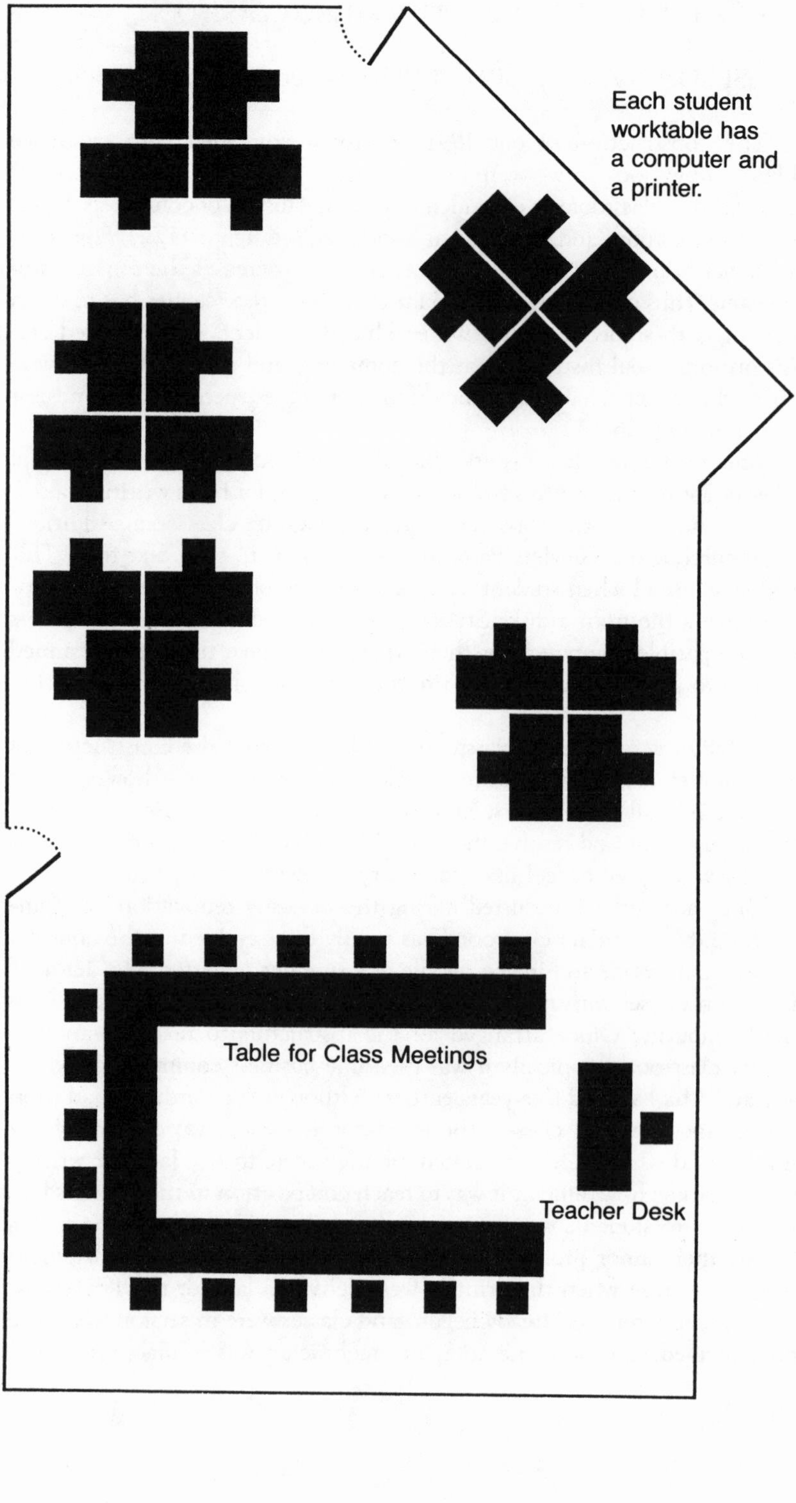

Each student worktable has a computer and a printer.

Table for Class Meetings

Teacher Desk

Fig. 11.2. 1991 Classroom

the twenty printers. We were desperate to have the printers for our students, so I spent the better part of a Thursday in the computer classroom working with the computer technician, unpacking and installing printers as Sandy taught her class.

Once we built this new classroom for basic writers, we were able to offer more computer-integrated first-year composition classes in our 1987 (circular) classroom. Inasmuch as these students generally do less writing in class, the computer room is used on a rotating basis, supplemented by the college's central computer lab. The schedule for the rotation of two classes in a three-hour time slot is negotiated by the faculty teaching those classes. We recognize that this is not ideal, but we feel that some computer instruction for many students in first-year composition is better than extensive instruction for only a few students.

Our 1992 computer writing classroom will be built in an existing classroom this summer. This classroom will have eighteen PS/2 386 computers, seventeen dot matrix printers, and one Laser Jet printer. The layout, which Sandy and I designed in just a few hours, will, again, consist of computers in clusters of four. (See figure 11.3.) Brookdale now has classrooms with permanent walls, so our only concerns with this renovation are layout, electricity (which is already in place), and security.

FACULTY TRAINING AND SUPPORT

Developing and upgrading the computer expertise of our faculty is an important concern. Sandy and I continue to provide workshops for faculty so they can learn word processing, and trouble-shooting workshops to help them learn how to resolve minor computer problems. We have adapted an approach similar to one developed at the University of Massachusetts (LeBlanc and Moran, 1989) to provide workshops to help faculty learn to provide responses to on-screen text. Additionally, we meet to discuss the use of technology and its impact on writing pedagogy. Many of the faculty who teach in the computer classroom have brought new ideas and approaches to their instruction, which has enriched the experience for all of us. Currently twelve full-time faculty teach at least one class in the computer classroom, and at least three more have expressed interest in doing so next fall. Only one or two of our adjuncts have taught computer-integrated writing classes, but we hope to be able to include more of them soon.

Teaching in this environment is exciting and dynamic, yet it also requires a tremendous investment of time and energy to keep computer classrooms up and running and provide faculty support. In addition to providing computer training, Sandy and I still change printer ribbons, unjam printers,

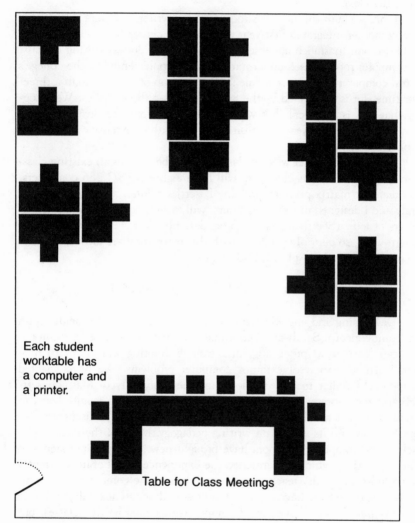

Each student worktable has a computer and a printer.

Table for Class Meetings

Fig. 11.3. 1992 Classroom

and resolve most minor computer problems. We also plan a computer budget and coordinate repairs, staffing, and supplies. A computer writing classroom that works well is more than a room full of machines: It is a fully integrated program of training and support. Therefore, it is crucial to have administrative support for released time for faculty to provide the direction and faculty support required for a successful computer-integrated writing program.

CLASSROOM RESEARCH

Teaching with computers continues to be challenging and enlightening. The "attitude of inquiry" that we brought to our original computer pilot project in 1986 has enabled us to design effective teaching environments and encouraged us to study its impact on instruction. In 1988 our computer-integrated approach to teaching writing and our classroom design were recognized as a Distinguished Curriculum Innovation by the EDUCOM/NCRIPTAL Software Awards Program.

The study of computer classroom pedagogy continues to intrigue us. Last year Sandy and I completed a classroom research project researching the nature of student and teacher interaction in the computer classroom, which was published in *Computers and Composition* (see D'Agostino and Varone, 1991). In 1991 Sandy received a teacher-researcher grant from the National Council of Teachers of English (NCTE) to support an investigation of peer interaction in the computer classroom.

We have been very fortunate to have strong support from our college in providing computer writing classrooms and to share a fine collaborative relationship. Teaching with computers had been very demanding but has also provided us with challenges unlike any others. As this goes to press, the computers for our newest classroom are arriving; thus, in many ways, our work has just begun.

REFERENCES

D'Agostino, Karen Nilson, and Sandra Varone. 1991. "Interacting with Basic Writers in the Computer Classroom." *Computers and Composition* 8(3): 39–49.

LeBlanc, Paul, and Charles Moran. 1989. "Adapting to a New Environment: Word Processing and the Training of Writing Teachers at the University of Massachusetts at Amherst." In *Computers in English and the Language Arts: The Challenge of Teacher Education*, edited by Cynthia L.

Selfe, Dawn Rodrigues, and William R. Oates, 111–30. Urbana, Ill.: National Council of Teachers of English.

Rodrigues, Dawn, and Raymond J. Rodrigues. 1986. *Teaching Writing with a Word Processor, Grades 7–13*. Urbana, Ill.: ERIC Clearinghouse on Reading and Communication Skills and National Council of Teachers of English.

Selfe, Cynthia. 1987. Creating a Computer Lab That Composition Teachers Can Live With." *Collegiate Microcomputer* 5(2): 149–57.

12

Students, Teachers, Computers, and Architects: Designing an Open Computer Writing Laboratory

Gordon Thomas

THE WRITING PROGRAM AT THE UNIVERSITY OF IDAHO

The writing program at the University of Idaho consists of courses at the introductory, intermediate, and advanced levels. The introductory composition sequence has as its primary goal the acquisition of academic writing skills, but instructors are encouraged to incorporate personal writing assignments that build to writing that is more transactional or referential. Although attention is paid to matters of correctness, the emphasis in these courses is on getting students to write in an engaged manner with a clear sense of purpose and of audience. In all courses, students are asked to examine their own writing process and further refine these processes in light of the response they receive from both the instructor and their fellow students. Except for the first-semester course, instructors have considerable autonomy in devising assignments and assignment sequences in light of these general goals, but most instructors try to design assignments and activities that enhance the social aspect of writing and reading.

When a university decides to use computers to help teach writing these days, it can follow one of several models. One is to build a computer classroom or to equip an existing classroom with a computer for each student, and radically restructure the activities of the class itself to take advantage of the computers. Another possibility is to build a computer lab, staff it with monitors and writing instructors, and invite or require students to do their writing on computers in this lab. The Department of English at the University of Idaho chose the second model when it planned a computer-assisted writing facility in the fall of 1984.

Today the English Computer Writing Lab contains fifty-six computers that are used primarily for straightforward word processing. Classes seldom meet in the lab itself; instead, the lab is open for ninety-five hours a week, to all students taking courses in English, and students can stay after hours if they arrive in the lab before it closes. During October 1991, 1,091 students made 5,183 visits to the lab, an average of 167 each day. While students appear to be benefiting from the computers, the decision to make the facility available to all the students in the writing program has hampered our efforts to teach more advanced methods of word processing and to use the computer for other functions such as synchronous or, especially, asynchronous communication. But as probably occurs to some degree in the development of every computer writing facility, many of our earlier decisions about the use of space and the choice of hardware and software have turned out to be beneficial for reasons we did not expect.

In our case, the decision to equip the lab with what was to become nonstandard equipment (DEC Rainbows), along with inflated expectations about the value of Writer's Workbench software, paved the way for the decision to acquire Unix-based minicomputers. With this kind of platform, our lab now offers students an easy-to-use and versatile electronic-mail system, a system that uses social constructionism to enhance learning.

Our writing facility has developed in three phases. The first involved establishing a permanent facility. This involved operating the lab for a year in some temporary quarters, while waiting for physical plant personnel to remodel the basement of an existing building. During the second phase, the writing program developed the pedagogical advantages of word processing for composing and revision. During the middle of this second phase, the original director resigned and I replaced him, so the lab was directed for the first time by someone with training in composition theory. During the third phase, the lab began to exploit the communication abilities of the newly acquired Unix-based hardware and software. Although most activity in the lab still involves word processing, students can now use asynchronous communication programs (E-mail in a variety of implementations) to extend the uses they make of written discourse.

PHASE 1—ESTABLISHMENT OF THE LAB

The impetus for developing some sort of computer writing facility came from the dean of the College of Letters and Science, who saw Writer's Workbench demonstrated at the Rocky Mountain Dean's Conference in 1982. The next year, he arranged for a delegation consisting of the assistant dean, the chair of the English department, the director of writing, and an English professor in charge of placing students into writing courses to visit the computer lab at Colorado State University, which used Writer's Workbench in a large number of its classes. Recognizing support from the dean's office, the English faculty were quick to accept the idea of a large-scale writing facility, but they wanted it to be a place where students could use computers to compose their papers, rather than just a place to run a style analysis program.

In the late spring, summer, and early fall of 1984, the department considered various schemes for implementing such a vision: Because Writer's Workbench would run only on a minicomputer that lacked the kind of word processors that were beginning to be developed for microcomputers, the faculty could not decide specifically what it wanted. Richard Hannaford, director of writing at the time, recalled this period as follows:

> We were trying to integrate computer technology, which was unfamiliar to us, into those aspects of writing pedagogy that were familiar, in order to create something new. All this was done before any of us had regular access to even word processing programs. We lacked any models of what had been done before, so it was difficult to decide the direction we wanted to take. (Hannaford, 1990)

The issue was resolved by a kind of deus ex machina: The university had inadvertently acquired far more DEC Rainbows than it could possibly sell in its computer store. In a kind of "let's cut our losses" decision, the financial vice president decided to give the English department seventy-five of these machines. "It was either that or nothing; the college had no money to purchase equipment," recalled Doyle Anderegg, assistant dean at that time. Fifteen of these computers were immediately put into faculty offices to acquaint the faculty with the technology. Thus, in spite of all the discussion and talk of style-analysis programs, the department acquired its computers almost by accident.

In 1984, however, it was not clear that the IBM PC would become the industry standard; in fact, the DEC Rainbow had many features that made it superior to the IBM PC. The DEC Rainbow was built around a different architecture, though, so it needed a special version of DOS and special versions of application programs, such as WordPerfect. Later the Rainbow's biggest liability was not its compatibility, but its fragile disk drives.

Fortunately, the college administration realized that a computer facility needed more than just computers, and they were willing to fund a space for the machines. In addition, the department requested and received approval to hire a computer specialist as computer lab director. In the summer of 1985, two unused faculty offices were remodeled to create the department's first computer lab, a nine-station facility that could provide word processing facilities for three or four sections of introductory composition (approximately one hundred students). Because of the large number of decisions involving computers that affected the department that year, the chair of our department appointed an ad hoc computer committee, consisting of the director of writing and four other professors, which included specialists in secondary education, composition theory, and technical writing. The committee's first order of business was to hire a director for the lab. The committee was willing to hire a composition instructor who knew a lot about computers, but given the needs of the lab, the most important attributes for such a position were administrative ability and expertise with computers. The first director of the lab was well qualified in both these areas, but had never taught composition.

Faculty involved in these early decisions were particularly interested in the potential of style-analysis programs to simplify the work of the teachers, although some had come to realize that word processing was likely to be the principal activity of the lab. Partially because of early interest in Writer's Workbench, the department purchased Punctuation & Style, a style-analysis program, to incorporate into the writing program. Meanwhile, selected introductory writing classes were encouraged to use this small lab for their papers. Because computers were scarce in other places on campus, the number of students from these classes who used the lab was high.

The most significant way that computers affected the pedagogy in these classes was that teachers found that they could expect revisions of papers more easily. Without having to retype their papers, students were able to revise quickly and were more willing to do so. It was this change in pedagogy, combined with a sense that we were keeping up to date in our writing instruction, and the absence of other software, that led the committee to plan the permanent writing lab as a large-scale version of this small lab.

By late fall of 1986, a full-time computer lab director was hired and began overseeing the establishment of the full-scale lab in temporary quarters—the large basement of the newly constructed Life Sciences Building. The new director put his efforts into making the software easily accessible to students through a series of batch files and menus that shielded the students from DOS. He also had the responsibility of urging the university architect and physical plant personnel to speed up the remodeling of the space that the permanent facility was to occupy. For the whole of 1986–87, the Ad Hoc Computer Advisory Committee considered plans for the new facility. The university architect consulted this committee on numerous occasions, especially with regard to the size and placement of the tables and the interior decor. These decisions were to have a permanent effect on how the department came to use computers in all the writing classes.

The university architect attempted to design a state-of-the-art computer facility. Her plan called for two adjacent rooms connected by a sliding door. The wall between the rooms had windows, so that with the door open and the venetian blinds rolled up, one could easily see from one side of the lab to the other. A lab monitor station overlooked both rooms. (See figure 12.1.) Because the lab was in a basement, there were no outside windows. Above the rows of computers themselves were fluorescent lights, each equipped with parabolic filters to diffuse the glare. To fill out the lighting in the aisles, there were recessed incandescent lights. The two outside walls in the lab were covered with acoustic panels to absorb sound; they would also provide a good surface on which to attach posters.

The architect consulted the committee several times on color schemes for the tabletops, the carpet, the acoustic panels, and the venetian blinds. The doors and the trim on the computer desks and lab monitor station were to be made of white oak. The committee settled on a rust color for the laminated tabletops and venetian blinds, a light brown for the nonstatic carpet, and beige for the acoustic tiles. I was a member of the ad hoc committee, and I remember feeling that we were really handling things well: The architect seemed very solicitous of our needs. Surely, we would end up with a facility that would serve our needs in every way.

No one on the Ad Hoc Computer Advisory Committee knew for sure exactly how many computers it would take to support sixteen hundred students, the maximum enrollment in all the introductory writing classes, but it soon became unthinkable to construct a facility that would not hold all of the computers that the department was already using for students. The space we had been allotted was in the Psychology Building, several hundred yards away from the building that housed all the English department faculty and graduate student offices. (This location was determined largely by the necessity to build the facility on the ground floor so that it could be easily accessible to the handicapped. The particular decision to put the lab in the Psychology

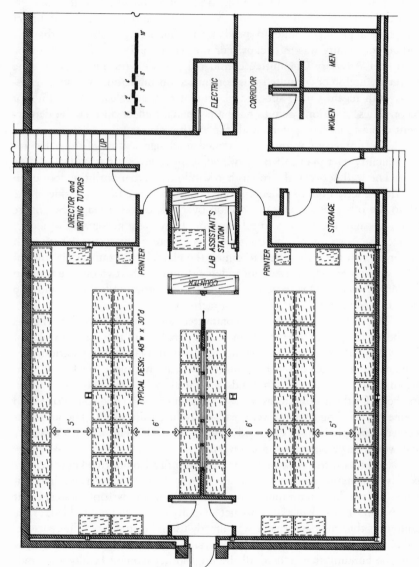

Fig. 12.1. English computer writing lab, University of Idaho.

Building was made by the Space Allocation Committee, an upper-level administrative committee upon which the English department had little influence.) In retrospect, these two constraints—the location of the writing lab in relation to the rest of the department, and the number of computers—had a powerful effect on the thinking of the computer committee, although at the time we felt that we were very much in control of the situation. The main decision the committee faced was whether the writing lab should function as both a classroom and a lab or just as a lab.

The most significant question that the architect asked the committee was whether the furniture (and by extension the electrical outlets and lighting fixtures) should be arranged to accommodate a computer classroom, with all the tables facing one direction, or a computerized writing lab. One member of the department spoke up forcefully for making at least one of the rooms of the computer lab a teaching facility, but the committee was moved by arguments to the contrary. It would be irresponsible, it was argued, to encourage instructors to use the lab as a classroom at times when students from all the classes needed to use it. The architect pointed out that arranging the furniture for a classroom would allow her to accommodate only twenty-five workstations, but positioning the computer tables around the edges of the room with two rows down the center of the room could accommodate twenty-nine workstations. Because sixty was the number of computers and printers that the department hoped to put into service, the two rooms were laid out in a "lab" rather than a "classroom" design.

Each room in the lab would hold twenty-nine computer desks, which were four feet deep and two and a half feet wide and stand twenty-six inches from the floor. Twelve of the desks were to be placed in an island in the center of the room, with the remaining eighteen facing the walls (eight on one, five on another, with four desks each on the two ends of the room—see figure 12.1). There was no extra space between desks, but the aisle running around the twelve computers situated in the center was six feet wide—wide enough that one could walk down the aisle even when students were seated at both rows of computers. Each desk had a recessed ledge underneath that was originally designed to hold paper for the printers, along with a compartment that could store the CPU of a microcomputer when the CPU was tipped on its side. This meant that the disk drives would be vertical, instead of horizontal, but the top of the counter would be free.

One issue that the ad hoc committee did not explore was ventilation. Fifty-eight computers and printers produce a lot of heat, especially when sixty people are in the rooms. The architect provided for an HVAC (heating, ventilation, and air conditioning) system that would be suitable for a room of this size. Most of this system involved air conditioning and ventilation, since the heat from the rest of the building and from the computers and bodies was enough for the building even in winter.

PHASE 2—SET UP HARDWARE, DEVELOP WORD PROCESSING SKILLS

From January 1987 through December 1990, the lab operated primarily as a center for word processing. Classes did not regularly meet in the lab during the regular school year; students would come to the lab any time they wished to use the word processing and style-analysis programs. The lab was open to students in all English courses during the day, when classes were meeting, as well as the evening hours. Its hours were 8:00 A.M. to 11:00 P.M. Monday through Thursday, 8:00 A.M. to 5:00 P.M. on Fridays, 10:00 A.M. to 5:00 P.M. on Saturdays, and 1:00 P.M. to 11:00 P.M. on Sundays. (Later these hours were expanded.) The lab became busiest during the mid- to late-morning hours on Mondays, Wednesdays, and Fridays—the most popular time for classes—and during the mid-afternoons on Tuesday and Thursdays. Nights before papers were due were naturally quite busy as well. During off-peak hours, the number of students might drop to only six or seven, but the lab was rarely completely empty.

When the lab first opened in its permanent facility in January 1987, all the problems that the committee had considered in detail seemed to vanish, and new ones arose to take their place. The most serious problem was the DEC Rainbows, a reliable enough computer except for the fragility of its disk drives. Eventually, repairs to the machines in the department were costing nearly six thousand dollars a year.

Another problem was that although the original HVAC system was powerful enough, fans hidden in the ceiling made enough noise for it to be difficult to address all the students in the room when they assembled for training sessions at the beginning of the semester. During these times, it was necessary to turn off the ventilation and air conditioning, which of course made the temperature and humidity rise as the training sessions progressed.

In spite of these difficulties, the first director of the lab, whose strengths were in the area of computing, devised an ingenious system so that students did not have to know how to use DOS to access the word processing programs. He assigned part of the 896K RAM of the DEC Rainbows to a RAM drive and started each computer up with special boot disks that copied a large number of interrelated batch files and the spelling checker for WordPerfect onto this memory drive. Students had then only to select an item from a menu in order to format their disks, load WordPerfect, or back up files. Upon entering the lab, a student would exchange her or his ID card for a "system

disk," which contained only the WordPerfect program. Because the computers were normally on all the time, the student had then only to insert the
system disk and a working disk, choose a menu item, and press Return to be
in the WordPerfect program. The computers would be powered down only for
vacations or long weekends. In this way, we kept training to a minimum.
Students learned most of what they needed to know in one seventy-
five-minute session at the beginning of the semester.

How did students use this lab? At first glance, it appeared to be one big
typing room. In fact, at the beginning of the semester the majority of students wrote their papers out by hand and then typed them into the computer.
However, interviews with students revealed that most of them would make
changes to their papers as they typed them. All writing teachers encouraged
revisions, and the computer lab figured more significantly into some students'
success when teachers demanded revisions. As the semester advanced, more
students learned to compose at the keyboard, but some found the atmosphere
of the lab, especially when it was crowded, to be inhibiting. In general, the
instructors were able to emphasize revision much more, since the computers
eliminated much of the drudgery involved with redoing a paper. Overall, the
pass rate in the introductory classes increased dramatically with the introduction of computers. Although other factors were obviously at work, it is
hard not to feel that the computers had some effect.

When the noisy ventilation system was replaced with a quieter system
after the first year, teaching became practical, and a few classes were taught
in the facility. Most students are obliged to look sideways at the instructor,
who must stand at one end of the room (see figure 12.1). When the students
are writing at the computers, however, which is the most natural activity
given the equipment in the room, the instructor can easily walk down the
aisles and look over the shoulder at what the students are doing. When used
as a classroom, the lab requires most instructors to alter their teaching styles.
Neither the instructor nor the blackboard (whiteboard in this case) is at the
center of the activity; instead, the computers themselves dominate the room.
No teacher-centered activity such as lectures or general class discussion can
be sustained for very long, but activities such as individual writing at the
computer or working in small groups work exceptionally well. The students
are almost automatically put into small groups when they turn their chairs
around; students seated at the computers in the center of the room are faced
with students seated at the edges of the room, and the distance is quite comfortable for group work.

Providing computer technology to large numbers of students does have
its disadvantages. Students are trained on the word processor by the computer lab staff—several writing instructors, the director, and the undergrad-

uate lab monitors. The training is seventy-five minutes long at the beginning of the semester; its purpose is to get students to master the basic functions of the word processor: loading the program, entering text, formatting a standard paper, saving a file, running the spelling checker, printing, exiting the program. The limited time does not allow students to learn how to move or delete blocks of text or even how to move the cursor in the most efficient manner. The lab provides a word processing manual especially written for students in these courses, and numerous handouts, but the students do not receive direct instruction about computers in the course itself. Consequently, the word processing skills of most students appear to fossilize at a low level. Each of the computers in the lab makes a slight electronic click when a key is depressed. When the key is held down, as people tend to do with the arrow keys, the sound is a little like a cricket chirping. When ten or fifteen students are at work in the lab, the lab sounds like a summer evening alive with the sound of insects, but this is really evidence of the low level of word processing skills that most students have acquired.

An obvious solution to such a problem would be to teach the students some of the advanced word processing commands in the classroom. However, since the classes do not meet in the lab, the students do not get an immediate chance to try out the new information. Consequently, they don't learn it very well. A more serious obstacle to teaching advanced commands is that only 50 to 60 percent of the students in any one class use the writing lab regularly. (Many have access to other computers.) Because of this mix of students, it is not feasible for the instructor to talk about a particular word processing package. So a more significant result has been that in our decision to make the lab accessible to all the students, we may have inadvertently limited the number of word processing skills that most students are able to master. We may be fostering the notion of the lab as a place where one goes to type the paper up, not where one engages in any significant thinking. It is even conceivable that the lab may encourage at least a few students to overemphasize the surface features of their writing to the detriment of the larger issues of rhetorical purpose, organization, and audience. For these students the word processing commands needed to properly format a paper become additional details that compete for students' attention, just as they must focus on the rules of spelling and punctuation.

Yet against these disadvantages must be balanced the fact that the departmental computers in the lab are available to all the students in the writing program. Substantial numbers of students have testified in follow-up interviews to the multiple-choice questions on our yearly evaluation that they use the computers for more than simple transcriptions and that they learned to do so in the introductory composition course that required them to use a computer. Throughout the history of our lab, we have experienced these contradictory results: Many decisions we made in room design, computer software, or lab policies turned out to be wrong when judged by the standards of how well the decision fulfilled goals that were then current. But in adapting to the decision, we were also able to fulfill new goals as the writing program evolved.

In 1986, a change in personnel brought in a director of writing whose specialty was composition theory. The writing program took on a different tone to better fulfill the administration's goal of retaining more first-year students. The new director encouraged the instructors to play a more supportive role with the students. Although standards were not compromised (a complex writing proficiency system that tested students and read the work of borderline students continued to operate), the instructors were encouraged to take a less adversarial role with the students. Revisions of every assignment were strongly encouraged, even after supposedly "final" grades had been given. The computer technology available to the students naturally made it easier for teachers to promote such revisions.

At the same time, the director of the lab moved ahead to purchase equipment that would bring about the original vision that the faculty in 1983–84 had for the lab. In the fall of 1988 he heard about AT&T's offer to sell universities one of its 3B2 series of computers and give the university another one for free. The 3B2 was well suited to running Writer's Workbench in its "Collegiate Edition," a version of the program that had been slightly modified by Colorado State's experience with the program. In practice the promotion turned out to be just another way to discount a lot of expensive hardware (the offer was good only for a stripped-down 3B2, lacking the memory or external ports it would need to be useful). Although the total cost of the entire acquisition was going to be almost fifty thousand dollars, the university administration approved the purchase surprisingly quickly, probably because it appeared that the new equipment would create the ideal facility. But what was considered ideal in 1989 had changed from what was considered ideal in 1983.

In the midst of the transition to the new Unix hardware in 1989, the director of the lab resigned for a better position, and I replaced him. (One of the difficulties of a department's hiring its own computer specialists is that, as employees who are exempt from the classified system for staff positions, there is no opportunity for advancement.) During my first year as director, I was able to consolidate the word processing phase. Although the software and hardware were well under control, the overall atmosphere of the lab was somewhat sterile, which may have contributed to the attitude that the lab was primarily a facility for students to type the final drafts of their papers, rather than a place for composing. I learned that some of my predecessor's policies were to blame: The lab assistants, for example, had been instructed to encourage students to exhaust other methods before asking a lab assistant for help, methods that included using the on-screen Help feature of Word-Perfect or reading the manuals. While such practices may have helped some students become more self-sufficient, many students were inhibited from us-ing the computers effectively because they simply did not feel comfortable in the lab.

I changed this policy by instructing the lab assistants that students were to look to them as a first (rather than last) resort and that the lab assistants were to show themselves very willing to go out to the student's computer for all but the very simplest of questions, instead of remaining in the lab assistant station. At the same time, the department used some of the money that it captured from the previous director's salary (my teaching load was cut in half, whereas the previous director had not taught any courses) to fund four sec-tions' worth of individual tutoring for students in the lab. Because the uni-versity did not have a writing lab at the time, the computer lab came to be the only place on campus where students could get individually tutored. Changes such as these, along with posters on the walls and handouts that were better suited to the particular assignments students were facing, slowly transformed the lab into an environment that was more nurturing to writing. It also distinguished our lab from the other general-purpose labs on campus.

PHASE 3—ELECTRONIC MAIL AND UNIX

Even before the department acquired the 3B2 computers, composition theory had begun to emphasize the social nature of writing, and pedagogical methods based on social constructionism were affecting many writing pro-grams. Although Writer's Workbench is impressive in some ways at analyzing the surface features of a student's text, few would argue that it does much to promote the principles of social constructionism. But the 3B2 computers needed to run Writer's Workbench use Unix as their operating system, and this fact opened the door to a new kind of pedagogy.

Unix is extraordinarily well suited for communications; much of the software is built in, and the protocols in use make the computers easy to con-nect to outside systems. At the same time, WordPerfect has developed a Unix version of its program, so it became feasible to run the computer lab in a Unix-based environment rather than a DOS-based one. Although the lab does not have all the technical features of a DOS-based computer network, the Unix environment enables students to send and receive mail within their own class and between other classes. It is now possible for an instructor to plan writing activities that depend on asynchronous communication. And although the Unix operating system is rather difficult to learn, compared to DOS, it is a relatively easy programming task to use Unix shell scripts to provide students with complete menus for all the tasks they need, including help screens for more complex procedures (a Unix shell script is roughly analogous to a DOS batch file, but the programming capabilities of the shell rival those of the standard languages, while DOS commands comprise a programming language that is quite limited).

In this way, we have been able to encourage a pedagogy that builds on the principles of social constructionism. After logging on, each student is faced with a menu that looks like this:

Date: November 28, 1990.   Home Directory
Time: 9:30 pm.   /usr/students/103–11/G. Thomas
                                 You have mail.

Choose one of the following:

W - Load WordPerfect
B - Run Writer's WorkBench on Your Text

M - Class Mail Menu
G - Group and Individual Mail Menu
N - Read the News

L - List Directory
D - Delete a file
T - Transfer a file from Unix to DOS
C - Display Calendar

Q or X - Log Off

Enter your choice:

Under each one of these menu choices, students get further menus, each of which displays a detailed help screen. The Class Mail Menu option allows students to participate in one or two electronic conferences with other members of their class. Although a "signature" is always appended to each student's contribution to these conferences, students can control what this signature says. They may adopt a pseudonym, or even represent themselves as more than one person (with differing opinions). Under the Group and In-dividual Mail option, students can send individual mail to each other or to members of other classes. This mail is always signed with the student's own name (to prevent one student from harassing another) and offers students a means to communicate with each other privately. Students may also send "group mail," which on this system means mail that is similar to individual mail, but that goes out to several people in their own class. Students may form two different groups consisting of any group of students within their own class; they may reconstitute these groups whenever they wish.

Students still use the Unix system for basic word processing. Thus, the lab retains the pedagogical advantages brought about in Phase 2. However, new capabilities brought about by Phase 3, in particular the easy use of elec-tronic mail, allow instructors to create special assignments that stimulate discussion. For example, in preparation for writing on a complex or con-troversial topic, students can be asked to write at least one contribution to the class mail collection on a particular subject but to first read the contri-butions of the other students before doing so. The result is a kind of out-of-class conversation that can greatly stimulate discussion in class when the issue is raised.

The mail system has been particularly successful at enhancing the writ-ing component of literature classes. Instead of only producing two or three traditional literary analyses, students in courses that have required them to participate in electronic conferences write more text, and they are more en-gaged with their topics. One colleague of mine required sixty students in two sections of a survey course to make two or three contributions a week to their class's electronic conference, usually in response to a specific question she had posed in class. Some of their answers did not differ much from what they would have written if they had been asked to hand in the assignment in a more traditional manner, but students would often include remarks that showed them responding to what their classmates had contributed earlier. Students were instructed to make their contributions at least a half hour be-fore the class met. I then wrote a program that would run automatically a half hour before class every day and print out all the contributions to that par-ticular conference. Lab assistants would then deliver the hard copy to the professor, so that she could read and annotate it and use it in the course of the class discussion. (She could have read it on the screen, but having the hard copy made preparing for class much easier.)

In order to facilitate class discussion, all of these students were asked to sign their contributions with their own names rather than pseudonyms. In another literature class, students were told simply to make one contribution a week and to sign these texts with pseudonyms. Both the teacher and the students were surprised at the depth and range of the subject matter that the class explored. Many students apparently used the electronic conference to explore topics that they felt uncomfortable discussing in class. The students would be much more frank about their religious beliefs and how they corresponded to ideas they discovered in the literature. A brief discussion of Walt Whitman's homosexuality in class prompted an extensive exploration of the general topic in the electronic forum. At least one of the students created two personas, both of which were arguing positions that the student did not personally agree with, a fact that the student revealed to the class only toward the end of the semester. Many of the students felt obliged to reveal their identities, even though there was no requirement that they do so. However, the professor in this class complained that his students appeared unusually taciturn in class. In contrast, in the class where students had been required to sign their own names, the electronic conference seemed, if anything, to make the students more talkative. By the end of the semester the typical student in the class had generated approximately eight single-spaced pages of text, which usually consisted of responses to comments other students had written.

RECOMMENDATIONS

It is only in its general aspects that the story of how a particular lab developed can be instructive to those who are planning a new facility. In this section I briefly mention some lessons from our experience that could be applied to other situations:

1. Integration of lab with existing facilities. Any computer facility that is run by an English department will serve only a limited number of students, usually not even the full number of students who are taking English courses. Most of these students will use this facility only when they are taking an English course. I would urge the planners of any new facility to consider carefully what kinds of computer systems the students will use *after* they have finished their English courses. A departmental facility should have a place in the institutions' general plan for allocating computer resources. Hardware and software should be selected not only with an eye as to how well they fill pedagogical goals within a particular writing program, but also with some consideration as to the general computing environment that students will be using later. Ideally, an English department's computer classroom or lab should be similar enough to other facilities for it to serve as the site where students are introduced to these other facilities. For this reason, it is crucial in the long run for the lab

director to work closely with centralized computer services, not only to keep informed about institution-wide computer goals regarding instruction, but also to influence those central services as they plan general-use facilities.

Another reason for cooperating as much as possible with computer services is to insure that the English lab benefits from local expertise available to everyone on campus. Most institutions have some kind of campus-wide E-mail system; the English lab or classroom should be part of that system. It is sometimes the case that these E-mail systems are not particularly easy to use, but I would argue that in the long run, the energies of a lab director are better spent in getting students to use a campus-wide E-mail system (and so exert pressure to make these facilities useful to the largest number of persons) than they are in creating a special environment in the English lab that does not resemble the larger computing environment and that students can use only while taking an English course.

2. Administration of the lab. Cynthia Selfe's (1989) advice that the director of the lab should be a composition specialist is even more valid today. Knowledge of computers is only one skill that a director needs, and many people working in composition these days have that kind of knowledge. The more difficult aspect of directing a lab is knowing how to introduce the value of the computers to students.

The alternatives to such an approach are for an English department to hire its own computer specialist or for the department to depend on the institution's central services to supply such expertise. The former approach is rather expensive and will ultimately prove unfair to anyone so employed, for opportunities for promotion will be limited. Furthermore, such computer specialists will always have difficulty understanding the instructional needs of students in a writing course, unless they teach or have taught themselves. The latter approach is always necessary to some degree (Computer Services at my own institution can frequently give me valuable advice on technical matters, and some things such as equipment repair could probably be done better by them), but it is essential, I believe, for a computer facility that is used to teach writing to retain its own identity with the department that does this teaching.

3. Lab Environment. The director should pay considerable attention to the way lab assistants interact with students, particularly those apprehensive about working with computers. But even the majority of students, who are already somewhat familiar with computers, need to work in an environment that is conducive to *writing* and not just *word processing*. This is the difference between training students in the use of particular operating

systems and word processing packages (the role that many in business would like higher education to assume) and educating them to be at home in a world that asks them to use computers as a composing tool and as a medium of communication.

CONCLUSION

The writing program at the University of Idaho has yet to exploit all the possibilities brought about by Phase 3 of the lab's development. Plans are now under way to connect the lab to the university's computer backbone, which will allow students to log on to the lab's computer system from other labs on campus. This backbone connection will also give students access to the library's computer system and the university registration system. The most significant advantage of this connection, though, is that students will have access to Internet (a wide-area computer network, similar to Bitnet, that provides electronic links to a vast number of colleges and universities). With this connection, students will be able to participate in electronic forums with students from other institutions, making possible a wide variety of pedagogical activities that should serve to broaden considerably the intellectual experience of students in a region of the country that is otherwise somewhat isolated.

This kind of development runs counter to the prevailing wisdom about integrating computer technology into a curriculum. Writing programs are usually encouraged to determine their pedagogical goals before deciding how some of these goals can be achieved by means of computer technology. In this way, it is argued, the technology can be prevented from driving the pedagogy. The experience of our lab, however, suggests that it is difficult to prevent this from happening. It is certainly true that computer technology by itself will not help a writing program that lacks pedagogical goals. However, particular hardware and software does encourage some pedagogies more than others, and it is hard to know, at the time when funds are allocated, just what effect the technology will have. The pedagogical needs of the writing program, indeed of the entire profession, may change, but the equipment and rooms will still be there. The only way to avoid such a problem is for those in charge of the computer facility to be constantly planning for new ways to use and adapt computer technology as our language theories revise our pedagogical goals.

REFERENCES

Barber, David. 1990. Personal interview with the author, November.

Hannaford, Richard. 1990. Personal interview with the author, November.

Judge, Mary Ann. 1990. *The Computer Writing Lab: Integrating Theory with Operation.* Master's thesis, University of Idaho.

Olsson, Kurt. 1990. Personal interview with the author, November.

Selfe, Cynthia. 1989. *Creating a Computer-supported Writing Facility: A Blueprint for Action.* Houghton, Mich.: Computers and Composition.

CONTRIBUTORS

VALERIE M. BALESTER, an Assistant Professor of English at Texas A&M University, earned a Ph.D. in Rhetoric from The University of Texas and a Masters in English from The Pennsylvania State University. Her research interests revolve around literacy and rhetoric. She has written on attitudes toward minority dialects, especially Black English Vernacular, on using computers in writing instruction, and on studying the style of novice writers. In computer classrooms, she encourages collaborative learning and frequent communication through electronic conferencing. Her most recent work has centered in integrating computers—particularly for conferencing and text sharing—into a writing center setting.

TRENT BATSON has worked within deaf education, at Gallaudet University in Washington, D.C., for twenty-five of the thirty years he has been in academia, but he has also taught at Michigan State University, George Washington University, and, most recently, Carnegie Mellon University. Though his doctorate is in American Studies, he has been involved with computers and writing since the early 1980s and developed the ENFI Project with Joy Peyton in 1985. ENFI became a consortium project, involving four universities other than Gallaudet under Batson's direction, that was funded by the Annenberg/CPB Project. In 1987–88 Batson was a Dana Fellow at Carnegie Mellon, in 1989 he won an EDUCOM award for best computer application in writing, in 1990 and 1991 he was a finalist in the Smithsonian Computerworld computer awards, and in 1991 the ENFI Project was named one of the 101 best computers and education projects in the United States by EDUCOM. He has written numerous articles, book chapters, and conference presentations about computers and writing and recently coedited, with Bertram Bruce and Joy Peyton, *Network-Based Classrooms: Promises and Realities*.

KAREN NILSON D'AGOSTINO is Associate Professor and Cochair of the Writing Department at Brookdale Community College in Lincroft, N.J. She and her frequent collaborator-colleague, Sandra Varone, have published on computers and writing and have published articles on teaching with computers in *Composition Chronicle and Computers and Composition*. They received a Distinguished Curriculum Innovation Award from EDUCOM/NCRIPTAL in 1988 for their successful integration of computer technology into basic writing instruction.

LISA GERRARD is on the faculty of the UCLA Writing Programs, where for the past twelve years she has taught with mainframe, mini-, and personal computers. Her publications include articles on such issues as courseware design, software ownership, and the politics of computer-assisted instruction; and the books *Writing with HBJ Writer* (Harcourt Brace Jovanovich, 1987) and *Writing at Century's End: Essays on Computers and Composition* (Random House, 1987). She coauthored the software *HBJ Writer* (Harcourt Brace Jovanovich, 1986), the *Prewriting Stacks* (Chariot Software, 1992), and *La preescritura* (Chariot Software, 1992) and is currently developing a computer program that explores issues of language and gender.

ROBERT C. GREEN began teaching English at the community college level in 1967. Presently he is a Professor of English at Harrisburg Area Community College (HACC) in Pennsylvania, where he has been a member of the faculty since 1972. He has taught mainframe or microcomputer courses at HACC since 1979. In addition to his normal load of English and computer courses, he taught graduate-level computer courses in a state-funded program to promote computer literacy among school teachers in Pennsylvania. Beyond his work in credit courses, he has a range of experience as a trainer in English and in the computer field, both at HACC and—as an independent consultant—for local school districts and state government. Currently, his course load includes English in the Communication and Arts Division at HACC and Computer Information Systems in the Business/Management Division there.

CAROLYN HANDA teaches composition and literature at American River College in Sacramento, California, where she chairs the English Department's Computer Committee. She helped plan and design the department's first computer classroom, installed in the spring of 1991. She has edited a collection of essays entitled *Computers and Community: Teaching Composition in the Twenty-first Century* Boynton/Cook. In addition, her chapter entitled "RE: Structure, Class, Room . . . and Technology" appeared in book *Vital Signs 3: Restructuring the English Classroom*, edited by James L. Collins. Handa serves on the editorial board of *Computers and Composition* and is an associate editor of *Writing on the Edge*. Her other research interests include the poetry of Elizabeth Bishop and of Seamus Heaney. She tries to relax by reading mysteries, especially ones with strong female protagonists and exceedingly mean streets.

GAIL E. HAWISHER is Associate Professor of English and Director of the Center for Writing Studies at the University of Illinois, Urbana-Champaign. She serves on the NCTE College Editorial Board and is also Chair of the NCTE Instructional Technology Committee. Her recently published work includes the coedited collections *Critical Perspectives on Computers and Composition Instruction, On Literacy and its Teaching, Evolving Perspectives on Computers and Composition Studies: Questions for the 1990s,* and *Re-Imagining Computers and Composition: Teaching and Research in the Virtual Age.* She has published widely in computers and composition studies, and her work has appeared in such journals as *Research in the Teaching of English, College Composition and Communication, Collegiate Microcomputer,* the *English Journal* and *The Writing Instructor.* With Cynthia Selfe, she also edits *Computers and Composition,* a journal devoted to examining issues related to writing, writing instruction, and the new technologies, and the CCCC *Bibliography on Composition and Rhetoric.* She is currently at work on a book with Cynthia Selfe, Paul LeBlanc, and Charles Moran on the history of computers and composition studies.

DEBORAH HOLDSTEIN has since 1985 directed the writing program at Governors State University, an upper-division institution located just south of Chicago. She teaches undergraduate and graduate courses in literature, composition, and theory. From 1980–85, she taught at the Illinois Institute of technology, where whe was associate professor of English. Holdstein received her Ph.D in Comparative Literature (in 1978) from the University of Illinois, her A.M. in Comparative Literature (in 1975, also from the University of Illinois), and the B.A. in English and French (in 1973) from Northwestern University. Her publications include *On Composition and Computers* (1987) and *Computers and Writing: Research, Theory, Practice* along with numerous essays. In addition to her work in computers and composition, Holdstein's research interests include the relationship between critical theory and theoretical and pedagogical issues in composition: She has recently written several essays on such topics as assessment and evaluating teachers who use technology in the classroom and is also at work on a collection of essays and an anthology of literature for composition.

JOHNDAN JOHNSON-EILOLA is a Ph.D. candidate in the Rhetoric and Technical Communication Program at Michigan Technological University. His work on hypertext and computer-supported writing has appeared in *Comput-*

ers and Composition, Collegiate Microcomputer, Writing on the Edge, and several books and conferences. His work on this essay was supported by a fellowship from Ford Motor Company and the Department of Humanities at Michigan Technological University.

FRED KEMP is an Assistant Professor of English and Director of Composition at Texas Tech University. He received his Ph.D. in English at the University of Texas at Austin in 1988 with emphases in Rhetoric and Composition and Computer-Based Rhetoric. As a graduate student at the University of Texas he was the cofounder of that English department's Computer Research Lab and its Associate Director from 1985 to 1988. In 1988 he joined with other academics to form The Daedalus Group, Inc., a software development company and the originator of the Daedalus Instructional System, collaborative groupware for computer networks that won the EDUCOM/NCRIPTAL award for the best writing software of 1990. In 1989 he initiated the Computer-based Writing Instruction Research Project at Texas Tech and received a $119,000 grant from Apple Computers, Inc., to establish a state-of-the art network writing classroom. In 1990 Kemp began "Megabyte University," or MBU-L, a national Bitnet list currently serving approximately 230 members from sixty-five campuses interested in computers and writing. In 1991, he was elected Chair of the CCCC Committee on Computers in Composition.

MICHAEL A. PEMBERTON is Assistant Professor of English and Associate Director of the Center for Writing Studies at the University of Illinois, Urbana-Champaign, where he also serves as Director of the Writers' Workshop, the campus drop-in tutorial center. His work has appeared in such journals as *College Composition and Communication,* the *Writing Lab Newsletter,* and the *Writing Instructor,* on topics ranging from modeling theory and composing process models to teacher research in computers and composition studies. He is coeditor of *The Journal of Language & Learning across the Disciplines,* a journal that engages and explores issues of language use and knowledge construction in a variety of disciplinary communities. He is currently working on a book that investigates the relationship between representation and knowledge in composition studies.

CYNTHIA L. SELFE is a Professor of Composition and Communication in the Humanities Department of Michigan Technological University. Currently a coeditor (with Gail Hawisher) of the CCCC *Bibliography on Composition and Rhetoric,* Selfe has authored journal articles and book chapters on computer use in composition classrooms, included in *Computer-Assisted Instruction in*

Composition: Create Your Own (NCTE) and *Creating a Computer-Supported Writing Facility* (Computers and Composition Press). Selfe has also coedited several collections of essays on computers, including *Evolving Perspectives on Computers in Composition Studies: Questions for the 1990s* (with Gail Hawisher; National Council of Teachers of English and Computers and Composition Press), *Computers in English and Language Arts: The Challenge of Teacher Education* (with Dawn Rodrigues and William Oates; National Council of Teachers of English), *Critical Perspectives on Computers and Composition Instruction* (with Gail Hawisher; Teachers College Press), and *Computers and Writing: Theory, Research, and Practice* (with Deborah Holdstein, Modern Language Association).

In 1983, Selfe founded the journal *Computers and Composition* with Kate Kiefer; she continues to edit that journal with Gail Hawisher. In 1989, Selfe and Hawisher founded the Computers and Composition Press to support the publication of books on computers and their uses in English classrooms.

RICHARD J. SELFE is a Technical Communication Specialist and an Instructor in the Scientific and Technical Communication program at Michigan Technological University (MTU). He currently is the chief administrator of Michigan Tech's communication-oriented computer facility (Center for Computer-Assisted Language Instruction), video production lab, and print production lab. He teaches courses in first-year English, publications management, video production, and print production. Selfe is currently working on his Ph.D. in Rhetoric and Technical Communication at MTU.

Selfe's major interest is in composition pedagogy and the social, political, and cultural influences of electronic media on that pedagogy. He has authored chapters on computer literacy ("Terms You May Want to Know," forthcoming in *Re-Imagining Composition in the Virtual Age*, edited by Gail E. Hawisher and Paul LeBlanc) and educating technical communicators about computer-based citizenship ("Educating Technical Communicator as Citizens in a Democracy: Politicizing and Inhabiting Virtual Landscapes as Discursive Spaces," forthcoming in *Multidisciplinary Research in Non-Academic Writing: Challenging the Boundaries*, edited by Ann Hill Duin and Craig J. Hansen).

BARBARA SITKO is Assistant Professor of English and Director of the Avery Microcomputer Lab at Washington State University. Because this Macintosh lab is fully integrated into the introductory composition courses, she works with thirty teachers each year to design instruction in writing with computers. An affiliate of the Center for the Study of Writing and Literacy at

Berkeley and Carnegie Mellon Universities, she researches writers' revising processes and develops models of writing instruction based on cognitive process research. Her work has appeared in *Constructing Rhetorical Education* and in *Hearing Ourselves Think: Studying Cognitive Processes in the College Classroom*, which she coedited.

GORDON P. THOMAS is Associate Professor of English at the University of Idaho, where he directs the English Computer Writing Lab and teaches courses in writing, composition theory, introductory literature, and linguistics. He has published articles in *College English*, *Computers and Composition*, and the *Journal of Advanced Composition*. He has also written a series of computer programs for writing students inexperienced with computers who are working in a Unix environment. His current research interests center on the uses of electronic mail and electronic forums in the teaching of writing.

GLOSSARY

This glossary defines the computer terms used in these essays and identifies software and hardware packages most often mentioned in the essays.

Apple. Apple is one of the largest personal computer manufacturers. Apple products include the Macintosh, which contains innovations in graphics, word processing, and ease of use.

Application program. Any computer program that performs useful work not related to the computer itself, carrying out specific applications such as word processing, spreadsheet calculations, or data base operations. In contrast, *see* **Utilities; Operating system.**

Applications programmer. A person who writes programs that use computers as tools to solve particular applied problems. In contrast, *see* **Systems Programmer.**

ASCII file. ASCII (American Standard Code for Information Interchange) is a standard code for representing characters as binary numbers as is used on most microcomputers, computer terminals, and printers. Creating an ASCII file, or a *text file,* removes the special codes for margins, underlining, and so on that word processors insert. Thus, the file can be read by almost any processor, computer screen, or printer.

Asynchronous transmission. Because the processes within the computer are not synchronized (during real-time conferencing, for example), the terminal or the computer is free to transmit any number of characters at any time. In contrast, *see* **Synchronous transmissions.**

Auxiliary storage. A storage device that is under the control of the computer, but not directly a part of it—disks and tapes, for example. The computer has its own storage device called *internal storage.*

Bandwidth. An indication of the range of frequencies that an electronic system can transmit. In data communication, high bandwidth allows fast transmission or the transmission of many signals at once and so provides a sharp image on the screen.

Bit. Binary digit. A single, small piece of electronic information.

Bitnet. A wide-area network linking university computer centers all over the world. It is most commonly used to transmit electronic mail between students and scholars who are working together.

Boot. To boot a computer is to start it up.

Broadband. Pertaining to a wide band of electromagnetic frequencies. Communication media (wires, cables, microwave transmissions, etc.) are generally grouped by speed into three grades (also known as *bandwidths*). The width of the frequency band is proportional to the speed of transmission the medium allows. A *LAN* configured with broadband technology, because it uses cable that can carry a wider range of frequencies, is capable of supporting not only data and voice but also video transmissions.

Bridge. A combination of hardware and software that connects two or more networks in an internet. Bridges are used to increase the number of devices and the distances covered in a network.

Bug. An error in a computer program.

Bus. The main communication avenue in a computer. A set of parallel wires to which the CPU, the memory, and all input-output devices are connected.

Byte. The amount of memory space needed to store one character, usually eight bits.

Central processing unit. *See* **CPU.**

Character. Any symbol that can be stored and processed by a computer. The ASCII coding system is one way of representing characters on a computer.

Click. To click on a mouse is to press one button briefly. In contrast, *See* **Press; Double-click; Mouse.**

Comment. A comment is information in a computer program that is ignored by the computer and is included only for the benefit of human readers. Comments remind us that programs are written to be read by human beings as well as computers.

Compatible. Two devices are compatible if they can work together. For example, a particular brand of printer is compatible with a particular computer to which it can be connected; this is hardware compatibility. Software compatibility is supposed when two computers can run the same programs. Be cautioned though, that there are degrees of compatibility. Many computers claim to be compatible with the IBM PC, but some IBM PC programs contain hardware-dependent features that will not run correctly on non-IBM computers.

CompuServe. Users can communicate with the CompuServe Consumer Information Service by phone or computer terminals with modems (*See* **Modem**). CompuServe offers information on a wide range of topics, including weather forecasts, airline schedules, the stock market, and a medical question-and-answer service. Subscribers can send information to each other either individually or en masse via special-interest conferences where anyone can read and respond to the messages.

Configure. To configure a computer program is to set it up to be used in a particular way. Many commercial software packages have to be configured, or installed; this involves setting them up for a particular machine and for a particular user's preference.

Curtis clip. A plastic arm with a clip, which is attached to a monitor with velcro. The clip is designed to hold paper next to the monitor and thereby reduce the eyestrain that can result from working from hard copy at the computer.

Command-driven software. Any program that the user operates by typing commands at the keyboard rather than by selecting commands from a menu.

Computer projection panel. Any information (text, graphics, etc.) on a computer's screen can be magnified severalfold and viewed by audience with the aid of a computer projection panel. The panel is connected via a cable to a computer and set atop an ordinary overhead projector. Cost of the panel and cable runs $1,200 and up.

CPU. Central processing unit. This is the heart of any computer system—where the actual computing gets done, where arithmetic and logical operations are performed and instructions are decoded and executed. All information is processed in this part of the computer and is then sent out to the screen (or terminal), the printer, disk drives, or another computer.

Crash. A computer or computer system is said to "crash" when a hardware failure or program error causes the computer to become inoperable.

Data projectors. Devices that, in various ways, allow what shows on an individual monitor to be projected to a large public screen.

Debug. To debug a system is to remove errors from it.

Desktop publishing. The use of personal computers to design and print professional-quality typeset documents, using operations more complex than word processing.

Directory. The area on a disk where the names and locations of files are stored. *Subordinate (sub) directories* are listed in the directory in which they are stored.

Disk. A magnetic disk is a computer storage device. *Floppy disks* or *diskettes* are portable and can be used with any compatible computer. A *hard disk* is permanently mounted in the computer and cannot be removed. The *disk drive* is the part of the computer that reads and writes on the disk.

Document. The file containing the text to be printed.

Disinfectant. A virus-detection application developed to help with the detection and removal of Macintosh viruses.

Document-sharing software. Software that allows for collaborative writing. When this software is in use, any keystroke performed on one computer will have the same effect on all computers on the same network.

DOS. Disk operating system. This is the name for various operating systems used by many computer manufacturers.

Dot matrix printer. A relatively low-cost impact printer that produces character impressions on paper by positioning tiny rods (pins, dots) to form the image of the character, then pushing the image through a ribbon. The least-expensive dot matrix printers use nine pins to form the image of a letter. The more-recently developed twenty-four-pin technology costs more, but produces better print.

Double click. To depress the button on a mouse twice in rapid succession. In contrast, *see* **Click; Press.**

Down. A computer is down when it is not available to users for some reason.

Download. To transmit a file or program from a central computer to a smaller computer or to a disk.

Electronic mail (E-mail). An electronic mailing system allows the user to type a message at one computer or terminal and send it to someone at another computer or terminal. The message is stored until the receiver opts to read it and either respond to, delete, or store the message.

Ergonomics. The science of designing machines and working elements to suit human needs regarding such features as vision and posture.

Ethernet. A type of local-area network on which communication is conducted by radio frequency signals carried through coaxial cable.

Fax. Facsimile (fax) machines have been used to transmit text and graphics over phone lines since the 1950s. With a fax board installed in a computer, you can communicate with similarly equipped computers or with fax machines, and your system printer can print faxes. With the addition of a compatible scanner, you can input and send printed material and graphics.

File server. A computer that can be accessed by other computers and on which files can be stored and shared by those computers. A combination of software, one or more hard disks, and a computer that allows users to store and share documents, folders, and applications over a network.

Footprint. The physical area occupied by a personal computer or computer terminal, including the height and width.

Gateway. A combination of hardware and software that provides a link between LANs, or from a LAN to a mainframe or minicomputer.

Glitch. An erroneous response that occurs inside the computer because signals that are supposed to be simultaneous actually arrive at slightly different times.

Graphics. The use of computer output devices, such as screens and plotters, to produce pictures.

Hardcopy. The printout of a text; the physical paper-copy.

Hardware. The physical chips, machines, and systems that contain and process software applications.

HyperCard. A program of data management for the Apple Macintosh. Information is arranged in stacks, which consist of collections of cards. When a card is displayed, a button appears that, when pressed (via the mouse), causes an indicated function, such as moving to the next card.

Hypertext. Computer-based writing that allows readers to select a word or phrase and open a further text expanding on that word or phrase, and so forth through an unlimited number of "windows" in the text. Hypertext therefore provides a kind of three-dimensional extension to linear text.

IBM. International Business Machines, the largest computer manufacturer.

Icon. A picture on a computer screen that indicates a particular object or command.

Impact printer. A printer that produces characters on paper by striking an inked ribbon against the paper. Dot matrix printers and letter quality printers are the most common types of impact printer. Some teachers find impact printers useful because they can be used to produce ditto masters. Impact printers tend to be noisy.

Ink jet printer. A nonimpact printer that sprays drops of ink through a nozzle onto the page to form a character. An ink jet printer produces a relatively high-quality image, is less expensive than a laser printer (but more limited in function), and is quieter in operation than an impact printer. An ink jet printer cannot be used to cut a ditto master.

Input. The data fed into the computer for it to process.

LAN. A combination of hardware and software that allows connected PCs, terminals, or workstations to share information and computing resources such as printers, storage, software, and other computers.

Laptop. A small, lightweight computer (under eight pounds) with a flip-up screen that can be powered by batteries and is easily portable.

Laser printer. A nonimpact printer that uses a laser beam to activate a photoconductor, which then electrostatically attracts particles of toner that are fused onto paper to produce an image. Though relatively expensive to buy and maintain, the laser printer produces very high quality output that can produce characters and graphics in various sizes and types. It is considerably less noisy than an impact printer, but lacks the impact to cut ditto masters.

LCD. Liquid crystal display, the type of display found on many portable computers and overhead projector viewers.

Letter quality printer. An impact printer that produces higher-quality output than a dot matrix printer will. Unlike dot matrix, a letter quality printer pushes a fully formed solid character image against the ribbon to print on the paper. The daisy-wheel printer is the most common kind of letter quality printer used with microcomputers.

Local-area network. *See* **LAN.**

Macintosh. Introduced by Apple, this was the first personal computer to use a graphical interface with a mouse. Users operate the software by clicking on icons rather than by typing commands.

Macro. An instruction that stands for a sequence of simpler instructions.

Mainframe computer. This term has commonly come to mean any computer that can run several terminals at once. Usually it means very powerful individual computers that serve large systems such as those found on campuses. It is the largest class of computers in terms of computing power, speed of the central processing unit (CPU), and size of the memory (RAM).

Memory. The space within the computer where information is stored while being actively worked on. Memory can be expanded by adding *memory chips* into sockets, allowing the user to operate larger software packages and programs.

Menu-driven software. Programs that offer the user on-screen menus from which the user selects commands. This design philosophy began as a response to user demand that software operations should be easier to learn. The *menu* allows the user to view all of the operation choices and to select the desired command by pressing the corresponding letter and number.

Microcomputer. Computers of this class are the smallest in terms of computing power, speed of the central processing unit (CPU), and size of the memory (RAM). A microcomputer almost always operates as a single terminal and can sit on a desktop.

Minicomputer. A computer of intermediate size and power between the microcomputer and the mainframe. Almost all minicomputers are capable of running several terminals at the same time—anywhere from four to several hundred.

Modem. A communication device that converts electrical signals from a computer into an audio form that can be transmitted over regular (analog, nondigital) phone lines. With a modem, you can access electronic bulletin boards and various on-line services.

Network. A set of computers connected together. *See also* **LAN; WAN.**

Nonimpact printer. A printer that forms characters by any means other than by striking a ribbon against the paper. Ink jet printers and laser printers are the most common kinds of nonimpact printers currently in use. Thermal printers are also nonimpact in nature.

Null modem. A cable with pairs of wires crossed so that, without actual use of a modem, two computers that are physically close to one another can be connected.

On-line system. A system in which data entered into the terminal is connected directly to the computer.

Operating system. A program that controls the computer and allows users to enter and run their own programs. The operating system runs "underneath" the user's program. It organizes the data on disks, arranging it in files. It keeps track of the data in these files and contains commands that allow the users to save, delete, rename, or move these files.

Password. A secret character string that is required in order to log on to a computer system, thus preventing unauthorized persons from obtaining access to the computer. *See* **Security.**

PC. Personal computer. PCs are designed for use either at home or at business.

Pin. The pins on a dot matrix printer press into the ribbon to form to dots (characters) on the paper. *See* **Impact printer.**

Press. To depress and hold down a mouse button. In contrast, *see* **Click.**

Print server. A combination of hardware and software that stores documents sent to it over a network and manages the printing of those documents on a printer.

Public domain software. Programs that are not protected by copyright. Essentially, this is "free" software that may be legally copied and used.

RAM. Random access memory. This is a memory device by which any location in memory can be found as quickly as any other. It is usually expressed in terms of numbers of kilobytes (1 K = 1,024 bytes) or megabytes (1 MB = approx. 1 million bytes), as in "640 K of memory" or "16 MB of memory."

Real time. Real-time processing involves systems that help control real-life activities as these activities are actually going on. It eliminates delays that put people out of sync with one another as each goes through the process of decoding the received message, thinking about it, and constructing a written response to it. *See* **Networking; Synchronous transmissions.**

Resolution. The measure of image sharpness on a printer or a screen.

Scanner. A device that enables a computer to read, and copy to a disk, hardcopy images—including pictures, graphs, handwriting, and printed text.

Security. Computer files with public or confidential data are open to loss, sabotage, and misuse. Hazards from which computers need protection include the following: *Computer tampering:* When many machines are using the same software packages, the ease with which someone can enter into another's files is increased. Change passwords regularly and make a note whenever you make a change to any of your files. *Easily guessed passwords.* Avoid using the name of a significant other (including a pet), a birthdate, an address, or a telephone number. Also, do not leave your terminal unattended or neglect to log out of the system you are using. *Machine failure.* Make backups of all important files frequently. *Operator error.* Information may easily be deleted accidentally. Try to obtain software that retains the original files while copies or alterations are being made. *Physical hazards.* Protect computers from theft, fire, flood, and similar hazards; store backups at a remote location.

Server. A combination of hardware and software that provides specific services to a number of connected computers (such as giving all of them access to a data base).

Shareware. Software that, though protected by copyright, is being marketed on what is sometimes called the "honor system." Shareware can generally be copied freely for the purpose of trying it out before buying it. If you continue using a piece of shareware after testing it, you are asked or required to send the author some payment. Registration is often available at a fee as low as $15 per program.

Shell. A computer program that stands between the user and the heart of the operating system (called the "kernel"). It interprets the user's commands for the kernel so that the computer does what the user wants it to do.

Software. Electronically encoded instructions that inform hardware functions; a set of programs that tell the computer what to do.

Spooling. The process of storing the computer output before sending it to the printer.

Surge protector. A device that absorbs brief bursts of excessive electrical voltage coming from an AC power line. Note that surge protectors do little if the power line is not properly grounded. Be certain that the computer is plugged into a three-wire outlet meeting modern standards.

Synchronous transmissions. Transmission of data in packets of more than one character. This is faster than *asynchronous transmission*, because there is no need for a start bit or stop bit on each individual character.

Systems programmer. A person who writes the programs needed for a system to function; such as operating systems or language processors.

Text file. *See* **ASCII.**

Token-ring network. A network in which all computers are connected in a ring. A special message, called a "token," is passed from one machine to another around the ring, and each machine can transmit only while holding the token. *See* **LAN.**

Unix. An operating system for minicomputers and large microcomputers. Analogous to DOS, Unix is a more complex operating system but performs basically the same functions as DOS.

Utilities. Programs that assist in the operation of a computer but do not do the main work for which the computer was bought. By contrast, programs such as word processors do the work for the user; these are *application programs.*

Vaccine. A computer program that offers protection from viruses *See* **virus** by making additional checks of the operating system's integrity. No vaccine can offer complete protection from all viruses.

Virtual space. (1) Additional storage space available when the main or real storage (RAM) is full. This memory area is stored on auxiliary storage (a disk) and is managed by the computer system so that the software program that is running can easily access this extra space. (2) By analogy to its meaning in the computer field, the term *virtual space* is also used to emphasize the human dimensions of technology. A computer network is not just circuitry and cables linking various keyboards and screens; for the humanist, a computer network is a meeting place without physical walls.

Virus. Software designed to replicate itself and "infect" the user information or storage media of computing systems, such as LANs and networks.

WAN. Wide-area network. This is a set of widely separated computers connected together; a WAN spans one or several states or continents. (LANs provide access to WANs for many network users.)

Wide area network. *See* **WAN.**

Window. An area of a screen set aside for a special purpose. With some software, the user can control the size, position, and the shape of the window, which allows several texts to be seen simultaneously.

INDEX

A

Access
 computer 21, 31, 39, 44, 47, 59, 68,
  69, 71–73, 77, 78, 80, 99,
  106, 110, 114, 117. *See also*
  Scheduling
Acoustics 14, 139, 141. *See also* Sound;
  Noise
Administration 61, 111, 196
Air conditioning 26, 75, 76, 152, 155,
  171, 187, 188
 See also Ventilation
Alliances 54, 56, 57, 61, 66
 administration 56, 61, 66, 120, 162,
  183, 191
 alumni 61
 committee 36, 61, 111, 120–122,
  184–185, 187
 computer services 196, *see also* Computer specialists/technicians
 faculty 56, 58, 61, 62, 66, 184. *see*
  also Consulted teachers
Apprehension/fear
 student 58–59, 129
 teacher 56, 59
 See also Attitude
Approaches, pedagogical
 cognitivist 39, 43
 collaborative 136
 environmental 10
 expressivist 39, 43, 46
 portfolio 69, 165
 presentational 10
 process 55

social constructivist 39, 43, 45, 86,
  106, 182
social epistemic 140
traditional 2, 7–9, 11–14, 16, 25–29,
  33, 61, 71, 92, 96, 106, 109,
  116, 121, 127, 139, 150, 120,
  127, 132, 133, 136, 140, 142,
  147, 150, 151, 166, 174, 194
variety 150
workshop 140. *See also* Collaboration
Architects/architecture 5, 7–9, 48, 50,
  56, 181, 184, 185, 187
Atmosphere/ambiance 109–110, 126,
  139, 140, 142, 144, 162, 185,
  189, 191
Attitude 22, 106
 faculty 166, 174, 177
 student 115, 129–130, 133, 155,
  166, 167–168, 173, 175, 191–
  192, 196
 worker 116
Authority 6, 8, 16, 22, 27, 29, 33, 42,
  43, 56, 91, 107
 computer 38
 student 27, 42, 107–108, 131, 136,
  147, 151
 teacher 12, 27, 43, 104, 115, 136–
  137, 140–142, 147, 150

B

Benefits 45, 61, 74, 76, 78, 130–133
 for student 29, 130
 for teacher 29, 132